Mysticism of East and West

Se tu segui tua stella,
Non puoi fallire al glorioso porto.
INFERNO XV. 55.

Mysticism of East and West
Studies in Mystical and Moral Philosophy
William Loftus Hare

With an Introduction by
J. Estlin Carpenter, D.Litt.

New York
Harcourt, Brace and Company

Works by the same Author

The World Religions	1905
An Essay on Prayer	1918
The Dreamer and the Butterfly, a Chinese Phantasy	1919
Parables for the Times	1920

All rights reserved

Printed in Great Britain by Butler & Tanner, *Frome and London*

AUTHOR'S PREFACE

DURING the course of many years' study of Comparative Religion and Philosophy I have often been urged by my friends to put the results of my pleasant labour into a book. True, I have not been altogether idle, and have expressed myself in a transitory way to a public which I had opportunities to address by voice and pen. But so vast is the field of Comparative Religion and Philosophy that no one writer could do justice to it; even if he had the ability and the means at his disposal, his life would have to be prolonged before he could complete the necessary cycle. The best work is now done by concentration and specialization; and such a world-book as my friends have asked for, and as the hungry public needs, is gradually being produced by the hundreds of scholars in many countries, whose work will reach its synthetic stage from generation to generation. I have sat at the feet of such scholars and am grateful to them. My own aim has been to absorb as much of their erudition as was possible to me and represent it to readers and hearers who have little opportunity for original research, and who, on account of their intense preoccupation with daily labours characteristic of our age, need a certain guidance through the maze.

The contents of this book may, therefore, be explained as being such part of my studies, not hitherto published in permanent form, as I consider most valuable. I desired the book to contain not much which can be found in the works of greater status on Comparative Religion and Philosophy, and I have attempted to handle the material in an original manner. Some of the matter I think I can claim as unique.

AUTHOR'S PREFACE

The book is not divided formally into parts reserved strictly for different religions, although a glance at the Table of Contents will reveal that the general branches of study are the Philosophy of Religion, Chinese Philosophy, Indian Philosophy, Buddhism, Greek Philosophy and Christianity. A perusal of its pages will, I hope, show that the material chosen supports a fairly consistent philosophy which will, perhaps, steal into the heart of the reader without asking his final assent to formal intellectual propositions. It will leave him as free at the end as he was in the beginning to go his own way in the further study of the important subject of religion which, if I judge aright, is now asking for a renaissance at a very critical stage of the world's history.

The order of the twenty sections in general is chronological except in the cases of a few which belong to no particular epoch or nation. "The Origin of Evil," for instance, follows the Chinese sections because of a philosophical connection which the reader will perceive. Again, "Krishna's Advice to Arjuna" follows best "Buddhism and War," because, as I believe, the *Bhagavad Gītā* was a post-Buddhistic revival of Brahminism in its best form. And "Nietzsche's Critique of Buddhism" is not placed last on account of his modernity but in juxtaposition to the Buddhist essays.

I call attention to a special cycle of studies which is spread over the pages rather than united in one place. Sections III, VII, XII, and XV may be read together, subsequent to the general perusal of the book, in order to realize the wide diffusion of the "Philosophy of Egoism" not only over the world, but through historical time. It will give to moralists some sense of the strength of the antagonist they are languidly opposing, and will warn them not to be surprised if the dragon should suddenly spring to life again in the days that are to come.

Perhaps, then, the central thought of my book, not expressed specifically in any of the essays, may be placed

AUTHOR'S PREFACE

here. It is that Religion is essentially a mystical process which has its roots deeply set in the metaphysical Life-Unity; that it rises and spreads, where it will and when it can, over the surface of human life, but that it meets with opposition at the hands of our Natural Egoism which, in its turn, is rooted in Life-Diversity. The strife is a long one, and its issue depends upon how we throw our will to one side or the other. It is not wrapped up in inevitable destiny, as some have believed, but rests with the decision of Man and Humanity.

Not as a conventional gesture, but as a sincere acknowledgment, I here express my thanks to the large body of scholars and translators, too numerous to mention by name, to whose works I am indebted as the basis of my own modest researches. I have given reference to all quotations.

In conclusion, I hope I may be allowed to use Dr. Estlin Carpenter as the symbol of learning and kindness, and to thank him here for the Introduction he has so graciously supplied to this book.

1923.   WILLIAM LOFTUS HARE.

INTRODUCTION

THE study of the higher forms of religion is one of the most interesting of historical inquiries. Religion may be approached from the side of doctrine and belief in its creeds and scriptures; from that of emotion and action in its ceremonies and rituals; or from that of social and moral force in its institutions. These are all, of course, intertwined in the great historic faiths, and each reacts upon the others.

But there is yet another aspect, where religion assumes the character of what Matthew Arnold called the "criticism of life." This definition assimilates it to poetry. Others may set it beside philosophy. It implies a view of the worth of existence, of its aptitudes and powers, in the presence of the world of men, their rivalries, their claims, and their opportunities. The questions that arise here are not concerned with the authority of sacred books, the size or structure of an altar, or the ranks and powers of a priesthood. They gather round the values which we assign to different classes and levels of objects, the purposes which we form in dealing with them, the aims which we set ourselves, the helps and hindrances which we meet upon the way from one another or from Powers beyond ourselves. What are our relations to our fellows, to the events of the natural world, or to agencies above them? How do we interpret their action, and how does it modify our own?

These are some of the themes which the author of this little book desires to illustrate. From China to the Mediterranean different races have discussed them. Centuries of literature before Christianity are full of them. In the following pages the inquirer will find a rich selection of

INTRODUCTION

examples patiently gathered from translations by accredited scholars, and illumined by long reflection as well as by frequent experience in teaching. Not every reader, perhaps, will feel able to accept all the author's inferences, or follow all his suggestions. But even an occasional adventure into unfamiliar fields may be full of interest. And to many who have scanty time for independent investigation, and only occasional access to good libraries, this small work, packed full of matter, should open wider horizons of knowledge and provoke independent activity of thought.

J. E. C.

OXFORD,
March 28, 1923.

TABLE OF CONTENTS

		PAGE
Author's Preface		9
Introduction by J. Estlin Carpenter, D.Litt.		13

I Religion and the Soul.   21

Religion as the Inward Process of Universal Spiritual Evolution—Religions as the Historical Forms which Religion assumes in Time and Place—Three Aspects of Religion: Metaphysical Process, Discipline and Doctrine—Three Theories of Religion: The Downward Theory, the Upward Theory and the Inward Theory—A Definition of Religion.

II The Age of Perfect Virtue.   28

The Chinese View of Remote Antiquity—A Theory of the Migration of the Ruling Race from the West—The Distinction between the Primitives and the Civilizers—The Origin of the Two Faiths of Taoism and Confucianism to be found in Racial and Psychological Elements—Description of the Men of Perfect Virtue by the Chinese Historians—The Cause of their Disappearance—The Polemical Purpose of the Legends.

III Chinese Egoism.   46

The Four Chief Schools of Moral Philosophy in China—Yang-chu an Outgrowth from Taoism—His Metaphysic and Psychology—Life according to Natural Impulse—Sociological and Political Inferences—The Attempts at Refutation of his Doctrines by Confucians, Taoists and Rationalists.

TABLE OF CONTENTS

		PAGE
IV	The Origin of Evil.	67

    Three Periods Considered—Outlines of Eight Views on the Subject—Hebrew Tradition in Two Forms—Indian Tradition of Brahmins and Buddhists—Western Tradition as Formulated by St. Augustine and Plotinus—The Solution Lies in the Search for the Psychological Source of Evils rather than the Origin in Time of Evil itself—The Possible Oblivion of Evil.

V   The Teachers in the Upanishads.   86

    The Entry of the Aryans into India—Royal Philosophers and their Priestly Disciples—The Fundamental Doctrines of the Vedānta Upanishads Traced to the Ruling Caste—Later Expositors.

VI An Outline of the Sānkhya Philosophy.   92

    Philosophic Change from the Rig-Veda to the Vedānta Upanishads—The Sānkhya a Declension from Idealism—Its Atheistic Character—Diagram of its Elements: a Dualism—The Three Qualities or Moods of Nature—Restoration of God to the System in the *Bhagavad Gītā*.

VII Indian Egoism and Materialism.   101

    The many Minor Schools of Egoism, Materialism, Atheism and Determinism—Various Attempts at their Refutation by Brahmins, Buddhists, and Jains—A Widely-diffused Hedonism—Chānakya, the Indian Machiavelli.

VIII The Buddha's Personality.   125

    Doubts as to the Truth of the Legends—The Origin of the Sākya Clan and its Probable

TABLE OF CONTENTS

PAGE

Non-Aryan Source—Gotama possibly of Mongolian Stock—Abundant Details as to his Personal Appearance, his Charm, and his Psychology—His Method of Teaching, his Logic and his Humour—His Great Faith in Man's Power to Attain Salvation.

IX BUDDHISM AND WAR. 142

The New Dharma and its Implications—How it Undermined the Brahmin Social System—The Strict Ethic of Love and its Consequences—Asoka's Great Experiment of Peace Based on Compassion and Remorse for the Suffering he had Caused.

X KRISHNA'S ADVICE TO ARJUNA. 159

The Character of the *Bhagavad Gītā*: its General Aim and Literary Devices—The Conventional Military Ethic of the Warrior Caste Affected by Asoka's Pacifism—"The Distress of Arjuna"—Misapplied Truth—Dogmatic Esoteric Doctrine on War Inconsistent with the Prevailing Sound Philosophy of the *Gītā*.

XI NIRVĀNA. 174

The Place of Nirvāna in the Buddha's System—Its Simple Origin in Ethics and Psychology—The "Moral Nirvāna" for this Life and the Consequent "Metaphysical Nirvāna" Hereafter—Māhayāna Developments and the Logical Strength of the Doctrine.

XII NIETZSCHE'S CRITIQUE OF BUDDHISM. 191

Nietzsche's Claims to be the First Immoralist Refuted—His Attack on Religion Examined—His Exposition of Buddhism and Misunderstanding of its Purpose—His Unfounded

TABLE OF CONTENTS

PAGE

Speculations—His Appreciation of Buddhism as Compared to Christianity.

XIII A VIEW OF KARMA. 209

The Origin in the Upanishads of a Doctrine of the Significance of Deeds: In Buddhism and Jainism—The Vedānta View and its Implications—Desire, Will, Deeds and their Results in Character—Three Possible Hypotheses for Karma.

XIV THE KEY TO PYTHAGORAS. 231

The Place of Pythagoras in the Cycle of Physical Philosophy—A Law of Motion Needed—Misunderstanding of the Fundamental Discovery of Pythagoras which was not a Law of Numbers, but a Law of Rhythm—Solution Found for Most of the Problems by a Single Idea—Rhythm in Sound, in the Body, in the Soul, in Society and in the Cosmos.

XV SOKRATES THE MORAL INNOVATOR. 243

Prevailing Hedonism at the Time of Sokrates—Fragments from Greek Literature Exhibiting a Strong Philosophic Nihilism, Egoism and Materialism—The Attempt of Sokrates to Refute these Doctrines and to Found an Ethic on the Universals of Morality and Justice.

XVI NEO-PLATONISM. 267

Religion Combined with Philosophy—The Genealogy of the System—The Three Great Schools of Alexandria-Rome, Syria and Athens—Fundamental Changes in the Doctrine of the Soul and its Transmigration from Plato to Proclus.

TABLE OF CONTENTS

                                                                       PAGE

XVII   BETWEEN THE TESTAMENTS.   302

        The Period Immediately Preceding the Coming of The Christ—The Failure of the Prophetic Hopes—A New Philosophy of History—Apocalyptic Literature—Sophia and Logos—The Messiah.

XVIII   THE EUCHARIST.   318

        The Supersession of Sacrifice by Sacrament—The Christian Love Feast and the Last Supper—Communion and Thanksgiving—Two Divergent Views Observed in the Historical Documents—The Rite as Symbolical and the Rite as Magical—Emergence of the True View.

XIX   "THE UNPARDONABLE SIN."   330

        Grave Misunderstanding of the Phrases in the Gospels—The Meaning of Certain Key-words—The Ideas of Sin and Exorcism—Reconstruction of the Discourse in which the Text Occurs—Emergence of the Important Doctrine of the Defensive Power of "The Holy Spirit"—The Law of the Expulsion of Evil.

XX   THE ETHIC AND PSYCHOLOGY OF FORGIVENESS.   339

        The Burden of Nemesis and Karma—The Difference between Justice and Mercy, Pardon and Forgiveness—The Development of the Doctrine of Human Forgiveness from the Old Testament to the New—The Stages and Elements of an Act of Forgiveness—Its Consequences: the Oblivion of Evil, the Remembrance of Good.

Errata

Page 34, line 2, read Yang-Chu
,, 100, ,, 17, ,, Keith
,, 112, ,, 13, ,, *Samgraha*
,, 119, ,, 33, ,, Magadha
,, 123, ,, 34, ,, Shamasastry Pilay
,, 127, ,, 20, add to reference Vol. II, p. 881
,, 137, ,, 21, read *Kūtadanta*
,, 183, ,, 20, ,, Parinirvana
,, 211, ,, note ,, Keith
,, 269, lines 28, 29, read Eudoras, Thrasyllus, and Maximus
,, 270, table, read Cyrenaics
,, 274, line 9, read *Bibliotheca*
,, 283, ,, 27, ,, Speusippos
,, 284, table, read Gedalius
,, 304, line 24, ,, older Canon
,, 310, ,, 26, ,, *Hokma*

I : *Religion and the Soul*

THERE is hardly one of us who has not heard, during recent fateful years, murmurings of distrust of religion, and impatience with the churches. On all sides it has been said: "the churches have failed" or "Christianity has failed" or "Religion has been tried and found wanting"; and indeed the professed expositors of Religion have been hard pressed to know what defence to make against these reproaches. Impartial and critical defenders of Religion, however, standing aside from religious institutions or teaching bodies, might oppose these hasty judgments, by pointing out that Religion itself must not be identified with any particular dogma, customary morality, ancient scripture, or indeed with any system combining all of them; if *they* fail to meet the world's need in days of trial, Religion itself is still left —natural, unqualified, undifferentiated, unrestricted. I believe there is force in this argument, but do not propose to pursue it until I have examined more closely into the nature of Religion itself. If we can form a concept of Religion harmonious to common experience, we may then come back to our question, and admit that there has been put upon Religion the hard task of surviving in the breasts of men while they have been engaged, at the world's demand, in such activities of strife as make Religion seem a caged and impotent prisoner of war.

1. A CONCEPT OF RELIGION

Our first concept of Religion may be formed, I think, by the help of two analogies. The first is the idea of Involution and Evolution; the two parts of a great cyclic process of development which is conceived to be in action within the confines of Time and Space. Involution is the downward and outward movement of Spirit towards Matter, at the lowest point of which Spirit reaches the maximum degree of its material manifestation. This is conceived to be but one-half of a cosmic process, the other being Evolution, the return of Spirit to its pure supremacy, disentangled from all limitations. I mention this without further elaboration now, to help those who are familiar with it, and also those who meet it for the first time, to recognize that Religion may be conceived of as none other than this *return journey of the human soul* to its source.

Here it will be helpful to turn to the Latin dictionary, which sometimes throws light on the essential meaning of a word. We find there two adjectives, which stand in opposition to one another. The first is *negligens* (= negligent, careless, heedless, reckless), which may be considered as representing the downward and outward course of our egoistic life ; the second is *religens* (= pious, holy, devout, religious), which may be regarded as the upward path of return. The Latin noun is *religio, religionis* (= religion, piety, devotion to God), and our English word preserves the early and essential meaning of both *religens* and *religionis*.

We may employ, secondly, the analogy of *speech* and *language*, in order to help us to discriminate between *Religion* and *religions*. Speech is the universal human function, languages are the differing and sometimes entirely different forms into which speech is moulded.

2. RELIGION AND RELIGIONS

Further, Religion may be described as a universal process through which the souls of *all* men pass, while religions are the historical and local forms which, in several civilizations, Religion assumes, both in relation to doctrines, discipline, and social ethic.

I will now attempt a closer examination of Religion, and propose to look at it in three aspects.

RELIGION AND THE SOUL

First; it is, as we have seen already, a part of the general progress of the soul, corresponding to the evolutionary ascent, or second great phase of human cyclical experience. It has often been likened to a journey, an odyssey, a voyage, a battle, or a path which has its beginnings, its crises, its obstacles, and its goal. All historical religions have expressed in some striking terms the nature of this goal, or final aim. The ancient Chinese spoke of it as "possessing the Tao," a state which a man might attain as the result of some special discipline, a state corresponding to the highest spiritual condition of the Brahmins—*Mōksha*, or Liberation, *Kaivalya*, Aloofness, *Apavarga*, the Highest Bliss. The Buddhist *Nirvāna* corresponds to the Christian *Salvation*.

In our own language there was in use in the seventeenth century a very beautiful and concise phrase to the effect that such and such a man "has religion," Religion here being regarded as a coveted possession or as the end of the journey itself, its final meaning.

The above facts would seem to indicate that Religion is primarily *experience*, and only secondarily *belief*; beliefs are contradictory, but it is in the realm of experience that we notice religions begin to touch one another closely and often to attain a unity which, despite all our efforts, we cannot affirm on their doctrinal and philosophical side.

If we examine carefully the beautiful literature of the Upanishads, of Taoism, Plato, Aristotle, Philo, the Christians and Plotinus, we shall find that they all lead the soul to this consummation by means of appropriate disciplines, and that each one makes use of an intellectual apparatus appropriate to its own time, country, temperament and philosophic outlook. But this apparatus is not Religion itself, with which it is often confused.

Secondly; every end needs means for its attainment, and religious discipline, whether primitive or advanced, may be regarded as an experimental means to aid the soul to make the journey to its goal. One may perhaps be better than another, or more suitable to some persons than to others. The discipline, however, whether it be that of the Church, the Buddhist Order, the Pythagorean Brotherhood, or the Witch-doctor's taboo, is not Religion itself, but its instrument and servant.

Thirdly, since there is an aim, and a means devised to its attainment, there is naturally an intellectual aspect of the process. This is the religious philosophy, the creed, the dogmatic teaching of the school; which, again, is not Religion itself, but its intellectual reflection.

Coming now to the consideration of religions, we may regard them as the particular types or forms which, in given lands and times, Religion has taken. These types vary according to circumstances, such as the intensity of the religious life itself, the external conditions, institutions and political channels through which the spiritual life flows, the degree of intellectual and philosophic development reached by any people.

3. THREE THEORIES OF RELIGION

I now turn to the chief theories as to the growth of form in Religion. First, I distinguish two, which I call respectively the Downward Theory and the Upward Theory, about each of which I will say a few words, after which I shall propose for consideration a third.

(*a*) The results of a comparative study of religions, philosophies, customs and folk-lore give countenance to the widely-diffused tradition of a Golden Age or Age of the Gods, " the Age of Perfect Virtue," variously referred to in the ancient Jewish scriptures, the Mohammedan sacred books, the Taoist literature, and called in India the *Krita-Yuga*. This tradition suggests that in very early times the heads of the human race shared intimate relationship with celestial powers, and received from them a teaching, or a revelation of ultimate mysteries. It also declares that this

Divine Wisdom was the fountain head of all sacred traditions. It supposes that as long as men have walked by its light, evolution has advanced, but when they have forsaken it, they have become ignorant and degenerate.

One objection to the claim of any one religion to have been thus communicated by a semi-divine teacher or man of great authority—Moses from Sinai, Apollo on Olympus or Jesus on the mountain-side in Palestine—is that all such claims are resented and disputed by rival custodians of tradition, and the tendency has been for the faith to become nationalistic and separative rather than universal.

(*b*) The other theory, more harmonious to modern evolutionary ideas, is the basis of all recent scholastic study of religions and philosophies, and has yielded much fruit by the adoption of scientific and critical methods, not only in Europe and America, but in the East. It does not assume an original deposit of wisdom, but traces by historical methods what it conceives to be the upward and outward expansion of religious impulse and belief. It therefore takes particular note of the terrestrial conditions in which any given religion is found, that is to say, of physical and political geography, ethnology, language, economic conditions and changes in political supremacy. It then examines without bias the content of the religion on its psychological, ethical and philosophic sides, and puts us into possession of all obtainable data.

But there is one aspect of this Upward Theory which is unsatisfactory. Many of its exponents, particularly of the rationalist type, make out Religion to be a kind of "by-product" of physical evolution. Spencer, Grant Allen, Frazer, Robertson and a host of German scholars seem to show Religion rising from the mud of superstition and illusion, and they make considerable play with the fact that they can discover in primitive beliefs and institutions the origins of our modern forms of faith.

It will be seen that, in a general way, the Downward Theory is held in the East and with regard to the more ancient, perhaps prehistoric, phases of religions, while the Upward Theory has been adopted with regard to religions expressed in written literature and living tradition. I should like to say, though I cannot elaborate the point here, that the two theories, though seemingly different, are not entirely and mutually exclusive. For even supposing there had been in very ancient times an original deposit of wisdom, placed in the hands of the leaders of the human race, and that this had become broken, corrupted and partially lost, the work of collecting its remnants, regaining by various means some of the beauties assumed to belong to the whole body of Divine Wisdom, would be the upward movement in question, by the critical and historical method.

In historical times, at least, we should be able to trace the general advance and upward tendency from comparatively primitive, degenerate and restricted an outlook towards the universal outlook now reached by most of the great living religious impulses.

(c) It is true that, as a rule, the exponents of the Upward Theory do not look with favour upon the older view ; for the reason that the alleged data are not in their hands ; they prefer to collect all possible facts from literary and customary sources and to draw deductions from them such as seem reasonable.

Let it be always remembered, however, that we are studying something *real*, the inner movement of the souls of men as it has expressed itself in historical forms of religions. Consequently we need an Inward Theory which explains Religion, neither as a gift or gifts, nor as a man-made product of the evolutionary struggle. Religion is not handed down from heaven nor has it grown up from the mud ; it is itself the inmost process of the journey of the soul.

RELIGION AND THE SOUL

4. A DEFINITION OF RELIGION

I now offer a definition of Religion which I think may be derived from the foregoing considerations. *Religion is the assimilation of the Soul to the Universal Order.* I may remark that in these pages I have not yet considered the Soul in its scientific aspect ; and I must not leave my present theme to discuss so great a topic. One may, however, contemplate the contact between the human and the Divine as an " assimilation," a becoming like, a re-linking of two natures properly one. The Divine Spirit, essentially one with that divine portion which is each man's " self," touches the element below it and illuminates the Intuition ; likewise the Reason becomes clear and pure, the Will ordered into harmony with the Divine Will, the Feelings or Emotions disciplined and quieted, and even the Sensations—the outermost part of the " Soul "—corrected and sharpened, so that the Body derives from all the higher transformations a corresponding health otherwise unobtainable. To become thus assimilated is, as Plato says, to be just and holy, like the Gods.

The beautiful parable of the Prodigal Son is a perfect dramatic symbol of *negligens* and *religens* ; of the outward, self-affirming, separative life which leads, on repentance, to a return to the soul's spiritual home. With the words " his father ran towards him and fell on his neck and kissed him " Muhammad, the prophet of Islam, was deeply struck, and it is said he remarked : " When man walks towards God, God runs towards him." This deeply mystical view of Religion is most precious to us, for it supports us with the thought that whatever we do to effect an assimilation of the soul to the Universal Order, the Universal Order blesses, and adds its own energy to ours. Religion, then, is not merely Man's search for God, but God's search for Man.

II : *The Age of Perfect Virtue*

THE legends of a golden age preserved by Chinese historians have about them a peculiar fascination and philosophical import which amount to a challenge to most of our well-established ideas. The Chinese have few myths of the creation of the world by gods as other nations have; what they do instead is to push beyond historical times to a time of which little record exists, and to people that period with men whose characteristics, as some of them think, are admirable. These men they call "the Ancients" or "the men of perfect virtue." We are able provisionally to place this long-forgotten age in its relation to more recent times by the following tables of rulers whose names the Chinese writers have preserved. Of the men in the first list, nothing is known but their names; of the second list, Fu-hsi is, by some scholars, placed as far back as the year 3322 B.C., but, with greater probability, he flourished about 2900 B.C. Hirth, in *The Ancient History of China*, gives a list of seven legendary dynasties before Fu-hsi.

I. "THE AGE OF PERFECT VIRTUE." (? 3500 B.C.)

Yung-Ch'ang, Ta-t'ing, Po-hwang, Chang-yang, Li-lu, Li-Ch'u, Hsien-yuan, Ho-hsu, Tsun-lu, Chu-yung.

II. "THE THREE EMPERORS."

Fu-hsi	began to reign B.C.	2943
Shan-nang	,, ,, ,,	2828
Hwang-ti	,, ,, ,,	2688

THE AGE OF PERFECT VIRTUE
III. "THE FIVE RULERS."

Shao-hao	began	to reign	B.C.	2588
Chuen-hia	,,	,,	,,	2504
Ti-ko	,,	,,	,,	2424
Yao	,,	,,	,,	2355
Shun	,,	,,	,,	2253
Yü	,,	,,	,,	2208

1. PRIMITIVES AND CIVILIZERS

I believe it is possible to admit some historical basis for the very remarkable claims the Chinese make on behalf of their "ancients." Some modern sinologists seem to be agreed that there was an important migration of Mongolian tribes from the point where, late in the fourth millennium B.C., the Mongolian race came into closest contact and conflict with the older Akkadian race; that is, the land of Elam, the northern portion of which (Anshan) was conquered by Gudea, the *patesi* of Shirpula, in lower Babylonia, 3000 B.C. The Akkadians were a highly civilized people, and had built great cities and invented a system of writing. The less civilized Mongolians on their borders were driven to the N.E., and continued their trek along the southern shores of the Caspian Sea and far beyond, ultimately reaching the upper valleys of the Yellow River (Hoang-ho) and the Wei River. This important migration was, so to speak, a return of a more cultured tribe from a point on its circumference towards the centre and across the diameter of the Mongolian race as a whole. It cut the primitive Mongolians in two as with a wedge, driving the northern section towards Siberia and the southern towards Indo-China and Malaya. Adopting the many hints that are given by the Chinese historians, we must therefore think of the Age of Perfect Virtue as preceding this disturbing migration. "The men of remote antiquity" are not those who came slowly Eastward from Elam, but those who belonged to the primitive proto-Mongolian race. The history of ancient China is the record of the gradual supersession of the primitives by the more civilized Mongolians from the West.

I believe we have in the above historical hypothesis the key to the opposition of the two " religions " which in earlier ages divided the allegiance of the Chinese people. The differences between them were political and temperamental. Taoism professes in a hundred of its pages to be identified with the primitive people ; it belongs to nature rather than to art. On the other hand, Confucianism is historically connected with the *civilizers* of the ancient people. Its progress marks the gradual supremacy of the Chu-hia (or small nucleus of federated states on the banks of the Yellow River) over the less civilized peoples. Confucius himself claimed descent from the old ruling family of Shang, while Lao-tze, the chief expositor of Taoism, belonged to the one-time barbarian state of Ts'u. Confucius exalts the " superior man," the aristocrat ; Taoism speaks for the people, and remonstrates continually with the rulers.

For these reasons I venture to place the so-called " age of perfect virtue " historically at an epoch antedating the above-mentioned migration to the Valley of the Yellow River, that is to say, any time before the date of Fu-hsi, 2900 B.C., or, at latest, Hwang-ti, 2688 B.C. As to the location of " the men of perfect virtue " we have some clue ; they would have lived in the modern south Shen-si, south Shan-si, north Ho-nan, south Chih-li and west Shan-tung —precisely those parts that Fu-hsi and his successors are represented as having civilized—and probably more or less distributed over the unknown mid-China of that day.

Ethnologists may find much interest in thinking of the Mongolian race as a whole—containing the *ancestors* of the Finns, Esquimos, Lapps, Magyars, Samoyeds, Turks, Manchus, Inland Chinese, Malays, Tibetans and Burmese— as psychologically *Taoist*, possessed of intuitive contact with Nature, and showing reverence for her cryptic and hidden

THE AGE OF PERFECT VIRTUE

orders. This was followed by contact with and influences from the Akkadians, substituting the more personal and individual rule of the *man* for the diffused authority of the inner and feminine *Tao*. Then ensued a period of preoccupation with the social order, rationalistic, utilitarian and humanistic in the best sense.

The Chinese nation is, then, as a whole, the result of the elevation of a portion of the proto-Mongoloids, basically Taoist, and slowly evolutionary, by a superficial, volitional and progressive impulse received from the Akkadian civilization.

2. PERFECT VIRTUE DESCRIBED

Having said so much by way of historical theory, to which of course I do not tie either myself or my readers, I now proceed with some quotations from the Chinese writings. My authorities are the Confucian Classics, the *Tao-teh-king*, the writings of Chwang-tze, Lieh-tze and Yang-chu. From them I shall quote at some length, adding only explanatory comments.

> Are you, Sir, unacquainted with the age of perfect virtue? Anciently there were Yung-Ch'ang, Ta-t'ing, Po-hwang, Chang-yang, Li-lu, Li-Ch'u, Hsien-yuan, Ho-hsu, Tsun-lu, Chu-yung, Fu-hsi, and Shan-nang. In their times the people made knots on cords in carrying on their affairs. They thought their simple food pleasant, and their plain clothing beautiful. They were happy in their simple manners, and felt at rest in their poor dwellings. The people of neighbouring states might be able to descry one another; the voices of their cocks and dogs might be heard all the way from one to the other; they did not die till they were old; and yet all their life they would have no communication together. In those times perfect good order prevailed.
> (CHWANG-TZE, *S. B. E.* X. II. iii. 4.)

It will be noticed that Chwang-tze brings down the age of perfect virtue into the time of the second of " the three Emperors "—Shan-nang.

Formerly the ancient kings had no houses. In winter they lived in caves which they had excavated, and in summer in nests which they had framed. They knew not yet the transforming power of fire, but ate the fruits of plants and trees. They knew not yet the use of flax and silk, but clothed themselves with feathers and skins.
(*Li-yun*, VII. i. *The Li-Ki., S.B.E.*)

In the time of Ho-hsu, the people occupied their dwellings without knowing what they were doing, and walked out without knowing where they were going. They filled their mouths with food and were glad ; they slapped their stomachs to express their satisfaction. This was all the ability which they possessed.
(CHWANG-TZE, XI. II. ii.)

The people had their regular and constant nature ; they wove and made themselves clothes ; they tilled the ground and got food. This was their common faculty. They were all one in this, and did not form themselves into separate classes ; so were they constituted and left to their natural tendencies. Therefore in the age of perfect virtue men walked along with slow and grave step, and with their looks steadily directed forwards. At that time there were no footpaths on the hills, nor excavated passages ; on the lakes there were no boats nor dams ; all creatures lived in companies ; and the places of their settlement were made close to one another. Birds and beasts multiplied to flocks and herds ; the grass and trees grew luxuriant and long. In this condition the birds and beasts might be led about without feeling the constraint ; the

THE AGE OF PERFECT VIRTUE

nest of the magpie might be climbed to, and peeped into. Yes, in the age of perfect virtue, men lived in common with birds and beasts, and were on terms of equality with all creatures, as forming one family;—how could they know among themselves the distinctions of superior men and small men? Equally without knowledge, they did not leave the path of their natural virtue; equally free from desires, they were in the state of pure simplicity. In that state of pure simplicity the nature of that people was what it ought to be.

(Ibid., IX. II. ii. 2.)

In the age of perfect virtue they attached no value to wisdom, nor employed men of ability. Superiors were but as the higher branches of a tree; and the people were like the deer of the wild. They were upright and correct, without knowing that to be so was "Righteousness"; they loved one another, without knowing that to do so was "Benevolence"; they were honest and leal-hearted, without knowing that it was "Loyalty"; they fulfilled their engagements, without knowing that to do so was "Good Faith"; in their simple movements they employed the services of one another, without thinking that they were conferring or receiving any gift. Therefore their actions left no trace, and there is no record of their affairs.

(Ibid., XII. II. v. 13.)

The words "Righteousness," etc., are, as we shall learn hereafter, the technical terms of the system of morality taught by Kung-fu-tze, his predecessors and successors. There was a twinkle in the historian's eye, surely, when he wrote "there is no record left of their affairs." It is a striking fact that the normal flow of life is not generally recorded, but when some interruption occurs, some evil or good event, then history begins to be written. To the same effect writes Yung-Chu.

> The memory of things of the highest antiquity is faded. Who recollects them? Of the time of the generations of the three Emperors, something is preserved, but the rest is lost. Of the five rulers, something is still known, the rest is only guessed at. Of the events during the time of the three Emperors, some are veiled in deep obscurity, and some are clear, yet out of the hundred thousand not one is recollected. Of the things of our present life some are heard, others seen, yet not one out of ten thousand is recollected. It is impossible to calculate the number of years that have elapsed from remote antiquity to the present day. Only from Fu-hsi downwards there are more than three hundred thousand years.
> (*Yang Chu's Garden of Pleasure*, Wisdom of the East Series.)

This last sentence, even according to Chinese chronology, is exaggerated about a hundredfold! But perhaps the sense is not vitiated.

> The ancients knew that all creatures enter but for a short while into life, and must suddenly depart in death. Therefore they gave way to their impulses and did not check their natural propensities. They denied themselves nothing that could give pleasure to their bodies; consequently, as they were not seeking fame, but were following their own nature, they went smoothly on, never at variance with their inclinations. They did not seek for posthumous fame. They neither did anything criminal, and of glory and fame, rank and position, as well as of the span of their life, they took no heed.
> (*Yang Chu's Garden of Pleasure*.)

THE AGE OF PERFECT VIRTUE

The relations between animals and men are beautifully depicted in a number of passages.

In the earliest ages, the animals dwelt and moved about in company with man. It was not until the age of emperors and kings that they began to be afraid, and broke away into scattered bands. And now, in this final period, they habitually hide and keep out of man's way so as to avoid injury at his hands. Yet at the present day, the Chieh-shih people in the Far East can in many cases interpret the language of the six domestic animals, although they have probably but an imperfect understanding of it.

In remote antiquity, there were men of divine enlightenment who were perfectly acquainted with the feelings and habits of all living things, and thoroughly understood the languages of the various species. The latter assembled at their bidding, and received the instruction imparted to them, exactly like human beings. . . . These sages declared that, in mind and understanding, there was no wide gulf between any of the living species endowed with blood and breath. And, therefore, knowing that this was so, they neglected or passed over none that came to them for instruction.
(LIEH-TZE, II, Wisdom of the East Series.)

And, moreover, I have heard that anciently birds and beasts, were numerous, and men were few, so that the men lived in nests in order to avoid the animals. In the day-time they gathered acorns and chestnuts, and in the night they roosted on the trees; and on account of this they are called "the people of the Nest-builder." Anciently the people did not know the use of clothes. In summer they collected great stores of faggots, and in winter kept themselves warm by means of them; and on account of this they are called the people who knew how to take care of their lives. In the age of Shan-Wang, the people lay down in simple innocence, and rose up in quiet security. They knew their mothers, but did not know their fathers. They dwelt along with the elks and deer. They ploughed and ate ; they wove and made clothes ; they had no idea of injuring one another—this was the grand time of Perfect virtue.

(CHWANG-TZE, XXIX. III. vii. 1.)

The above reference to the custom of matriarchy, or rule of the mother, is interesting, and suggests a very ancient practice which even in the time of the legendary Shan-nang had not passed away ; the practice of polyandry would apparently have co-existed with matriarchy.

The True men of old could not be fully described by the wisest, nor be led into excess by the most beautiful, nor be forced by the most violent robber. Neither Fu-hsi nor Hwang-Ti could compel them to be their friends. Death and life are indeed great considerations, but they could make no change in their true self ; and how much less could rank and emolument do so ? Being such, their spirits might pass over the Thai mountain and find it no obstacle to them ; they might enter the greatest gulfs, and not be wet by them ; they might occupy the lowest and smallest positions without being distressed by them. Theirs was the fulness of heaven and earth ; the more they gave to others, the more they had.

(*Ibid.*, XXI. II. xiv.)

3. HOW THE GOLDEN AGE WAS LOST

The Chinese historians are precise in their information as to how the age of perfect virtue passed away. The declension from primitive simplicity was accomplished gradually, and was hastened by the attempt to set up the

THE AGE OF PERFECT VIRTUE

rule of one man over many. Government, in fact, even though beneficent, had in it the seeds of social decay. The four ages are described by Lao-tze in words that are brief and significant.

> In the highest antiquity, the people did not know that there were any rulers. In the next age they loved them and praised them. In the next they feared them; in the next they despised them. Thus it was that when in the rulers faith in the Tao was deficient, a want of faith in them ensued in the people.
> (*Tao Teh King*, XVII. S.B.E.)

This dictum seems to place the initial responsibility on the shoulders of the Three Emperors, who secured love and praise from the people of their day, and thus detached them from the perfect assimilation to the Universal Order which belonged to the earlier time.

> When the Great Tao ceased to be observed, "benevolence" and "righteousness" came into vogue. Then appeared wisdom and shrewdness, and there ensued great hypocrisy. When harmony no longer prevailed throughout the six kinships, "filial sons" found their manifestation; when the states and clans fell into disorder, "loyal ministers" appeared.
> (*Ibid.*, XVIII.)

Lao-tze regarded "benevolence," "righteousness," "filial affection" and "loyalty" as specific virtues, which were called into being simultaneously with their opposite vices. He wanted to do away with both virtue and vice, and revert to the natural harmony with the Tao, i.e., the Universal Order. To rulers who want to stamp out evil by the hand of authority he says confidentially:

> If we could renounce our "sageness" and discard our "wisdom," it would be better for the people a hundredfold. If we could renounce our "benevolence"

and discard our "righteousness," the people would again become naturally filial and kindly. If we could renounce our artful contrivances and discard our scheming for gain, there would be no thieves nor robbers.
(*Ibid.*, XIX.)

These are thoughts that cannot be lightly or easily refuted. There is tremendous power in the words of the old philosopher, whose critique might well be levelled at the forceful moralists of the present world, who, with sword and gun, airship and submarine, have lately attempted to enforce righteousness and peace with the most futile exhibition of energy the world has ever known. Lao-Tze's brilliant disciple, Chwang-tze, describes an interview which his master granted to Kung-fu-tze, who was much his junior.

Lao Tan said, "Come a little more forward, my son, and I will tell you how the Three Hwangs and the Five Ti's ruled the world.

"Hwang-Ti ruled it, so as to make the minds of the people all conform to the One simplicity. If the parents of one of them died, and he did not wail, no one blamed him.

"Yao ruled it so as to cause the hearts of the people to cherish relative affection. If any, however, made the observances on the death of other members of their kindred less than those for their parents, no one blamed them.

"Shun ruled it, so as to produce a feeling of rivalry in the minds of the people. Their wives gave birth to their children in the tenth month of their pregnancy, but those children could speak at five months, and before they were three years old, they began to call people by their surnames and names. Then it was that men began to die prematurely.

"Yü ruled it, so as to cause the minds of the people to become changed. Men's minds became scheming,

THE AGE OF PERFECT VIRTUE

and they used their weapons as if they might legitimately do so, saying that they were 'killing thieves' and not killing other men. The people formed themselves into different combinations;—so it was throughout the kingdom. Everywhere there was great consternation, and then arose the Literati. I tell you that the 'rule' of the Three Kings and Five Ti's may be called by that name, but nothing can be greater than the disorder which it produced. The 'wisdom' of the Three Kings was opposed to the brightness of the sun and the moon above, contrary to the exquisite purity of the hills and streams below, and subversive of the beneficent gifts of the four seasons between. Their 'wisdom' has been more fatal than the sting of a scorpion or the bite of a dangerous beast. Unable to rest in the true attributes of their nature and constitution, they still regarded themselves as sages :— was it not a thing to be ashamed of? But they were shameless."

(CHWANG-TZE, XIV. II. vii. 7.)

The above passage concludes by the words "Kung-fu-tze stood quite disconcerted and ill at ease." Well might he do so while the old dragon poured subtle scorn on his own system and its typical representatives.

Chwang-tze on his own authority amplifies the story of the declension from the age of perfect virtue, pointing again at the ancient Emperors, who were, by the Literati, acclaimed as patterns of wisdom.

The men of old, while the primitive condition was yet undeveloped, shared the placid tranquility which belonged to the whole world. At that time the Yin and Yang [1] were harmonious and still; their

[1] The two primal elements of the world, opposites and complementaries.

resting and movement proceeded without any disturbance ; the four seasons had their definite times ; not a single thing received any injury, and no living being came to a premature end. Men might be possessed of the faculty of knowledge, but they had no occasion for its use. This was what is called the state of Perfect Unity. At this time there was no volitional action on the part of any one, but a constant manifestation of spontaneity.

This condition of excellence deteriorated and decayed, till Sui-zan and Fu-hsi arose and commenced their administration of the world ; on which came a compliance with their methods, but the state of unity was lost. The condition going on to deteriorate and decay, Shan-nang and Hwang-ti arose, and took the administration of the world, on which the people rested in their methods, but did not themselves comply with them. Still the deterioration and decay continued till the lords of T'ang and Yü began to administer the world. These introduced the method of governing by transformation, resorting to the stream instead of to the spring, thus vitiating the purity and destroying the simplicity of the nature. They left the Tao and substituted the " Good " for it, and pursued the course of Haphazard Virtue. After this they forsook their nature and followed the promptings of their minds. One mind and another assimilated their knowledge, but were unable to give rest to the world. Then they added to this knowledge external and elegant forms, and went on to make these more and more numerous. The forms extinguished the primal simplicity, till the mind was drowned by their multiplicity. After this the people began to be perplexed and disordered, and had no way by which they might return to their true nature, and bring back their original condition.

(CHWANG-TZE, XVI. II. ix. 2.)

THE AGE OF PERFECT VIRTUE

A general summary of the theory and history of the most ancient times down to his own "present day" is given by the composer of a most interesting document now lying at the Temple of Lao-tze; it has some new features, in that "the age of perfect virtue" is connected with certain cosmic processes of creation, in the manner of the later thinkers:

After the Primal Ether commenced its action, the earliest period of time began to be unfolded. The curtain of the sky was displayed, and the sun and moon were suspended in it; the four-cornered earth was established, and the mountains and streams found their places in it. Then the subtle influences of the Ether operated like the heaving of the breath, now subsiding and again expanding; the work of production went on in its seasons above and below; all things were formed as from materials, and were matured and maintained. There were the multitudes of the people; there were their rulers and superiors.

As to the august sovereigns of the highest antiquity, living as in nests on trees in summer, and in caves in winter, silently and spirit-like they exercised their wisdom. Dwelling like quails, and drinking the rain and dew like newly-hatched birds, they had their great ceremonies like the great terms of heaven and earth, not requiring to be regulated by the dishes and stands; and also their great music corresponding to the common harmonies of heaven and earth, not needing the guidance of bells and drums.

By and by there came the loss of the Tao, when its "Characteristics" took its place. They in their turn were lost, and then came "Benevolence." Under the Sovereigns and Kings that followed, now more slowly and anon more rapidly, the manners of the people, from being good and simple, became bad

and mean. Thereupon came the Literati and the moralists with their confused contentions ; names and rules were everywhere diffused. Yet the 300 rules of ceremony could not control men's natures ; the 3,000 rules of punishment were not sufficient to put a stop to their treacherous villainies. But he who knows how to cleanse the current of a stream begins by clearing out its source and he who would straighten the end of a process must commence with making its beginning correct. Is not the Great Tao the Grand Source and the Grand Origin of all things ?
(*The Stone Tablet in the Temple of Lao-tze.*)

As may perhaps be expected, in spite of the efforts of the "sagely men" to civilize the men of perfect virtue, the race had not entirely disappeared in the days of Chwang-tze (300 B.C.). He says :

In the southern state of Yüeh, there is a district called "the State of Established Virtue." The people are ignorant and simple. Their object is to minimise the thought of self and make their desires few ; they labour, but do not lay up their gains ; they give, but do not seek for any return ; they do not know what "righteousness" is required of them in any particular case, nor by what ceremonies their performances should be signalised ; acting in a wild and eccentric way as if they were mad, they yet keep to the grand rules of conduct. Their birth is an occasion for joy ; their death is followed by the rites of burial.
(CHWANG-TZE, XX. II. xiii. 2.)

Another writer makes the land of perfect virtue to be a place full of mystery and magic, a place which only the soul may reach in dreams. It was the Emperor Hwang-ti who had the good fortune so to reach it, and he learned the obvious moral :

THE AGE OF PERFECT VIRTUE

The Yellow Emperor then fell asleep in the daytime, and dreamed that he made a journey to the kingdom of Hua-hsu, situated I know not how many tens of thousands of miles distant from the Ch'i State. It was beyond the reach of ship or vehicle or any mortal foot. Only the soul could travel so far. This kingdom was without head or ruler; it simply went on of itself. Its people were without desires or cravings; they simply followed their natural instincts. They felt neither joy in life nor abhorrence of death; thus they came to no untimely end. They felt neither attachment to self nor indifference to others; thus they were exempt from love and hatred alike. They knew neither aversion from one course nor inclination to another; hence profit and loss existed not among them. All were equally untouched by the emotions of love and sympathy, of jealousy and fear. Water had no power to drown them, nor fire to burn; cuts and blows caused them neither injury nor pain; scratching or tickling could not make them itch. They bestrode the air as though treading on solid earth; they were cradled in space as though resting on a bed. Clouds and mist obstructed not their vision, thunderpeals could not stun their ears, physical beauty disturbed not their hearts, mountains and valleys hindered not their steps. They moved about like gods.

(LIEH-TZE, Bk. II.)

4. THE POLEMICAL PURPOSE OF THE LEGENDS

Chwang-tze at last seems to tell us that the man of perfect virtue is that *rara avis* who, belonging to no time or place, constitutes *a promise* of what mankind shall be.

The man of perfect virtue cannot be burnt by fire, nor drowned in water, nor hurt by frost or sun, nor torn by wild bird or beast. Not that he makes light of these; but that he discriminates between safety and danger. Happy under prosperous and adverse circumstances alike, cautious as to what he discards and what he accepts;—nothing can harm him. Therefore it has been said that the natural abides within, the artificial without. Virtue abides in the natural. Knowledge of the action of the natural and of the artificial has its root in the natural, its development in virtue. And thus, whether in motion or at rest, whether in expansion or in contraction, there is always a reversion to the essential and to the ultimate.

(Dr. Giles' *Chuang-tzu*, XVII.)

The man of perfect virtue, has in repose no thoughts, in action no anxiety. He recognises no right, nor wrong, nor good, nor bad. Within the Four Seas, when all profit—that is his pleasure; when all share—that is his repose. Men cling to him as children who have lost their mothers; they rally round him as wayfarers who have missed their road. He has wealth and to spare, but he knows not whence it comes. He has food and drink more than sufficient, but knows not who provides it. Such is a man of virtue.

The divine man rides upon the glory of the sky where his form can no longer be discerned. This is called absorption into light. He fulfils his destiny. He acts in accordance with his nature. He is one with God and man. For him all affairs cease to exist, and all things revert to their original state. This is called envelopment in darkness.

(*Ibid.*, XII.)

In closing our series of extracts from the ancient writings of the Chinese we have to make up our minds as to the ultimate value of the thoughts contained in them. They are the product of a philosophy which has appeared, not

THE AGE OF PERFECT VIRTUE

only in China, but in different guise, in other lands. We may well turn sharply upon the smiling celestial and ask him point-blank whether his Age of Perfect Virtue is really in the past, the present, or the remote future. Is it only the soul that can travel thus far in dreams? Does he seriously expect us to believe his fables and follow his advice? Are ours the days and are we the men to begin life all over again, and can we be sure, if we let go what we hold, that we shall find a richer treasure in our hands?

III : *Chinese Egoism*

1. YANG-CHU'S RELATION TO TAOISM

THE earliest Chinese records, preserved in the *Shu-king*, represent a patriarchal system of government under the beneficent rule of Shun, Yao, Yü, and their successors (B.C. 2300). In the sixth century B.C., Lao-tze and Kung-fu-tze (Confucius) are found expounding divergent ethical systems. That of the older age may be aptly called, "The Chinese Vedānta." Since everything is One, there is no specific distinction between good and evil. This "identity of opposites," taught in the *Tao-teh-king* was carried later to extreme degrees. Hence the Taoist fathers did not teach their disciples to do good and avoid evil, for they recognized neither good nor evil. In their eyes man has but one great duty, that is, to unite himself to Tao, the Principle, of which he is the temporary end ; to desire what the Tao desires, to do what the Tao does. (Egoism is thus impossible to him.) Since the Tao determines the course of all beings, it is man's duty not to interfere with anything, but to let the universe go on its way. For him nothing can happen wrongly, if it be the work of the Tao.

It is otherwise with the ethic of Kung-fu-tze, which is essentially an interference. He invites men to follow *teh*, or volitional morality ; he codifies it by thousands of rules and regulations, which are practically so many inroads upon free action, or what is the same thing, upon Tao. True, he strives to maintain an equilibrium between egoism and altruism by his "Doctrine of the Mean" ; and as contrasted with Taoism, his teaching is practical common-sense untrammelled by metaphysics.

CHINESE EGOISM

Yang-chu, of whom I have now to speak, is undoubtedy connected with Lao-tze by the "Back-to-Nature" thought, but he simply drops the Tao out of his system, and all his metaphysics are compressed into a sentence. He deftly substitutes "Man's impulses," for the Tao, and erects a thoroughgoing system of egoism upon that basis. Who, on the Taoist hypothesis, can deny him the right to do so? One of the proofs that his system is linked to Taoism, is the fact that the fragments of his discourses are preserved with the collected writings of Lieh-tze, as if they were the sayings of a Taoist sage, and they close with a dictum of Lao-tse himself, as a benediction.

The sources for my exposition of Yang-chu are : (1) the above-named work of his own ; (2) the criticisms of Meng-tze, the Confucian ; (3) the criticisms of Chwang-tze, the Taoist.[1] But before referring to them it will be necessary to take account of that extreme form of altruistic philosophy, against which Yang-chu seems to have protested ; he mentions it by name. The relation, both in time and character, of the rival teachers of China may be formally presented by the following table :—

Period.	Extreme Altruism.	Rationalistic Dualism.	Mystical Monism.	Extreme Egoism.
530 B.C.	—	—	Lao-tze	—
500	—	Kung-fu-tze	—	—
400	Mo-tze	—	Lieh-tze	—
325	—	Meng-tze	—	Yang-chu
300	—	—	Chwang-tze	—
265	—	Hsün-tze	—	—

I am inclined to regard Mo-tze's as an off-shoot from Confucian philosophy, in spite of the fact that the

[1] See (1) Dr. Forke's *Yang-chu's Garden of Pleasure* (Wisdom of the East Series), (2) Dr. Legge's *Chinese Classics*, and (3) *S. B. E.*, vols. 39 and 40. I have sometimes preferred Dr. Legge's translation to Dr. Forke's.

Taoists, out of respect for him, called him an "imperfect Taoist." Yang-chu may be regarded, as already explained, as an offshoot from Taoism and a critical revulsion from Mo-tze, whose famous dictum is a summary of his ethics: "The principle of making distinction between man and man is wrong; the principle of universal love is right." Yang appears implicitly to say the reverse: "The principle of universal love is wrong, that of self-love is right, because men are by nature different." I turn now to the exposition of his philosophy.

2. METAPHYSICS AND ETHICS

Yang's metaphysical principle is briefly stated, and to it is conjoined, as it should be, his leading ethical principle:

> The people of antiquity knew both the shortness of life and how suddenly and completely it might be closed by death, and therefore they obeyed the movements of their hearts, refusing not what it was natural for them to like, nor seeking to avoid any pleasure that occurred to them . . . they enjoyed themselves according to nature; they did not resist the common tendency of all things to self-enjoyment.
> (Chapter III.)

> Being once born, take your life as it comes, and endure it, and seeking to enjoy yourself as you desire, so await the approach of death. When you are about to die, treat the thing with indifference and endure it; and seeking to accomplish your departure so abandon yourself to annihilation. Both death and life should be treated with indifference; they should both be endured —why trouble oneself about earliness or lateness in connection with them?
> (XI.)

Life, however, is to be cherished—it suffices to give it

its free course, neither checking nor obstructing it. The eye, the ear, the nose, the mouth, the body, the mind are to be allowed to have "what they like," without obstruction or morbid vexation. Thus life is to be cherished on beauty, music, perfumes, fine food, bodily comfort and mental peace —and after death, no matter! Yang-chu is very careful to deduce his ethic from the nature of man ; he is not satisfied with his own or other sages' authoritative dicta, and his estimate of the function of intelligence is singularly Bergsonian.

> Of all creatures man is the most skilful. His nails and teeth do not suffice to procure his maintenance and shelter. His skin and sinews do not defend him ; by running he cannot escape from harm, and he has neither hair nor feathers to protect him from cold and heat. He is thus compelled to use things to nourish his nature, to rely on his intelligence and not to put confidence in brute force. Therefore intelligence is appreciated because it preserves us, and brute force is despised because it encroaches on things.
>
> (XVI.)

The final sentence seems to place Yang-chu in close harmony with the Taoists, who decried the use of force in accordance with their doctrine of *wu wei*, or non-striving. It strikes one as rather strange on the lips of an egoist.

3. LIFE ACCORDING TO IMPULSE

So far the metaphysical and ethical principles of our philosopher have led to nothing startling, but we are not to be left in doubt as to their possible developments in the family, society and politics. Yang-chu's method of enforcing his views is biographical ; he gives short accounts of certain Chinese worthies, so far as they illustrate the way in which their lives have been lived " according to Nature," or otherwise. In the examples I shall now quote, the moral in each case is obvious.

A famous minister of Cheng (about 550 B.C.) had an elder and a younger brother, who were addicted respectively to feasting and gallantry. The one was always so under the influence of wine that he neglected all the traditional duties and equally suffered no remorse or fear of any kind. The other surrounded himself with a harem filled with damsels of exquisite beauty. He likewise neglected all friends and family duties. The minister sought advice as to how he should deal with his brothers and was told : " Administer exhortations based on the importance of Life and Nature or admonitions regarding the sublimity of Righteousness and Propriety." He did so by saying to them : " That in which man is superior to beasts and birds are his mental faculties. Through them he gets righteousness and propriety, and so glory and rank fall to his share. You are only moved by what excites your sense, and indulge only in licentious desires, endangering your lives and natures."[1] His brothers Chow and Mu replied : " Long ago we knew it, and made our choice, nor had we to wait for your instruction to enlighten us. You value proper conduct and righteousness in order to excel before others, and you do violence to your feelings and nature in striving for glory. Our only fear is lest wishing to gaze our fill at all the beauties of this one life, we should be unable to drink what our palate delights in, or to revel with pretty women. . . . Your system of regulation by external things will do temporally for a single kingdom, but it is not in harmony with the human heart, while our system of regulating by internal things can be extended to the whole universe, and there would be no more princes and ministers. We always desired to propagate this doctrine of ours, and now you would

[1] This address represents generally the Confucian ethic.

CHINESE EGOISM

teach us yours." The minister went back to the person who had advised him and reported the interview, and this was their conclusion : "*We are living together with real men without knowing it. Who calls us wise?*"

No one can deny that Chow and Mu, the happy voluptuaries, were following the ethic of nature as elucidated by Yang-chu. Tuan-mu-shu, of Wei, carries the matter a stage further in extravagance, but it is hard to detect the inconsistency, once we grant the principle.

> He had a patrimony of ten thousand gold pieces. Indifferent to the chances of life, he followed his inclinations. What the heart delights in he would do and delight in : with his halls and pavilions, verandahs, gardens, parks, ponds, wine and food, carriages, dresses, women, and attendants. . . . Whenever his heart desired something, or his ear wished to hear something, his eye to see, or his mouth to taste, he would procure it at all costs. . . . When Tuan reached the age of sixty his mind and body began to decay, he gave up all his household and treasures. Within a year he had disposed of his fortune . . . and when he died there was not even money to pay for his funeral.
>
> (*Yang Chu's Garden of Pleasure*, X.)

Here, again, the conclusion is a bold one. The Mohist declares : "Tuan was a fool, who brought disgrace on his ancestors," but Yang's decision is : "Tuan was a wise man ; his virtue was much superior to that of his ancestors. The common-sense people were shocked at his conduct, but it was in accord with the right doctrine. They surely had not a heart like his!"

4. ALTRUISM CONTRARY TO NATURE

It is now possible to see the direction in which the quietist doctrine of the Taoists is being extended by Yang-chu ;

but he goes still farther, and that is, to the absolute denial of the altruistic motive. He will have none of it at any cost :

> Po-cheng would not part with a hair of his body for the benefit of others. . . .
>
> If the ancients could have rendered service to the world by injuring a single hair, they would not have done it. As nobody would damage even a hair, and nobody would do a favour to the world, the world was in a perfect state. (*Ibid.*, XII.)

Yang seems to be anxious to nip altruism in the bud. He sees that if he gives the altruist an inch, he will take an ell. So he explains :

> A hair may be multiplied till it becomes as important as a limb. A single hair is one of the ten thousand portions of the body—why should you make light of it ?

Ch'in-tze replied :—

> I cannot answer you. If I could refer your words to Lao-tze or Kwan-Yin, they would say that *you* were right ; but if I were to refer my words to the Great Emperor Yü, or to Mo-tze, they would say that *I* was right.
>
> (*Ibid.*, XII.)

We are told that the sage on that famous occasion escaped the dilemma by turning round and entering into conversation upon another subject.[1]

---

[1] If those scholars are right who trace Chinese Taoism to an Indian Vedāntic source, i.e., to the Upanishads, then the ethic of non-interference with Nature in the hands of the Taoists, as exemplified in this story, corresponds to *ahinsa*, " non-injury " of the Indian ascetics. The philosophical basis appears to be the same ; namely, the work of Tao or of Brahman must not be interfered with. It is strange to find that with the later Jains and Buddhists *ahinsa* rests upon compassion, but with Yang-chu upon self-interested egoism.

CHINESE EGOISM

5. REALITY *versus* REPUTATION

In passing to the next topic, I will recall a phrase, already quoted, that is invested with deep significance. The happy voluptuaries are called " real men." The well-known Chinese ideal, so emphasized by Kung-fu-tze, of remembering, revering and worshipping the ancestors both for their own sakes and for that of the worshipper, was totally rejected by Yang-chu. Having affirmed annihilation, he was bound to make a clean sweep of Heaven and its myriads of spiritual inhabitants. The words " fame," " glory," and " reputation " represent to the Confucian all that wealth of good that comes to the departed ancestor from the hands of his descendants. To Yang-chu it is all illusion, worse than nothing. Its true antithesis is " reality," the one present life, in all its fulness of sensuous pleasure. Reality *versus* Reputation is therefore a constant and quite intelligible theme with our philosopher. He says :

> The ignorant, while seeking to maintain *fame*, sacrifice *reality* ; they will have to learn that nothing can rescue them from danger and death, and know the difference between ease and comfort and sorrow and grief.
>
> (*Ibid.*, I.)

Any one acquainted with Chinese history knows that the names Shun, Yü, Chow-kung, and Kung-fu-tze stand for men universally respected and revered. The first three are noted for their wise and energetic administration in patriarchal days, while the fourth is China's outstanding sage. Hear what Yang-chu thinks of these great heroes :

> The world agrees in considering Shun, Yü, Chow-kung, and Kung-fu-tze to have been the most admirable of men and in considering Ch'ieh and Chow to have been the most wicked.

Then follows a detailed account of the excessive labours, privations, and sacrifices which these great men undertook for the sake of their countrymen. If they had been Hebrew kings, their historian would have told us, that "they did that which was good in the sight of the Lord." Yang measures them by another criterion.

Of Shun : Of all mortals, never was one whose life was so worn out and empoisoned as his. Sorrowfully he came to his death.

Of Yü : Sorrowfully he came to his death. Of all mortals never was one whose life was so saddened and embittered as his.

Of Chow-kung : Sorrowfully he came to his death. Of all mortals never was one whose life was so full of hazards and terrors as his.

Of Kung-fu-tze : Sorrowfully he came to his death. Of all mortals never was one whose life was so agitated and hurried as his.

Those four sages, during their life, had not a single day's joy. Since their death they have had a reputation that will last through myriads of ages. But that reputation is what no one who cares for what is *real* would choose. Celebrate them—they do not know it. Reward them—they do not know it.

(*Ibid.*, XIII.)

The reader will now be prepared to hear that the *real* is what the two villains, Ch'ieh and Chow, enjoyed.

Ch'ieh came into the accumulated wealth of many generations ; to him belonged the honour of the imperial seat ; his wisdom was enough to enable him to set at defiance all below ; his power was enough to shake the empire. He indulged the pleasures to which his eyes and ears prompted him ; he carried out whatever it came into his thoughts to do. He was

CHINESE EGOISM

gay and merry till death. Of all mortals never was one whose life was so luxurious and dissipated as his. It was the same with Chow; his will was everywhere obeyed; he indulged his feelings in all his palaces; he never made himself bitter by the thought of propriety and righteousness. Brightly he came to his destruction.

These two villains, during their life, had the joy of gratifying their desires. Since their death, they have had the evil reputation of folly and tyranny. Yet the *reality* of enjoyment is what no infamy can take away from them. Reproach them—they do not know it!

To the four sages all admiration is given; yet were their lives bitter to the end, and their common lot was death. To the two villains all condemnation was given; yet their lives were pleasant to the last, and their common lot was likewise death.

(*Ibid.*, XIII.)

If anybody cares for one hour's blame or praise, so much that by torturing his spirit and body he struggles for a name lasting some hundred years after his death, can the halo of glory revive his dried bones, or give him back the joy of living?

(*Ibid.*, XV.)

6. YANG'S PSYCHOLOGY

Thus does Yang-chu give the death-blow to "reputation" and all that it involves. He appears, too, to refute the Confucian doctrine that all men are "naturally good" and the Mohist belief that "the principle of making distinctions between man and man is wrong." Yang's psychology is based on the fact that men are by nature different and cannot be made alike. He says:

Wherein people differ is the matter of life; wherein

they agree is death. While they are alive, we have the distinctions of intelligence and stupidity, honourableness and meanness ; . . . yet intelligence and meanness, stupidity and honourableness are not in one's power ; neither is that condition of putridity, decay and utter disappearance—death. A man's life is not in his own hands ; nor is his death ; his intelligence is not his own, nor his stupidity—all are born to die . . . the virtuous and the sage die ; the ruffian and the fool also die. Alive they were Yao and Shun, Ch'ieh and Chow, dead they were so much rotten bone. While alive therefore let us hasten to make the best of life ; what leisure have we to be thinking of anything after death ?

(*Ibid.*, IV.)

Yang's system of psychology notes not only the differences inherent in man, regarding them as real, but admits of changes in individual men. " One cannot always be satisfied with these pleasures," he says ; " one cannot always be toying with beauty and listening to music " (III.). Quite so ; the distractions and business of life, besides one's varying moods, will constantly invade the territory of pleasure, and reduce, as Yang estimates it, a life of a hundred years' duration down to no more than ten years of pure pleasure —" but I reckon that not even in them will be found an hour of smiling self-abandonment, without the shadow of solicitude." This dictum seems to take the edge off the rollicking life of the Happy Voluptuaries, Tuan the Joyous, and the two villains, Ch'ieh and Chow. Surely *they* got more than an hour's smiling self-abandonment !

The relativity of pleasure, a Taoist tenet, is accepted by Yang, and makes possible a life in which some men are enjoying themselves in the manner of Tuan, and others in quite a simple way. By a fortunate provision of Nature there could not be a world full of Chows and Ch'iehs ! .

CHINESE EGOISM

There was once an old farmer of Sung, who never wore anything else than coarse, hempen clothes; even for the winter he had no others. In spring, when cultivating the land, he warmed himself in the sunshine. He did not know there were such things as large mansions and winter apartments, brocade and silk, furs of fox and badger in the world. Turning one day to his wife, he said: "People do not know how pleasant it is to have warm sunshine on the back. I shall communicate this to our prince, and I am sure to get a rich present."

(*Ibid.*, XVIII.)

7. REGULATION BY INTERNALS

Readers of Yang-chu must take as much notice of this humble farmer and his way of getting pleasure as of the Happy Voluptuaries. They will perceive that the criterion of value is not an arbitrary one. It lies in the individual psychology. *Whatever gives pleasure*—though not the same pleasure to each person, or pleasure to the same person at all times—*is the key to life*. I believe this is the meaning of a phrase already quoted from Chapter IX. and I shall reconsider it here in company with a passage that is still more explicit. Yang-chu says that there are four things which do not allow men to rest: long life, reputation, riches, and rank; they induce in their possessors fear of four kinds. The men of this type *regulate their lives by externals*, that is, by the exigencies of wealth, rank and fame; they live by laws external to their own nature. They are not self-directed. On the other hand, there is another kind of man:

Of this sort of man it may be truthfully said that they live in accordance with their nature. In the whole world they have no equal. *They regulate their life by inward things.*

(XVII.)

The old farmer of Sung, who discovered the pleasure of the warm sunshine on his back, *and* the Happy Voluptuaries, Chow and Mu, though so very different in æsthetic choice, all regulate their lives by inner and present claims, not by traditions, laws, conventional morality or Government. Yang-chu calls this " wisdom " and " virtue."

8. ECONOMICS AND GOVERNMENT

Every philosophy must have some extended implications, however personal and subjective its early operations may be ; therefore one expects to find Yang-chu relating his doctrines to the social order and to Government. There is not much under this head, but what there is is important. Yang himself had a garden of three acres and a house at Leang, in the State of Wei. In China every one seems to have had a house and lands from time immemorial. It is possible, therefore, that Yang may have regarded such material conditions as part of the order of Nature, and may not have concerned himself with economics. But he was penetrating enough to say : " If men could do without clothes and food there would be no more kings and governments," by which we must understand that he saw the dependence of the powers of civilization on the necessities dictated by Nature. We must also admit that, in the matter of property, as well as in other respects, Yang-chu's own personal preferences find their way into, nay, probably are, the basis of his philosophy.

> Poverty will not do, nor wealth either. But what will I do ? I will enjoy life and take my ease, for those who know how to enjoy life are not poor, and he who lives at ease requires no riches.
> *(Ibid., VI.)*

How can a body possessing four things, a comfortable house, fine clothes, good food and pretty women still long for anything else ? He who does so has an insatiable nature, and that is a worm that eats body and mind. (*Ibid.*, XIX.)

One does not expect from such an easy-going egoist a treatise on the economic implications of his philosophy. He contends, indeed (as the Taoists did), that the body belongs to the universe, not to man, and there is a dictum of his which, although it is a mere glimpse, points clearly in the direction of a very loose hold on material things. (The "joyous Tuan," it will be remembered, parted with every ounce of his goods before death.) Yang says:

> He who regards as common property a body appertaining to the universe, and the things of the universe which are essential to maintaining the body, is a perfect man. That is the highest degree of perfection.
> (*Ibid.*, XVI.)

On matters of Government Yang is mildly contemptuous; he expects life according to nature will sweep them away. Chow and Mu told their ministerial brother that if people would regulate their lives by internals there would be no more princes and ministers. Yang-chu said that when nobody would do the smallest injury, and nobody do the greatest good, "the world was in a perfect state." He told the King of Leang that to govern the world was as easy as to turn round the palm of the hand. His system, theoretically, seems to point to anarchism, the absence of central government altogether, and in this he is very closely allied to Laotze, who said: "The state should be governed as we cook a small fish."

9. CHINESE CRITICISM OF YANG-CHU'S PHILOSOPHY

(i.) By Meng-tze the Confucian

Our knowledge of any given philosophy is often increased by the criticism to which it is subjected; and when

I remark that the fragments of Yang-chu can be read through in half an hour, all possible additional information from other sources is desirable. The brevity of the discourses of Yang recorded by his disciple, Meng-sun-Yang, is no indication of slightness or lack of influence in the teacher himself. On the contrary, Yang seems to have raised quite a storm in philosophical circles in China during the fourth and third centuries B.C. Meng-tze expressly declares his own mission to be to " drive away " the doctrines of Mo-tze and Yang-chu. Having been accused of a fondness for disputing, that sage recounts the gradual decline from social order to confusion. Coming to his own day, he says:

> Once more sage kings do not arise and princes of the States give the reins to their lusts. The words of Yang-chu and Mo-tze fill the kingdom. If you listen to people you will find that if they are not adherents of Yang, they are those of Mo. Yang's principle is " Each one for himself," which leaves no place for duty to the ruler. Mo's principle is " to love all equally," which leaves no place for special affection due to a father. . . . If the principles of Yang and Mo are not stopped and the principles of Kung-fu-tze are not set forth, then those perverse speakings will delude the peoples, and stop up the path of benevolence and righteousness; the beasts will be led on to devour men and men will devour one another.
>
> I am alarmed by these things, and address myself to the defence of the principles of former sages. I oppose Yang and Mo, and drive away their licentious expressions, so that perverse speakers may not be able to show themselves.
>
> (Legge, *The Works of Meng-tze*, III. II. ix. 9–10.)

These father-deniers and king-deniers would have been smitten by the duke of Chow. I also wish to rectify men's hearts, and to put an end to those perverse speakings, to oppose their one-sided actions, and banish away their licentious expressions, and carry on the work of the sages. Do I do so because I am fond of disputing? I am constrained to do it. Whoever can by argument oppose Yang and Mo is a disciple of the sages.

(*Ibid.*, 12–14.)

It is a compliment to Yang's power that Meng-tze has to speak thus. Another passage brings us to the end of Meng's specific criticisms.

Though by plucking out one hair Yang-chu might have benefited all under heaven, he would not have done it. Mo-tze loves all equally. If by rubbing bare his body from crown to the heel, he could have benefited all under heaven, he would have done it. Tze-moh holds a medium between these, and he is nearer right. But without leaving room for *the exigency of the circumstances* it becomes like their holding to their one point. What I dislike in that holding one point is the injury it does to the way of right principle. It takes up one point and disregards a hundred others.

(*Ibid.*, VII. I. xxvi. 1–4.)

We are put in possession of the principle of Meng-tze's opposition to these extreme doctrines by a passage that elucidates the above, and has an interest of its own.

K'wan said: "It is the rule that males and females shall not allow their hands to touch in giving or receiving anything. . . . If a man's sister-in-law be drowning shall he not rescue her by the hand?" Meng said: "He who would not rescue her would be a wolf; for males and females not to allow their hands to touch is the general rule; to rescue by the hand a drowning sister-in-law is a peculiar exigency."

K'wan said: "Now, the whole kingdom is drowning and how is it that you, Master, will not rescue it?" Meng replied: "A drowning kingdom must be rescued by right principles, as a drowning sister-in-law has to be rescued by the hand. Do you, Sir, wish me to rescue the kingdom with *my hand*?"

(*Ibid.*, IV. I. 1–3.)

From these passages we may judge that Meng's philosophy sought to establish an ethic on what he called "right principles," but that these were not, in his conception, crystallized into arbitrary rules.

(ii.) BY CHWANG-TZE THE TAOIST

By the third century B.C. the rupture between Confucian orthodoxy and Taoism had become complete, and the philosophical world was witnessing a most brilliant battle of wit. Chwang-tse defends his ancient master, Lao-tze, with extraordinary power, and ridicules, refutes, and converts Kung-fu-tze again and again. *Inter alia*, he criticizes both Mo-tze and Yang-chu. He says:

If the mouths of Yang and Mo were gagged, and benevolence and righteousness thrown aside, the virtue of all men would begin to display its mysterious excellence.

(*S.B.E.* Vol. 39, p. 287.)

And now Yang and Mo begin to stretch forward from their different standpoints, each thinking that he has hit on the proper course for men. . . . What they have hit on only leads to distress—Can they have hit on the right thing? If they have, we may say that the dove in a cage has found the right thing for it!

(*Ibid.*, p. 329.)

CHINESE EGOISM

(iii.) By Hsün-tze (Seun-K'ing)

Although Yang-chu is not mentioned by name in the writings of Hsün-tze, his doctrines are. This philosopher is chiefly concerned to deny the doctrine affirmed by the orthodox Confucians that human nature is good; incidentally he sets forth what will be the consequences of a life according to impulse and the necessity of its overruling, even by the artificial control of "propriety and righteousness." But this control is not necessarily invalid on account of its being artificial. The triumph of Art over Nature is what Hsün-tze advocates.

> The nature of man is evil. There belongs to it even at his birth the love of gain, and as actions are in accordance with this, contentions and robberies grow up, and self-denial and yielding to others are not to be found; there belong to it envy and dislike, and as actions are in accordance with these, violence and injuries spring up, and self-devotedness and faith are not to be found; there belong to it the desires of the ears and the eyes, leading to love of sounds and beauty, and as actions are in accordance with these, lewdness and disorder spring up, and righteousness and propriety, with their various orderly displays, are not to be found. It thus appears that the following of man's nature and yielding obedience to its feelings will assuredly conduct to contentions and robberies, to the violation of the duties belonging to every one's lot, and the confounding of all distinctions till the issue will be in a state of savagery. . . .
>
> Now the man who is transformed by teachers and laws, gathers on himself the ornament of learning, and proceeds in the path of propriety and righteousness, is *a superior man*; and he who gives the reins to his nature and its feelings, indulges its resentments, and walks the contrary to propriety and righteous-

ness, is *a mean man*. Looking at the subject in this way we see clearly that the nature of man is evil; the good which it shows is artificial.

(Legge, *The Chinese Classics*, Vol. II.)

(iv.) Synthesis of Chinese Criticism

The Chinese criticism of Yang-chu just mentioned does not amount to much, nor does it materially add to our knowledge of the philosophy; I will, however, examine it. Meng-tze complains that Yang is an egoist—"each for himself"—and a king-denier, "the state of a beast"; that his teaching is sensuous, licentious, will delude the people, and destroy benevolence and righteousness; that it is hurtful to the conduct of business and to government. All this is true from Meng's point of view; the tradition he accepts makes obedience to elders and rulers the very essence of morality, the naïve assumption being that rulers are wise, though Meng knows quite well this is not always so. As to its sensuality and opposition to "propriety and righteousness," this is admitted by Yang himself.

Nowhere in the extant fragments of Yang does the formula "each for himself" appear. His egoism does not seem to equate with selfishness; its chief mark is the resistance to external control, and consequently, one would assume, the denial to oneself of the right of controlling others. This, with the explicit statement that rulers are not needed where life is "regulated by internals," constitutes him a king-denier.

Meng further declares that Yang's egoism is a fixed method which denies the more fluid "right principle" which he himself proposes. If this were so I should be inclined to support him; but it must be admitted that Yang's "regulation by internals," though a fixed principle, does not involve always the same kind of action, as has been seen. In practice, surely, for every one to act as his impulses lead him, does not mean that every one will act *alike*, or that one person will *always* act in the same way, though it may lead to the most extraordinary confusion, in spite of Yang's dicta to the contrary. It amounts precisely to Meng's own "right principle" of acting according to the exigencies of the moment. In a word, the man who rescues his drowning sister-in-law by the principle of Meng will be doing so because he wishes to, that is, because his impulses drive him, by the principle of "regulation by internals." The difference is mostly a matter of words so far as the formulæ are concerned.

Lieh-tze, a later Taoist, reports, but does not comment upon, several anecdotes in the life of Yang; these do but confirm the impression that this philosopher was always very close to Taoism. The moral of one story is that "the superior man is very cautious about doing good"; and of the other, that from the same indisputable phenomena of life divergent philosophies may be drawn, due to the difference in personal temperament. This is a point that has already been noted and shall receive further consideration.

Chwang merely asserts but does not prove that Yang's doctrines stand in the way of natural virtue. He has of course the Tao in mind. I see no appropriateness in his comparison of Yang to "a dove in a cage." "A parrot on the top of the cage" would better describe him!

Hsün is much more to the point. His criticism, which extends to considerable length, analyses the elements of man's nature and points to the germs of avarice, envy, antipathy and desire. His formula is: "as actions are in accordance with these," contention, robbery, violence, injury, lewdness and disorder spring up. Can Yang deny it? Nay, his very heroes exemplify it (Tuan, Chow and Mu), though possibly he himself lived decently. Hsün's next point is to prove, not that moral control is *natural*, but that it is, on the contrary, unnatural and artificial, the invention of sages, out of necessity, to save mankind from savagery. By the conquest of the natural by the artificial, man becomes the "Superior Man." Turning upon Hsün, however, and granting him his point so far, we may well ask him: How do you know that the organization of propriety and righteousness *is* artificial? May it not also proceed from profound elements in man's nature which you have not noticed? If so, Man's nature is neither wholly bad as you assert, nor wholly good as Meng asserts, but is a nature capable of yielding, as it develops, either good or bad impulses, actions, and social order. Given the alternative, the sage, by an effort of the will, chooses the one and rejects the other; he then seeks to stimulate in men the power of will to self-control, and according to his measure of success, constructs a social order appropriate to the dominant spiritual impulses he is seeking to organize. The fact that he often fails, as Yang truly said, does not vitiate the soundness of his effort. Let him try again!

IV : *The Origin of Evil*

IN relation to the subject of this chapter, and for its purposes, we may divide the history of mankind into three great evolutionary periods, in which the characteristics of moral consciousness may be respectively described as :
  (*a*) Non-recognition of good and evil ;
  (*b*) Knowledge of good and evil ;
  (*c*) Realization of good alone.

It need hardly be said that the middle period is that in which men, for the most part, now live, and that the earlier one belongs—if we consent to regard it as historical—to very remote times ; the third, of course, belongs to the future. It is true there are indications, usual in evolutionary processes, of the survival in the middle period of late types of the earliest, as well as early arrivals of types of the latest period. Indeed, most children exhibit non-recognition of good and evil, some few adults retain it, while some, even in our own day, are forerunners of the final form of consciousness which knows nothing but good. It would be a mistake, however, to suppose (*c*) to be a reversion to (*a*). It is hardly that ; on close analysis it will be found that the two forms are widely different.

Accepting, therefore, the actuality of the middle period, I will ask my readers to go back to a time in it when something like a *memory* of the former period was preserved by certain sections of humanity, and in addition to that memory, and possibly because of it, certain speculations were entered upon, which were in fact the beginning of moral philosophy. These speculations were part of primitive philosophy in general, which comprised many questions of a reflective character ; in the midst of them stands the question posed by the moral consciousness of the men of the early middle period : *How is it that evil appears in a world created by Divine power and sustained by Divine providence ?* Clearly such a question could only arise after the differentiation of good and evil had become distinct ; that is to say, after some quality common to all concrete evil things had become recognized, and abstracted from them as *Evil* itself. It was natural, therefore, that evil generally should be held to be the work of positively evil beings, or at least of beings capable of error of such a nature that its continuity led to evil at large. In other words, an origin in the *order of time* had to be found for a germinal evil, and its course in the *order of history* had to be traced, and finally some connection made between it and things currently experienced as evil.

The literature of the ancients contains various explanations of the existence of evil, which may be classified as follows :

(1) The existence of beings—demons, asuras, kwei, devils,—who, by their direct activity, caused evil to fall upon mankind, by invading and infesting the province of man. For a long time man was occupied with the practical concern of avoiding these beings, but at length he turned to consider the question :

(2) How did such beings come into existence ? Who are they ? This led to the legends accounting for evil spirits as the progeny of beings that were once good, but who, at a certain epoch, ceased to be good and set in train a series of events which led to the general distribution of evil in the world.

(3) A more advanced view, stated in a mythological manner, while still regarding evil as having its origin in time, finds its place in human psychology. A man, or some men, " sinned " and thus introduced evil into human life ; a man or some men demanded and obtained " a knowledge of good and evil " and passed from the state of

THE ORIGIN OF EVIL

innocence to that of power to choose both good and evil, and this power, by the exercise of free-will, led to the increase of evil.

(4) A similar, but less mythological view, and more strictly humanistic, is that preserved by the Chinese Taoists, who attribute all the evil of human society to the initial errors of certain individuals who so multiplied complexities, that civilization in time became a full-fledged evil. Section II has been especially devoted to this subject.

(5) More profound are those views, both primitive and late, which consider evil to belong *a priori* to the world, or to a certain part of the world, or to man. An instance of the primitive psychological evil may be given in the case of the Bagobos of the Philippine Islands, who think of an evil soul which dwells in the left part of the body. The Gnostics generally, and the Manichæans in particular, thought of evil as lying essentially in matter. It is clear that such views bring us nearer to another solution, which results from another kind of question : for we no longer ask for the *origin* of evil in time, but for its *source* and ground in the nature of things.

(6) To seek such a solution was repugnant to those who clung to the belief in a beneficent creator, but it was no trouble to those few who had dispensed with a creator, such as the Buddhists and the Sānkhyans of India. The former class, including certain Greek and Christian thinkers, invented the agency of a demi-creator, who shared the responsibility (on the creative side) with man (on the volitional side) for evil. Plato preserved a myth by which he exonerated God from all responsibility for evil by explaining it to be the negation or privation of His positive good work.

(7) Certain forms of mysticism appearing in religious philosophy of the East and West (traceable almost entirely to the East, however) get rid of evil as a reality by the introduction of the idea of illusion, *maya*, or *avidyā*, and thus do not have to explain either its *origin* in time or its *source* in

the nature of things, but merely the causes of its appearance in consciousness; their concern is with the practical question of how to transcend the consciousness of evil.

(8) There is another view, less exacting than the seventh type, more in harmony with general experience, and capable of continuous test, and this is advanced by modern philosophy and science. To begin with, it puts aside much that was formerly called evil merely because it was unpleasant. It notes that the surgeon's knife and the assassin's dagger both cause pain, and concludes that if pain is to be regarded as positive evil our search must be restricted only to the *bad*, or moral evil. It is that and that alone of which we need to find the origin or the source, and not merely for speculative but for practical ends. Modern philosophy thus finds the "origin of evil" or rather the "source of the bad" in the fundamental egoistic motive of the human will. Physical pain is generally regarded as a natural warning and protection to the organism.

Looking back from this point on the earlier solutions propounded, we observe that it is possible to translate some of the mythological-historical explanations of evil into psychological-metaphysical terms, so that, taken together, there is not a great variety of contradictory propositions, but only a few outstanding ones, of which we may now take notice.

I propose to ask my readers to collect for themselves, for the purposes of this study, all the explanations of the origin of specific or general evil of which they may have heard, and to draw from them, if possible, a unific idea. It will not be possible for me to print here more than a few.

1. THE HEBREW TRADITION

The general idea of "the fall" is expressed in several ways in the Hebrew literature, the most familiar being

THE ORIGIN OF EVIL

that in Genesis iii. It is probably the oldest recorded, and at the same time the highest in type, but it is by no means the earliest in point of development. A more primitive myth is that of Genesis vi. 1–7, which simply tells how men did evil continually after the marriage alliance between "the sons of God and the daughters of men."

VI. 1. And it came to pass, when men began to multiply on the face of the ground and daughters were born unto them, that the sons of God saw daughters of men that were fair, and they took them wives of all that they chose.

4. The giants were on the earth in these days and also after the time when the sons of God took the daughters of men, and they bare children to them. These are the mighty men, who were celebrated of old.

5. And Yahweh saw that the wickedness of man was great on the earth and that every device of the thoughts of his heart was only evil continually.

6. And Yahweh repented that he had made man upon the earth, and he was distressed in his heart.

7. And Yahweh said, "I will blot out men whom I have made from the face of the ground, since I repent that I made them." (Addis, *The Oldest Book of Hebrew History.*)

It is clear, however, that we have but part of this myth here, and for its completion we must turn to the Book of Enoch, an apocalypse commenced about 200 B.C. containing earlier traditional materials which Canon Charles believes to be fragments of a "Book of Noah." I quote the passages which describe how evil came into the world by the teaching of the fallen angels: now described as the "children of the heaven":

VI. 6. And they were in all two hundred who descended in the days of Jared on the summit of Mount Hermon.

MYSTICISM OF EAST AND WEST

VII. 2. And all the others together with them took unto themselves wives . . . and they bare great giants, whose height was three thousand ells:

3. Who consumed all the acquisitions of men. And when men could no longer sustain them,

4. The giants turned against them and devoured mankind.

5. And they began to sin against birds, and beasts, and reptiles, and fish, and to devour one another's flesh, and drink the blood.

6. Then the earth laid accusation against the lawless ones.
(Charles, *The Book of Enoch.*)

The way in which the angels, whose leaders are mentioned by name, taught specific evils is stated in an interesting manner. My readers will be glad, I am sure, to hear of the invention of military armaments!

VIII. 1. And Azazel taught men to make swords and knives, and shields, and breastplates, and made known to them the metals of the earth and the art of working them, and bracelets, and ornaments, and the use of antimony, and the beautifying of the eyelids, and all kinds of costly stones, and all colouring tinctures.

3. Semjaza taught them enchantments, and root cuttings, Armaros the resolving of enchantments, Baraqijal taught astrology, Kokabel the constellations, Ezeqeel the knowledge of the clouds, Araqiel the signs of the earth, Shamsiel the signs of the sun, and Sariel the course of the moon.

4. And as men perished, they cried, and their cry went up to heaven.
(*Ibid.*)

The moral of this story of the origin of evil is summed up in the words of judgment: "The whole earth has been corrupted through the works that were taught by Azazel: to him ascribe all sin" (x. 8). Again: "For men were

THE ORIGIN OF EVIL

created exactly like the angels, to the intent that they should continue pure and righteous, and death, which destroys everything, could not have taken hold of them ; but through this their knowledge they are perishing, and through this power death is consuming them" (lxix. 11). But in the same Book of Enoch, from the hand of a later writer, we have a practical rejection of the idea expressed in the myth of the fallen angels. It is a partial reversion to the older and truer conception contained in the myth of Adam's fall : "Sin has not been sent upon the earth, but man of himself has created it" (xcviii. 4).

We may now consider this familiar document without quoting it at length (refer to Genesis ii. 8-9, 15-17 ; Genesis iii. 1-7, 16-18).

It is almost certain that the myth of Adam's fall was already in existence when the Jehovist writer took up his pen to compose the oldest book of history. We are solely concerned, therefore, with the use that he made of it ; we recognize in his treatment a finer psychological insight than is displayed in the sister myths of his Semitic cousins the Babylonians and Assyrians. For him life is an uncertain term of penal servitude under the shadow of capital punishment. His experience makes him feel that man is under a curse, and he wants to say why this is so. He connects Adam's fall, through Cain's murder of his brother, with the progress of science, the building of Babel and the spread of civilization ; but this is not in order to explain *their* beginnings so much as to explain the beginnings of *sin* which runs through all their works. The story is not, in the hands of the old writer, so much the story of the first man, but of every man ; of the passage from primal innocence by disobedience to a knowledge and experience of good and evil. Disregarding the details of mythological machinery employed, we may say that the Jehovist writer's decision as to the origin of evil does not attribute it to the serpent, the woman, the angels, or to any primal necessity, but to the opposition of the freewill of man to the higher will of God. *This opposition is sin.* The subsequent history of mankind and of Israel illustrates these beliefs in long-drawn detail.

Before leaving the Hebrew writer, it is well to remark that, strange as it may seem, he is pessimistic, and offers his race no hope of a final victory over evil. This depressing view, never entirely lost, reached its lowest point in Roman times, and was expressed in the *Apocalypse of Esdras* in the following passages:

III. 21. For the First Adam bearing a wicked heart transgressed, and was overcome; and not he only, but all they also that are born of him.

IV. 30. For a grain of evil seed was sown in the heart of Adam from the beginning, and how much wickedness hath it brought forth unto this time and how much shall it yet bring forth until the time of threshing come.

VII. 46. But as touching them for whom my prayer was made, what shall I say? for who is there of them that be alive that hath not sinned, and who of the sons of men that hath not transgressed thy covenant?

(116) I answered then and said, This is my first and last saying, that it had been better that the earth had not given thee Adam: or else, when it had given him, to have restrained him from sinning.

VIII. 35. For in truth there is no man among them that be born, but he hath dealt wickedly; and among them that have lived there is none which hath not done amiss. (*Esdras II.*, Revised Version.)

This is surely the nadir of Jewish pessimism, for it means: *It were better not to have been*; it makes evil co-incidental with existence.

My readers will notice that the Origin of Evil in the

THE ORIGIN OF EVIL

Hebrew Tradition is explained in two ways. (1) The myths of the giants and the fallen angels exonerate *Man* from being the author of evil, and place the responsibility for it on the shoulders of beings once of a higher order. (2) The myth of Adam's fall exonerates God, and traces evil to the free-will of man being set in opposition to the will of God. Thus the first group of myths finds evil to have an *origin in time*, while the second finds it to have a *psychological source* in human nature. The first is the more primitive idea, the second the more developed, and they are both repeated *mutatis mutandis* in other cycles of thought on the subject.

2. THE INDIAN TRADITION

The Vedas, the oldest Hindu writings, contain no myth of a fall or of an *origin* of evil; this is evidence of their having been composed before the period of abstract philosophical thinking, in which the Hindus, in course of time, became so adept and which led them to endless speculations on the *nature* and *location* of evil. The earliest references to the subject that I can find are in the Brihadāranyaka and Chandogya Upanishads, and here we learn that Prajāpati was the father of two kinds of descendants, the Devas and the Asuras.[1] The Devas were the younger generation, and the Asuras the elder one; they struggled together in the earth continually, the good against the evil. A whimsical story is told of how Indra, the leader of the Devas, and Virochāna, the leader of the Asuras (Demons) went to learn from Prajāpati, who, in order to destroy the demons, taught them a doctrine that was false, saying to himself, "whoever will follow this doctrine will perish." Judging by present conditions, however, evil seems to have been communicated to mankind by an unhappy accident, before it had destroyed those whom it was designed to extirpate!

Although there is in the pre-Buddhistic writings abun-

[1] See Section VII for particulars of this myth.

dant evidence of distinct valuation of things good and evil, there is not, I think, until the Buddha's time, any philosophical theory indicating the origin and nature of evil; but when we come to his teaching we find, as we might expect, no speculative discussion and no myth, but a highly technical and penetrating psychological analysis, which results, not in a discovery of an *origin* of evil in the order of time, but a *source* of evil in man's nature, or, to be more precise, in certain aspects of his nature.

The doctrine is taught in the Buddha's " First Holy Truth about Suffering." All kinds of evil are traced to craving (*Tanhā*). We read :

> Without beginning or end is this *Samsāra* (wandering in the sea of rebirth and death). Unperceivable is the beginning of Beings buried in blindness, who, seized of *craving*, are ever and again brought to new birth, and so hasten through the endless round of re-birth.
>
> What think you, Brothers ? Which is greater, the floods of tears which, weeping and wailing, you have shed upon this long way, ever and again hastening towards new birth and new death, united to the undesired, separated from the desired ; this—or the waters of the Four Great Seas ?
>
> Long time, Brothers, have you suffered the death of a mother, a father, a son, a daughter, for long the death of brothers and sisters ; long time have you undergone the loss of your goods, long time have you been afflicted with disease. And because you have experienced all this suffering, you have verily shed more tears upon this long way—hastening from birth to death, from death to birth—more than all the waters that are held in the Four Great Seas.

(*Samyutta Nikāya*, xiv. 1, in " The Word of the Buddha.")

> There will come a time when the great world-ocean will dry up, vanish and be no more. There will come

THE ORIGIN OF EVIL

a time when the mighty earth will be devoured by fire, perish and be no more. But verily, there is no end to suffering of beings buried in blindness, who, seized by craving, are ever brought again and again to renewed birth and hasten through endless rounds of rebirths.
(*Samyutta Nikāya*, xxi. 10.)

The Buddhism of the Northern School, of Tibet and China, blending with the mythology of the countries which it penetrated, produced theories of the origin of evil which are historico-mythological reversions from the Buddha's psychological doctrine just quoted. Although the master discouraged speculation into relatively unprofitable questions, yet his followers could not resist the fascinating temptation to compose legends of the most remote ages; and we find, for instance, in the Tibetan *Dulva*, an account of the origin of evil. It is obvious that it is composed for edification in order to prepare a long historical background against which the Buddha may appear and give the appropriate corrective teaching. I will quote the salient passages of this interesting myth:

At the time when the world was destroyed, many of its inhabitants were born in the region of the *A'bhāsvara* devas, and there they had ethereal bodies, free from every impurity; their faculties were unimpaired, they were perfect in all their principal and secondary parts, of goodly appearance and of pleasing colour. Light proceeded from their persons; they moved through space and fed on joy, and they lived in this state to great ages for a long period.

In the meanwhile this great earth was mingled up with the waters and with the mighty deep. Then on the face of the great earth, of the water and of the ocean that were mingled together, there blew a wind, which solidified and concentrated the rich surface (*lit.* the cream); as when the wind, blowing over the surface of boiled milk which is cooling, solidifies and concentrates the cream, so likewise did this wind, blowing over the surface of the earth, the water and the ocean which were mixed together, solidify and coagulate it.

At that period there was neither sun nor moon in the world ; there were no stars in the world, neither was there night or day, minutes, seconds, or fractions of seconds ; there were no months, half months, no periods of time, no years : neither were there males or females ; there were only animated beings.

Then it happened that a being of an inquisitve nature tasted the rime with the tip of his finger, and thus he conceived a *liking* for it, and he commenced eating pieces of it as food.

Other beings saw this being tasting the rime, so they followed his example, and commenced eating pieces of it as food.

(Rockhill's *Life of the Buddha*, p. 1.)

That is how it began ! Then follows the long story of how, following the initial *liking*, came all the primitive psychological weaknesses of man ; his acquisitiveness, his sexual appetite, his differences, his caste distinction, his pride, his property, his houses, commerce, cities and boundaries ; and the warriors and all the necessary political institutions to keep the peace in a social world that had its origin based on *craving*. And at last, after millennial preparation, the Great Buddha Gautama was miraculously born to save men from the misery arising from their craving. I think this myth is an indication of the general character of such compositions, and warns us against interpreting them either literally or allegorically. They point to an *a priori* source of evil in character rather than to an origin in time. *Change the character, and the evil will be gone* ; that, ultimately, is their message.

THE ORIGIN OF EVIL

3. THE WESTERN TRADITION

It can hardly be said that the problem of the Origin of Evil, as a speculative one, is discussed at all in the records of the teaching of The Christ. True, there are references to specific evils—the man born blind and the fall of the tower of Siloam—but not to evil in the absolute sense.

But, as I remarked in the first part of this section, there were everywhere people who had considered the matter in this light, and amongst the Christian Gnostic sects the view was generally current that evil was inherent in matter or in the substance of the world. This led to two remarkable bi-products, one rather obvious, and the other surprising. The escape from specific evils was obtained by the escape from matter by a general disentanglement of the soul, by the adoption of a discipline usually designated "asceticism." The other result, attributed to the teachings of the Nicolaitans, was the complete and free immersion in matter, in the life of the body and its impulses, precisely *because* evil inhered to matter only, and could not touch the soul! Both these courses—extreme asceticism and reckless indulgence—were opposed by the criticism of the more philosophical Christian Fathers.

As a type of this criticism, with its new solution of the problem of evil, I quote St. Augustine, Bishop of Hippo (354–430 A.D.), who himself had been a Manichæan, that is, a follower of Mani, a Persian teacher who combined Zoroastrian and Gnostic Christian doctrines. I quote several passages from T. & T. Clark, 1872, *The Manichæan Heresy*.

> You ask me, *Whence is evil?* I ask you in return, *What is evil?* Which is the most reasonable question? Are those right who ask whence a thing is when they do not know what it is, or he who thinks it necessary to inquire first what it is, in order to avoid the gross absurdity of searching for the origin of a thing the nature of which is unknown? (*On Morals*, 2.)

In reply, several definitions of the nature of evil are attempted, the first and second of which we may pass by; the third is more interesting.

> I ask a third time, What is evil? Perhaps you will reply *Corruption*. Undeniably this is a definition of evil; for corruption implies opposition to nature and also hurt. But corruption exists not by itself, but in some substance which it corrupts; for corruption itself is not a substance. So the thing which it corrupts, is not corruption, is not evil; for what is corrupted suffers the loss of integrity and purity.
>
> (*Ibid.*, 7.)

The argument circles continually round the Manichæan idea that evil is a substance, and the Augustinian view that it is not. Augustine concludes that "Evil is not a substance, but a disagreement hostile to substance." He opposes the search for evil in the physical realm or in necessity, and he turns towards psychology to pitch upon free-will. This, then, is his decision.

> For, supposing men able to do a thing, to do which is right, while not to do it is great and heinous sin, their not doing it is their own choice. So, then, if they choose not to do it, the fault is in their will, not in necessity. *The origin of sin is in the will; therefore in the will is the origin of evil.* There is thus no reason why in your search for the origin of evil, you should fall into so great an error as that of calling a nature so rich in good things the nature of evil. The cause of this erroneous belief is your pride which you need not have unless you choose; but in your wish to defend at all hazards the error into which you have fallen, you take away the origin of evil from free-will, and place it in a fabulous "nature of evil." And thus you come at last to say, that souls became enemies

THE ORIGIN OF EVIL

to the sacred light, not from choice but from necessity. (*Reply to Faustus*, xii. 22.)

One more specimen of Western thought on the origin of evil may be taken from Plotinus, the founder of the Neo-Platonic School in Rome. He asks: "What can be the cause which has led the souls to forget God their Father? . . . The evil that has befallen them is due to a *tolma*, and to the desire of the souls to have a life of their own"

Tolma is one of the key-words of his whole system, and we must deal faithfully with it. The noun *tolma* is used by Pindar, Æschylus and Herodotus for "firm will," "bold daring," "courage in enterprise," and the verb *tolmáo* by Herodotus, Thucydides and Æschylus, for "to take on oneself," "to endure," "to hazard," "to venture on," "to have audacity to undertake anything."

We are asked to believe, then, that there was a time when all souls were denizens of Heaven and Eternity, and that there the desire came to them to gain an individualized life, and to forsake the group-spirit life which hitherto they had enjoyed.

"They began to revel in free will: they indulged in their own movement: they took the wrong path: then it was that they lost the knowledge that they sprang of that Divine Order. . . . They no longer had a true vision of the Supreme or of themselves. . . . Smitten with longing for the lower, rapt in love for it, they grew to depend upon it: so they broke away as far as they were able." (*Enneads*, V. 3, 9.)

Plotinus, like his Christian successor, St. Augustine (who was well versed in Neo-Platonic philosophy), connects evil with the exercise of the will, but removes the occasion of its exercise to a pre-earthly period and supposes that earthly evil is the hereditary consequence. The remedy is to reverse the decision of the earlier will and return to God by the path of philosophy.

4. CONCLUDING DISCUSSION

I think I have now given specimens or made references to all the types I outlined in paragraphs 1 to 6, and I have only 7 and 8 to conclude with. Readers will perceive that I have all along been trying to get away from an " origin in time " as an unsatisfactory explanation, and that I have been willing to consider that evil may have its source in nature *a priori*. But St. Augustine seems to have disposed of that explanation also, and very powerfully. He proposes to consider evil as lying in the operation of the will of man, and obviously not in all its operations, but only some of them. To put it plainly, he decides that a man is capable of originating a distinct cycle of evil by means of his personal free-will ; he is able to do a deed qualified by evil, not in virtue of the existence of any substantive reservoir of absolute evil, but to *create* it, so to speak, out of nothing.

It is well to remember that the word " evil " is fundamentally an adjective, and it is due to our having turned it into a noun that we have spent so much time in asking for its origin. We do not ask for the " origin of high " or the " origin of hot," for we recognize that the terms *high* and *hot* distinguish the qualities of certain things relatively to other things that are *low* and *cold*.

There appear to be well-defined scales of relativity by which we distinguish our experiences ; the sense of *sight* distinguishes infinite degrees from light to dark ; that of *touch* degrees of roughness and smoothness, heat and cold, etc., that of *taste* the sweet and the bitter, the *æsthetic* sense distinguishes degrees of beautiful and ugly. Our general body of *desire* makes its infinite distinctions between pleasure and pain, which, strictly speaking, should not be used as abstract nouns, but in their adjectival form as " pleasurable and painful experiences."

To what scale, then, do the words good and evil belong ? Surely to the scale of *value*. As we value a sight, a sensation, a taste or the possession of an object, we call it good in comparison with its opposite. But in doing this we may be going wrong, and falling into the pit of hedonism, which makes pleasure the criterion of value. Reflection shows us that though pleasure is always "good" on its own plane, yet it is a dangerous guide to follow for the person who experiences it; while, on the other hand, pain is always "evil" on its own plane of sensation, yet it really is a safe guide and a strong protection to the individual and the species. It is hardly possible to exaggerate the dangers into which we should fall as physical beings if we were insensitive to pain. Pain is a preserver.

This argument might be pushed still further, in regard to the more impalpable forms of pain—unhappiness, distress, despair or antipathy. All of these are symptomatic of unhealthy conditions, which would sooner or later bring our inner bodies to a dissolution, if we did not heed their warning note. We therefore conclude that pain is good, inasmuch as it stimulates us to search for its causes, and destroy them at their roots. This is surely what the Buddha meant when he said: "One thing I teach, Brothers; Suffering and the deliverance from Suffering."

But there is a scale which we have yet to inquire into —the scale of *moral value*—in which lie all the conceivable *deeds* of man, some at the highest octaves of sublimity and charm, others at the lowest octaves of malice. With what instrument are we enabled to distinguish them? The answer to this question is the long debate on the basis of morality, and I know of no more convincing answer than that of Schopenhauer, who puts his finger on the phenomenon of Compassion, which expresses the noumenon of Life-Unity. We feel with and for each other because we are really one with each other. In the valuation of deeds, then, Compassion is the touchstone which divides them into good and evil. It is no local, temporary, human code, nor even a divine law promulgated from Sinai or the Vedas. It is the voice of the Cosmos heard in the ear.

Having dismissed all those solutions to the problem of evil which find its origin in time, in matter, in nature, or in an evil entity or devil, we are left where Augustine brought us, namely, that "the origin of evil" is in the will. The formula may be extended and elucidated thus: In the human will lies the potentiality of deeds qualified or stimulated by compassion, and equally the potentiality of deeds qualified by egoism and malice. The origin of an evil deed is an evil choice, and upon that choice hangs a chain of evil consequences. For ages and ages men, under the stimulus of egoism, have been heaping up evil deeds, until they seem mountains high. But are they really so? Are these not the kind of mountains that can be removed and cast into the sea by the power of faith? This is the moral solution of the problem of evil, and those who adopt it may well be hopeful that when men contemplate the colossal mischief they have done, they will turn round and recognize themselves as the creators, moment by moment, of whatsoever evil there lies in their path. "The Kingdom of Hell is within you" is the complementary truth to the more famous dictum.

I want now, if I can, to go a step further in the direction of the mystical philosophers referred to in paragraph 7. According to certain thinkers, evil has no origin in time, no source in nature, and no potential existence in the will. Really, they say it has no existence at all, but belongs to the phenomena of illusion. Once break through that cloud, and evil things disappear forever. Such a view can only be finally valid for those who have made for themselves a demonstration of the unreality of matter and all the phenomena qualified by evil, and we do well to remember that many of the mystics upon whose revelations we wait talk in this paradoxical fashion about the "unreality of evil." Profiting by the suggestion implied by this term, I now suggest a harmony between what I have called the moral solution and this just-mentioned metaphysical solution.

THE ORIGIN OF EVIL

Surely, if according to the former (St. Augustine, to wit), *we need not do evil*, half its reality is gone already. If we were under necessity to do it the case would be hopeless, and there would be, moreover, no problem to solve.

In looking back to the beginning of this discussion, readers will observe that I there distinguished three evolutionary periods in which men express (1) the non-recognition of good and evil, (2) the knowledge of good and evil, and (3) the realization of good alone. This third position is the thing of the future. By argument we have already shown that much of what we formerly thought of as positive evil is really good ; that evil has no absolute existence, but can only be affirmed as a quality of specific deeds of men. The bravest thinkers now advise us to look upon evil as a form of error which, on penetrating scrutiny, fades away like a cloud.

There lie before us, then, two paths, not greatly divergent, which, as I suspect, will meet each other a little further on : the one is the path of moral effort, that of not adding more fuel to the fires of delusion, anger and desire ; the other is the metaphysical path of raising one's vision towards the real and only good, so much so that the search for the origin of evil gives place to the sense of the certainty of good.

V : *The Teachers in the Upanishads*

NOTHING is more interesting to the student of Indian literature than to observe the way in which the characteristic doctrines of the Upanishads gradually appear, and I propose now to sketch briefly the personages through whom the teaching was developed, the circumstances in which it was given, and the relations existing between these teachers.

In the first place, we must have before our mind's eye a map of Northern India, and a general concept of the dispersion of the Aryan people about the Upanishad period. The hymns of the preceding Rig-Veda were composed, for the most part, during the crossing of the rivers of the Panjab, when the Aryan tribes were passing slowly to the land which they called "Aryavarta," which lay beyond the Sutlej. After this period there followed a second one, which determined the character of the great civilization of the Kuru-Panchāla tribes. Meanwhile, probably passing to the north on the slopes of the mountainous country, over the heads of the Kurus, went the Rearguard which afterwards became the Vanguard of Aryan civilization, and founded the eastern kingdoms of the Videhas and the Kosālas, both on the north of the Ganges. An important group called the Kāsis settled round Benares.

We must picture the great war described in the Mahabharata as having ended, and a period of settled peace established over very wide areas, so far apart as to make possible independent religious, philosophical and political developments.

A rough division of the people and the country into two parts, made by the upper waters of the Jumna, will be useful

TEACHERS IN THE UPANISHADS

at this point, for, to the west lay the civilization entirely dominated by the sacrificial systems of the Priests of the Kuru-Panchālas, and to the east were independent nations that had only a small knowledge of these religious systems. It may be said that the contact between these two groups produced the early Upanishads, and besides, there is evidence of a contact, amounting to conflict, between the priestly caste, on the one hand, and the ruling caste on the other.

1. ROYAL PHILOSOPHERS

First, there is Ajātasatru of Kāsi, who is referred to in the *Brihadāranyaka Upanishad* (2. 11). There we find him discussing with "the proud Gārgya Bālāki, a man of great learning." And what is the discussion about? "Shall I tell you Brahman?" is the question which the priest puts to the King, and from this and similar questions we may conclude that there was already a considerable discussion, with no very fixed opinions as to what was meant by "Brahman." The King says that for such information he is willing to give a thousand cows, paying as good a price, in fact, as his rival and contemporary, King Janaka, of Videha, had paid. The point to notice for the moment is that Gārgya discovers that the king has a profounder knowledge of philosophical doctrine than he himself possesses, and he becomes his pupil. The story is also told in the *Kaushîtaki-Upanishad* (4. 1).

Prince Jaivali is the next teacher whom we have to notice. It is reported that he was present at one of the philosophical settlements of the Panchālas. He is called Pravāhana Jaivali, and was accompanied by some of his men when he accosted the youth Svetaketu. He also shows that he is better informed than the son and pupil of the famous Uddālaka, for he asks five questions which the youth cannot answer. This leads to a meeting between Uddālaka and Jaivali, and to the Brahmin becoming the pupil of "that fellow of a noble."

The King says to the Brahmin:

> "Do not be offended with us, neither you nor your forefathers, because this knowledge has never before now dwelt with any Brāhmana. But I shall tell it to you, for who could refuse you when you speak thus?"
>
> (*Brihad. Up.*, vi. 2. 8, *S.B.E.*)

It can hardly be denied that these words claim the teaching that is about to be imparted as the sole possession of the ruling caste. On another occasion the same prince is found in company with two Brahmins, whom he instructs as to the meaning of the symbol *OM*.

Uddālaka, again, in company with five members of the Brahmin caste, appears before Ashvapati Kaikeya, a member of the ruling caste, who makes them his pupils and teaches them many important doctrines about "the Self common to all." The meaning of this phrase ought not to escape us: *Atman Vaisvānara* was suggested by the earlier *Agni Vaisvānara*, as to which there is the following text of a teaching given to a Brahmin, not this time by a king, but by Yama, the first man to pass the portals of death. The "Self common to all" is like the fire common to all fires, or the air common to all airs.

> As the one fire, after it has entered the world, though one, becomes different according to whatever it burns, thus the one Self within all things becomes different, according to whatever it enters, and exists also without. As the one air, after it has entered the world, though one, becomes different according to what it enters, thus the one Self . . .
>
> (*Katha Upanishad*, II. 5. 9–10.)

Uddālaka's own teaching is expounded in the *Chāndogya Upanishad*, where he instructs his son in the fully-developed doctrine of the identity of the Self and Brahman. This

TEACHERS IN THE UPANISHADS

is the fundamental doctrine supporting all the greater Upanishads, the central idea of the Vedānta philosophy. We now come to Sanatkumāra, the King of Hastinapura, the ancient capital of the Pandus on the upper waters of the Ganges. The instruction given by him to Nārada is of the highest importance, and reveals him as being in possession of new and profound doctrines about Brahman.

We may now pass further east to the court of the famous Janaka. In the course of years, probably centuries, the kingdom of the Videhas rose in power and civilization, until it became the most prominent kingdom in Northern India. Janaka is probably the most prominent figure in the history of the Epic Period in India. This monarch had not only established his power in the farthest confines of the Hindu dominions in India, but had gathered round him the most learned men of his time; he entered into discussion with them, and instructed them in holy truths about the Universal Being. It is this that has surrounded the name of Janaka with undying glory. King Ajātasatru of the Kāsis, himself a learned man and a most renowned patron of learning, exclaimed in despair, "Verily, all people run away, saying 'Janaka is our patron.'" (*Brihad. Up.*, 11, 1, 1).

2. BRAHMIN PHILOSOPHERS

The great fame of Janaka is partly due to the high culture and learning of the chief priest of his court, Yājnavalkya Vājasaneyin. Under the encouragement of Janaka, this priest probably conceived the bold project of revising the Yajur Veda, as it then existed, of separating the formulæ from the exegetic matter, of condensing the former in the shape of the White Yajur Veda, and amplifying it into a vast body of the Brāhmana known as the *Satapatha Brāhmana*. Generations of priests laboured at this stupendous work, but the glory of starting it belongs to the founder of the school, Yājnavalkya Vājasaneyin, and his learned patron King Janaka of the Videhas.

But Janaka has a still higher claim to our respect and admiration. While the priestly caste was still multiplying rituals and supplying dogmatic and incredible explanations for every rite, the royal caste seems to have felt some impatience of the priestly supremacy, and also with the dogmas which were so authoritatively preached. Thoughtful and earnest Kshatriyas must have asked themselves if these rites and dogmas were all that religion had to teach. Rulers, while conforming to the rites laid down by the priests, gave a start to healthier speculations, and inquired about the destination of the human soul, and the nature of the Supreme Being. So bold, healthy and vigorous were these new speculations, that the priestly classes, who were wise in their own esteem, at last felt their own inferiority, and came to the Rulers to learn the wisdom of the new school. The Upanishads contain the speculations which were started at the close of the Epic Period, and King Janaka of Videha is honoured and respected,—more than any other king of the time,—as an original stimulator of these inquiries.

We now return to the most striking figure of the early sages of this group, namely, the already-mentioned Yājnavalkya. He was a priest who conducted the sacrifices, and held the rank of Adhvaryu. In the *Satapatha Brāhmana* there are many references to him, in which he is giving opinions about various details of the sacrifice. They are of no importance to us now; but we begin to touch matters of interest as soon as Yājnavalkya gives his views about Brahman. Thus, although he is constantly referred to as a person of importance and authority in the sacrificial practices of the Brahmins, there is *no sign* of the typical Upanishad Philosophy in the *Satapatha Brāhmana*. How can we account for this? Yājnavalkya learned the secret doctrines either from King Janaka, or from some other teachers of the ruling class who had taught it to other Brahmins—such rulers as Jaivali, Ashvapati, Ajatasatru and Sanatkumāra, already referred to. The answer to our

TEACHERS IN THE UPANISHADS

query is given in the genealogy of teachers of the *Brihadāranyaka Upanishad*. Evidently, after a long priestly career, Yājnavalkya was instructed in the doctrine of Brahman by none other than Uddālaka, the pupil of Prince Jaivali: and to some purpose; for it is to him that we owe the wonderful exposition about the Self, given at the court of King Janaka to a large number of learned priests and nobles, and also to famous women, including his own wife, to whom were addressed some of the most beautiful words in the whole of this most wonderful collection of writings.

It ought to be noticed that there is an evident contradiction between the texts of the Upanishads which attribute important teachings to the ruling caste, and some "stems" or genealogical lists of Brahmins through whom these teachings came to those who finally compiled them. Only in regard to the later generations can these lists have any authority. Forty teachers follow Yājnavalkya, for example, and twelve precede him, the first receiving the teaching from Âditya, the Sun. Another list, omitting Yājnavalkya, goes back forty-eight generations to Prajāpati and Brahman, the Adam and God of the Upanishad cosmogony. We can have no difficulty, therefore, in preferring the historical passages in the text and ignoring the formal stems except where they confirm the histories. But we would give much to know, if indeed it can be known, from whom, in their own order or outside it, the ruling caste of Northern India first received these great ideas. Here history seems to fail us, and leave us entirely in the hands of speculation.

VI : *An Outline of the Sānkhya Philosophy*

WHEN Indian Philosophy is spoken of, one turns immediately to the Vedānta system, that monument of speculation which took many centuries to build. It must not be forgotten, however, that India has produced many philosophies, and that these have differed from one another no less than have the systems of Western thought. The Sānkhya system, though now almost obsolete in India, has had a very important place in Indian thought, and may be taken as the oriental type of what is called " rationalism " in the West. Readers who are familiar with the several references to the Sānkhya system which are found in the *Bhagavad Gītā* may perhaps wish to hear more about this interesting school of thought.

In such a study, we must go back to the earlier stages of Indian life, and notice the successive phases of religion there exhibited. First came the Hymns of the *Rig-Veda*; then the *Brāhmanas*, or explanations of the sacrificial ritual of the Brahmin priesthood; then the *Āranyakas*, or forest books, for the use of those who had retired from household life and no longer needed any actual ritual, but resorted to a mental ritual instead. Finally came the *Upanishads*, wherein was begun a speculation, independent of the Brahmin priesthood, leading to the remarkable conceptions which formed the basis of the later Vedānta system. What were these ideas? Firstly, the idea—which manifested a growing strength—that all life is one; that one reality, called *Brahman*, lies behind all differentiated phenomena,

THE SĀNKHYA PHILOSOPHY

and is not only the first principle of the Cosmos, but also of the Soul. The further consequence, from which the Upanishad thinkers did not shrink, was that the Ātman, or self, of the universe and of man were one and the same. "I am Brahman" was therefore the philosophical formula of this brave system. We can imagine, however, that as such a towering thought penetrated the skies, none but a few would be able to reach its idealist summit. Even many who can in thought will not do so in life; and again, for many others, the effort to combat and contradict by reason the ever-pressing sense of surrounding actuality will be too great to make. They fall back, therefore, into realism, and provide themselves with a philosophical equipment which explains appearances, and satisfies the need of the intellect and the moral nature; both of which have, we may assume, long ago wearied of the Vaidic sacrificial ritual associated with the burdensome claims of the Brahmins.

Thus the Sānkhya philosophy, belonging generally to that type of thought which turned from superstition, aimed its arrow at Idealistic Monism, but missing that mark, fell into the outer ring of rationalistic dualism. I think I can make good this general statement in the following manner.

The early cosmogony of the *Rig-Veda* regards the development of the Universe as having occurred by means of a triad of principles: First, the Primal Being evolves from out of himself the Primitive Matter, and then takes form in the latter, illuminating it as the First Born of Creation.

The *Upanishad* thinkers had to account (I am using Western terms) for God, the Soul, and the World. They did so by making the second and third dependent upon, but still identical with, the first. Thus they had the following formulæ: Brahman = Ātman ("I am Brahman"); Brahman = The World; therefore Ātman = The World ("That thou art").

Expressed diagrammatically the formulæ would appear thus:

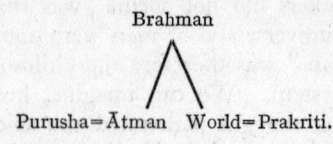

```
            Brahman
             /\
            /  \
Purusha=Ātman   World=Prakriti.
```

Brahman was *Purusha* in its higher and lower aspects, and Brahman also was *Prakriti* in its higher and lower aspects.

It was at this point that the Sānkhya philosophers decapitated, so to speak, the Upanishad monism, and left Purusha and Prakriti standing separate and alone, no longer connected, supported and explained by the invisible reality of Brahman.

Sānkhyan ideas appear in germ in the early Upanishads, particularly the *Svetāsvatara*, but the sage Kapila is credited with having founded the system, of which I will now give a brief account.

1. INEVITABLE DEVELOPMENT OF RATIONALISM

A word or two about chronology. We do not know when Kapila lived, but there are several strong reasons for believing that he and his system preceded the rise of Buddhism. The logical order, however, is what we want to realize, and that may be expressed in the following terms:

1. Vaidic Polytheism (admitting a plurality of Souls and Gods).
2. Upanishad Idealistic Monism (uniting all Souls and Gods).
3. Sānkhya Realistic Dualism (admitting the Soul, but denying God).
4. Buddhism (affirming morality, but denying both the Soul and God).
5. Materialism (denying God, the Soul and morality).
6. Vedānta (re-affirming the Upanishad philosophy against all the intervening schools).

(25) ETERNAL PURUSH
(Observing Prakriti)

(1) Aviyakta = undeveloped, chaotic
(2) Buddhi = cosmic perception, illumination
(3) Ahaṁkāra = individuality, differentiation
   Subjective ← → objective

Through (19) Manas = the mind
Central sense organ

The Three Qualities — SATTVAM | RAGAS | TAMAS

SATTVAM:
Ahaṁkāra (in rhythm) (vaikarika)
The Five Senses
(9) hearing (10) touch (11) sight (12) taste (13) smell

RAGAS:
Ahaṁkāra (in motion) (Taigasa)
Five Sense Organs
(14) ear (15) eye (16) nose (17) skin (18) tongue

Purusha through subjective Prakriti, perceiving the world

TAMAS:
Ahaṁkāra (inert) (Bhutadi)
The Five Subtle Essences of
(4) sound (5) touch (6) colour (7) savour (8) odour
The Five Gross Elements
(20) ether (21) air (22) fire (23) water (24) earth

Prakriti of the objective world

X The Point of Contact

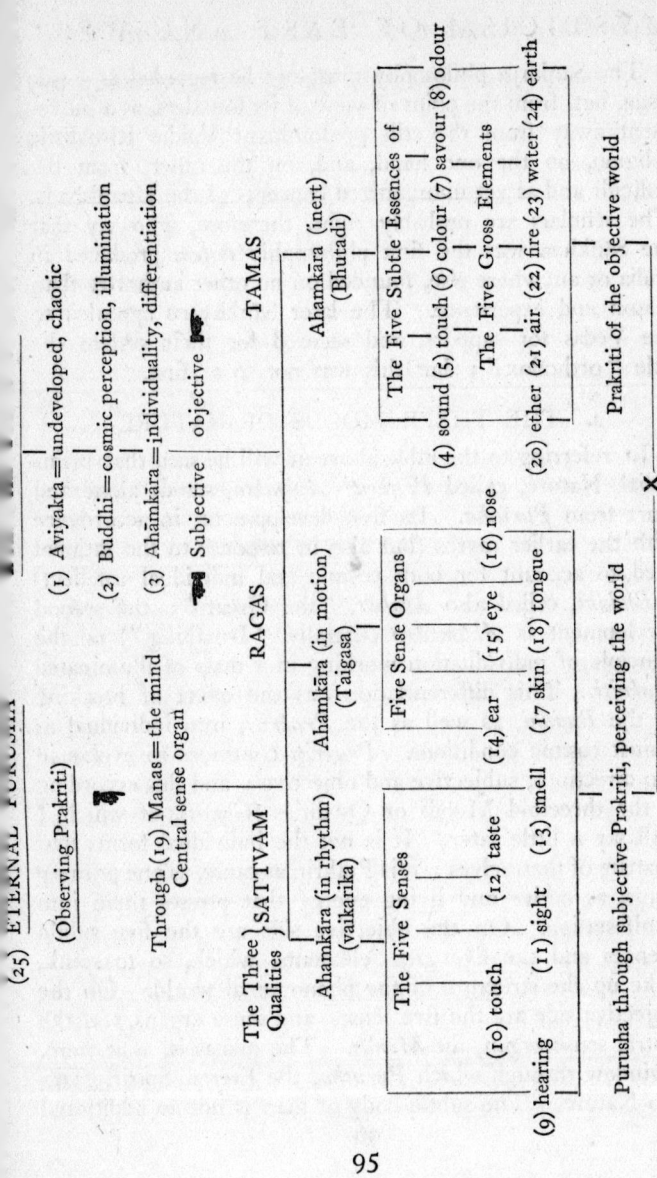

Diagram of the Sāṅkhya System based on the *Tattva Samāsa*

The Sānkhya philosophy must not be regarded as a side issue, but, from the point of view of its founders, as a movement away from the still predominant Vaidic Ritualistic religion, on the one hand, and, on the other, from the difficult and as yet unorganized concepts of the Upanishads. The scholars are probably right, therefore, who say that the Sānkhya was the first philosophic *system* produced in India or anywhere else, founded on no other authority than reason and experience. The later Sānkhyans appealed to the Vedas for support, and secured for their system the title "orthodox"; but this was not so at first.

2. THE THREE MOODS OF NATURE

In referring to the table above it will be seen that primordial Nature, called *Prakriti Aviyakta*, stands alone and apart from *Purusha*. Its first development, in accordance with the earlier myths (but also in response to the rational need to account for both cosmic and individual intellect) is *Buddhi*, called also *Mahāt*, "the Great"; the second development is *Ahāmkāra* (literally "I-making") or the principle of individuation working in a mass of illuminated *Prakriti*. This differentiation has the effect of breaking up the *Buddhi*, as well as the *Prakriti*, into individual as against cosmic conditions. *Prakriti* continues to evolve in two directions, subjective and objective; and this according to the threefold Moods or Qualities (*Gunas*), of which I shall say a little later. It is not the individual forms that emanate of themselves; it is Prakriti as cause, as one primary genus, as active and living energy that presses them into manifestation. On the objective side are the five subtle essences and the five gross elements, which, so to speak, make up the structure of the phenomenal world. On the subjective side are the five senses, and sense organs, *plus* the central sense organ, the *Manas*. The manas is, as it were, a window through which *Purusha*, the Eternal Spirit, gazes into Nature. The subtle body of man is not an additional

THE SĀNKHYA PHILOSOPHY

category, but a composite of the eighteen first products of Prakriti, from Buddhi, Ahāmkāra, the five subtle essences, to the five senses and five organs. It surrounds the soul, accompanies it on all its wanderings, and is called the *lingam*, because it is the "mark" by which each purusha is distinguished from the rest.

The existence of the soul is proved in the following remarkable manner:

(*a*) Every assemblage, every combination, has always for its object another being (*Sānkhya Pravachana*, i. 133). Just as a bed, which is an assemblage of bedding, etc. . . . is for another's use, not for its own, . . . so this world, which is an assemblage of the five elements, is for another's use; or there is a soul, for whose enjoyment this enjoyable body, consisting of intellect and the rest, has been produced. (*Gaudapada*.)

(*b*) We are conscious of a nature within us, which feels joy and woe; and this we infer is something different from matter, for we cannot conceive of mere matter as feeling and thinking—"therefore soul exists" (*Sānkhya-Karika*, 17).

There are further reasons, which I need not now quote, besides the proofs of the plurality of souls, in opposition to the older view of the unity of all souls. I will quote a few more passages about the Soul:

And from the contrariety of the soul (purusha) to nature (prakriti) it is concluded that the witnessing soul is isolated, neutral, perceptive and inactive by nature. It is thus from this union of the soul and body that the unintelligent body appears to be intelligent, and from the activity of the three qualities (*gunas*) the soul appears to be the agent. It is that the soul may be able to contemplate nature, and to become entirely

separated from it, that the union of both is made ...
and through that union the universe is formed.

(Sānkhya-Karika, 19–21).

The doctrine of the "Three Qualities of Nature" is a characteristic feature of the Sānkhya system. Its origin is derived from certain allusions in some of the Upanishads, where three forces of nature are referred to as "white, red and black." Obviously, Prakriti is not all of one homogeneous quality or mood, though it is difficult to understand, apart from tradition, why the number *three* should have been pitched upon, because the three qualities are themselves *degrees* in regard to each other and constitute an infinite number, in practice, rather than three only. It suffices to say, however, that Prakriti is said to have these three modes, and consequently every specific body is made up of a certain proportion of each of the three. They are *sattvam, rajas* and *tamas,* which correspond with the older classification, white, red and black. No one word will translate these terms, which may be taken to be (1) harmony, purity, equability, rhythm; (2) passion, desire, activity generally; (3) ignorance, darkness, dullness, inertness.

So far as the implied aim of life of the Sānkhya is concerned, it may be said to be either an equilibrium of the qualities, or an increase of the highest *(sattvam)* at the expense of the lowest *(tamas).* I have always felt this doctrine to provide peculiar difficulty, and, though I have no textual warrant for saying so, cannot see any need for it, unless we are to suppose that as the Purushas one by one become isolated (by knowledge) from Prakriti, each soul's allotment or share of Nature becomes harmonized, pure and at ease, whereas, in the lower states, it is inert, passionate and unhappy. In any case, is not this the experience promised by all philosophy to those who become enlightened?

THE SĀNKHYA PHILOSOPHY

3. THE AIM OF THE SYSTEM

This brings me to the avowed aim of the system : it is the discrimination (*Viveka*) of the Soul from Nature, and this is attained by knowledge ; the knowledge requisite is an understanding of the Sānkhya philosophy in its twenty-five topics. From increase of knowledge and quieting of the passions, there arises the destruction of all that is commonly considered as merit and demerit, and from this springs final beatitude, consisting of the soul's complete detachment from the world, and the concentration of Purusha in itself. I quote the authoritative texts.

> By the attainment of complete knowledge, virtue and the rest have become no longer a real cause ; yet a body continues to be held as a potter's wheel continues to revolve from the force of the previous impulse. This separation of body being obtained, when Nature ceases to act because her purpose has been accomplished, then the soul obtains an abstraction from matter which is both complete and eternal. (*Sānkhya-Karika*, 67–68.)
>
> The complete cessation of pain, which is of three kinds, is the complete end of man ; the effectuation of this is not by visible means, for we see its restoration after temporary cessation. . . . Therefore, though it be *not* easy, the knowledge of the truth is to be desired.
>
> (Ballantyne, *Sānkhya-Pravachana-bhashya*, i. 1 and 2.)

As is well known, the *Bhagavad Gītā* contains a good many references to the Sānkhya philosophy, and to Kapila, its reputed founder, and it may be useful to say a few words about them. The author of the *Gītā* has incorporated in his beautiful poem the materials at hand at the time, and the discerning reader can point to the well-known Sānkhya doctrines of the soul, its essential inaction in Nature, and the three qualities. It would indeed form a very interesting and useful task to extract from the *Gītā* all its characteristic Sānkhya ideas, and work at them unmixed with other doctrines. I ought to mention one thing that happened to the Sānkhya system when it entered the body of the *Gītā*. The "decapitated" portion of Upanishad Monism was restored to it! Brahman came back to unite Purusha and Prakriti with himself, and through himself, with each other. This fact, when recognised, will help the student to master the details of this most interesting and ancient view of life.

I give here a short list of the principal works of reference:
(1) *The Sānkhya-Karika* is translated by J. Davies in Trübner's Oriental Series ; (2) The *Sānkhya Pravachana* by J. R. Ballantyne in the same series ; (3) an excellent account is given by Max Müller (in his "Six Systems of Indian Philosophy") founded on the *Tattva-Samāsa*, the oldest and, as yet, untranslated document of the system.

Professor Berridale Kieth has recently issued through the Cambridge Press a rather stiff manual on the Sānkhya system.

VII : *Indian Egoism and Materialism*

WE so often hear the praises of the East, and particularly of India, as the upholder of a spiritual view of life, in contrast with what is vaguely called "Western Materialism," that the study, which here follows, of the origins of some of the most notable hedonistic and materialistic doctrines is of interest and historical importance. Incidentally, it will be noticed that hardly one aspect of such supposed modern ideas was absent from the thought of ancient India.

The plan of this section is to collect the references to materialistic teachings from authoritative documents, to exhibit their logical cohesion, and then to show the way in which the orthodox moralists of the time endeavoured to refute them. In the closing paragraphs I shall show the political implications of the machiavellian way of thinking, as it appeared in India. It will thus be seen that India cannot claim to be free from those peculiar philosophical vices which many of her champions attribute rather loosely to "the West."

1. FROM THE UPANISHADS

A doctrine of Egoism, philosophically expressed, is referred to in one of the oldest of the Upanishads. Therein Prajāpati is represented as teaching the famous Vedantic doctrine of the Self. Both gods and demons hear of it and send deputies to ask for further instruction. But the demons' representative, Virochāna, is deceived and misinformed by Prajāpati, from a desire to lead to their destruction.

> Satisfied in his heart, he went to the demons and preached that doctrine to them that the *body alone is*

> to be worshipped, that the body alone is to be served. . . .
> Therefore they call even now a man who does not
> give alms here, who has no faith, and offers no sacri-
> fices, a demon, for this is the doctrine of the demons.
> (S.B.E., Chandogya Up.: VIII. 8.)

In another of the Upanishads the legend is elaborated thus:

> Brihāspati brought forth that false knowledge for
> the safety of Indra and the destruction of the demons.
> By it they show that good is evil, and that evil is good.
> They say that we ought to ponder on the new law which
> upsets the Veda and the other sacred books. There-
> fore let no one ponder on that false knowledge; it is
> wrong, it is, as it were, barren. Its reward lasts
> only as long as pleasure lasts. . . . Let that false
> doctrine not be attempted, for thus it is said: "widely
> opposed and divergent are these two, one known as
> false knowledge, the other as knowledge."
>
> * * * * *
>
> On that self (i.e. the body) these deluded demons
> take their stand, clinging to it, destroying the true
> means of salvation, preaching untruth. What is
> untrue they see as true, as in jugglery.
> (S.B.E., Maitrayāna Up.: VII. 9.)

These two passages show us the existence of an egoistic way of thinking so objectionable to the compilers of the Upanishads that they represent it as fit only for demons; in reality it is no more than the ordinary view of life suggested by the egoistic impulses common to all men. We may regard the Upanishads as the work of men who wish to supply a speculative philosophy that will explain the phenomena of the individual life as related to those of the Cosmos, and a practical philosophy that will subordinate the first to the second—the assimilation of the soul to the

INDIAN EGOISM

Universal Order. To see " one life in all " is to see through the illusion of separateness, and to avoid its consequences ; to direct the will in accordance with that vision must lead to a reduction of the individualistic energies, and away from a sensuous, materialistic and egoistic social order. Such seems to have been the belief of the Upanishad philosophers. We can easily imagine that the egoism natural to man would become articulate in philosophic form, in India as elsewhere, and would rally to the defence of any system of thought based upon it. There is no doubt that such was actually the case.

2. FROM BUDDHIST AND JAINA SOURCES

In the days of the Buddha's mission (B.C. 520–485) there were many philosophers whose doctrines bring them within the general classification we call egoistic—and not philosophers only, as would appear from the following passage from one of the Buddha's discourses, but gods also !

There are certain gods (devas) called " Debauched by Pleasure." For ages they pass their time in pursuit of laughter and sport of sensual lusts. In consequence thereof their self-possession is corrupted, and through the loss of self-control they fall from that state (of devaship) . . . There are certain gods (devas) called the " Debauched in Mind." They burn continually with envy, one against the other, and being thus irritated, their hearts become ill-disposed towards each other, and being debauched, their bodies become feeble and their minds imbecile.

(*Brahma-jala-Sutta*, II. 7–10, in Rhys Davids' *Dialogues of the Buddha.*)

These devas are near relatives of the demons of whom we heard in the Upanishad ; their affinity to the " Fallen Angels " of Persian and Hebrew legend is also obvious ; but, as in the case of the demons, they are set as examples to men who may be in similar debauched states of body and mind. That there were men who openly taught a philosophy of sensuous indulgence like that attributed to the demons and the devas we can have no doubt. The Buddha says:

> There are also recluses and Brahmins who hold the doctrine of happiness in this life, who in five ways maintain the complete salvation in this visible world of a living being. And relying on what, starting out from what, do they do so? . . .
> Whensoever the soul, in full enjoyment, and possession of the five pleasures of sense, indulges all its functions, then the soul, they say, has attained in this visible world, to the highest Nirvāna. Thus do some maintain the complete happiness, in the visible world, of a living being.
> (*Ibid.* III. 19–20.)

An unnamed teacher is reported to have said:

> "Upwards from the soles of the feet, downwards from the tips of the hair on the head, within the skin's surface is what is called soul. . . . When this body is dead, it does not live. It lasts as long as the body lasts, it does not outlast the destruction of the body. . . . Therefore there is and exists no soul different from the body. Those who believe that there is and exists no such soul speak the truth. . . . Therefore you may kill, dig, slay, burn, cook, cut, break to pieces, or destroy! Life ends here; there is no world beyond. . . ."

The Jaina commentator connects this belief with its appropriate conduct. He says:

> "Thus they are given to pleasures, amusements and sensual lusts; they are greedy, fettered, passionate, covetous, the slaves of love and hate . . . they stick in pleasures and amusements. . . ."
> (*S.B.E.*, *Kritānga Sutra*, II. I. 15–19.)

INDIAN EGOISM

Another egoist teacher is reported as denying any distinction between right and wrong, upon the philosophical principle,—which the Jaina regards as particularly objectionable—of the right to take life.

> There are the five elements through which we explain whether an action is good or bad, meritorious or not, well done or not well done. Everything down to a blade of grass consists of them. . . . All living beings, all things in the whole world, consist of nothing but these five elements. They are the primary cause of the world, even down to a blade of grass. A man buys and causes to buy, kills and causes to kill, cooks and causes to cook, he may even sell and kill a man. Know that even in this case he does not do wrong.
>
> (*Ibid.*, 21–24.)

This doctrine is most probably the same as or very similar to that reported by King Ajātasattu to the Buddha, on the occasion of their memorable and only interview. It is that of a well-known teacher, Ajita Kesakambali, who, besides being a materialist, is a bit of a sophist as well. He was leader of the Ajivikas, who vainly sought to overcome the Buddha, and whose Order still existed in the time of King Asoka. Ajita teaches his "theory of annihilation" to the King. He says:

> "There is no such thing, O King, as alms or sacrifice or offering. There is neither fruit nor result of good or evil deeds. There is no such thing as this world or the next. There is neither father nor mother, nor beings springing into life without them. . . .
>
> A human being is built up of the four elements. When he dies the earthy in him returns or relapses to the earth, the fluid to the water, the heat to the fire, the windy to the air, and his faculties (five senses

and the mind) pass into space . . . and his offerings end in ashes. It is a doctrine of fools, this talk of religious gifts. It is an empty lie, mere idle talk, when men say there is profit therein. Fools and wise alike, on the dissolution of the body, are cut off, annihilated, and after death they are not."

(*Samanna-phala Sutta*, 23, in Rhys Davids' *Dialogues*.)

Next we hear Makkali Gosala state his "theory of purification through transmigration." He grants the existence of the soul, but allows it no free-will. There is no cause either for the rectitude or depravity of beings; consequently there is no conduct necessarily more moral than any other. Gosala is a determinist, a non-moralist and a fatalist. The "end of pain" comes when it is impossible to suffer any more. Though we are not told so directly, the ethic deduced from such a metaphysic would be an egoist one. Merit or demerit is impossible, for the reason that efforts to gain them lead to nothing; consequently one does what one likes. He says:

"There is, O King, no cause, either ultimate or remote, for the depravity of beings; they become depraved without reason and without cause. The attainment of any given condition, of any character, does not depend either on one's own acts, or on the acts of another, or on human effort. There is no such thing as power or energy, or human strength or human vigour. All creatures . . . are without force and power and energy of their own. They are bent this way and that, by the necessary condition of the class to which they belong, by their individual nature; and it is according to their position in one or other of the six species that they experience ease or pain."

The ease and pain measured out, as it were with a measure, cannot be altered in the course of trans-

INDIAN EGOISM

migration; there can be neither increase nor decrease thereof, neither excess nor deficiency. Just as when a ball of string is cast forth, it will spread out as far, and no farther, than it can unwind, just so both fools and wise alike, wandering in transmigration exactly for the allotted term, shall then, and only then, make an end of pain.

(Ibid., 20–22.)

The champion theoretical non-moralist of those far-off days was Purana Kassapa. He admits volition but denies the significance of deeds. The law of Karma, held very largely by his contemporaries, is entirely swept away by him, and when we ask what takes its place, the answer can only be : the law of impulse, namely, egoism.

To him who acts, O King, or causes another to act, to him who mutilates or causes another to mutilate, to him who punishes or causes another to punish, to him who causes grief or torment, to him who trembles or causes others to tremble, to him who kills a living creature, who takes what is not given, who breaks into houses, who commits dacoity, or robbery, or highway robbery, or adultery, or who speaks lies, to him thus acting there is no guilt. If with a discus, with an edge sharp as a razor, he should make all living creatures on the earth one heap, one mass of flesh, there would be no guilt thence resulting, no increase of guilt would ensue. Were he to go along the south bank of the Ganges striking and slaying, mutilating and having men mutilated, oppressing and having men oppressed, there would be no guilt thence resulting, no increase of guilt would ensue. Were he to go along the north bank of the Ganges giving alms, and ordering gifts to be given, offering sacrifices or causing them to be offered, there would be no merit thence resulting, no increase of merit. In generosity, in self-mastery, in control of the senses, in speaking truth, there is neither merit nor increase of merit.

(*Ibid.*, 17–18.)

In India, as elsewhere, egoism calls to its aid that peculiar instrument known as Sophistry. It is as if the debater were conscious of some weakness in his logical position, or of his inability to sustain his case; he therefore has recourse to Sophistry, which, by its very refusal to fight with equal weapons, prevents his opponent from gaining a victory. The Pyrrhonists of Greece and the " Eel-wrigglers " of India merely made philosophy impossible, and were proud of their achievement. The afore-mentioned Ajita was given to eel-wriggling, and according to the Buddha, there were four classes of these Sophists.

> There are some recluses and Brahmins who wriggle like eels; and when a question is put to them on this or that, they resort to equivocation, to eel-wriggling. They are clever, subtle, experienced in controversy, hair-splitters, who go about breaking to pieces by their wisdom the speculations of others; they will neither declare anything to be good or bad.
>
> (*Brahma-jala Sutta*, II. 23–29.)

The fourth type is familiar as the lazy and incompetent controversialist, who " by reason of his dullness and stupidity, resorts to equivocation and to wriggling like an eel."

3. SANKARA'S REFERENCES

Some few of the Vedānta Sutras, composed in the fifth century B.C., were employed in the refutation of the doctrine of materialism. We will quote one: *Some maintain the non-existence of a separate self, on account of the existence of the self where the body is only* (III. 3, 53). Sankara,

INDIAN EGOISM

the great Vedāntist commentator, has the following remarks on this Sutra :

"Here now some materialists, who see the self in the body only, are of opinion that a self separate from the body does not exist ; they assume that consciousness, although not observed in earth and other external elements—either single or combined—may yet appear in them when transformed into the shape of a body, so that consciousness springs from them, . . . that knowledge is analogous to intoxicating quality (which arises when certain materials are mixed in certain proportions), and that man is only body qualified by consciousness. There is thus, according to them, no separate self from the body, and capable of going to the heavenly world or obtaining release . . . but the body alone is what is conscious, is the Self. . . . The Self, therefore, is not different from the body. To this conclusion the next Sutra replies."

(*Vedānta Sutras S.B.E.*, Vol. 38, p. 269.)

4. MĀDHAVA'S EPITOME

Many centuries after the authoritative criticism by Sankara, the Vedāntist Madhava compiled an epitome of the heretical philosophies then in existence, that is, in 1331 A.D. He places in the forefront of his work an account of the Chārvāka philosophy, to which I will now refer. Although it is the fullest account of Indian materialism that can be found in ancient sources, I have postponed its consideration for two reasons ; first, in order to be chronologically sound, and second, because Madhava has been accused of romancing. I see no reason to accept this view. Doubtless in Madhava's day—though far removed from that of the mythical persons, Chārvāka and Brihāspati, with whom he connects the materialistic philosophy—there were traditions or documents that are not now at our disposal ;

but, having heard the undoubtedly authoritative fragments from Upanishad, Buddhist, Jaina and Vedāntic literature, I feel that Madhava has given a *résumé* that is very fair. He opens in ironic vein, thus:

> We have said in our preliminary invocation "salutation to Shiva"; but how can we attribute to the Divine Being the giving of supreme felicity when such a notion has been utterly abolished by Chārvāka,[1] the crest-gem of Brihāspati?[2]
>
> The efforts of Chārvāka are hard to be eradicated, for the majority of human beings hold by the current refrain:
>
> > While life is yours, live joyously;
> > None can escape Death's searching eye;
> > When once this frame of ours they burn
> > How shall it e'er again return?
>
> The mass of men, considering wealth and desire the only ends of man, and denying the existence of any object belonging to a future world, are found to follow only the doctrine of Chārvāka.
>
> In this school the four elements are the original principles; from these alone, when transformed into the body, intelligence is produced ... and when these are destroyed, intelligence at once perishes also.

[1] This Chārvāka is not a historical person but an ogre, a mythical character of the Mahābhārata, who appeared in the guise of a Brahmin; the views here attributed to him are those of the so-called Lōkayata system of philosophy. The origin of this term is much in dispute, but it appears to have meant originally Nature Lore (see Rhys David's *Dialogues of the Buddha,* where an interesting discussion occurs).

[2] Since Chārvāka is mythical we see no reason to doubt that his sensuous materialism can be identified with the false teaching given to the demons by Brihāspati in the *Maitrayāna Upanishad.*

INDIAN EGOISM

. . . Therefore the soul is only the body distinguished by the attribute of intelligence, since there is no evidence of any soul distinct from the body, as such cannot be proved, since this school holds that sense perception is the only source of knowledge, and does not allow inference.

The only end of man is enjoyment produced by sensual pleasures. Nor may you say that such cannot be called the end of man because they are always mixed with some kind of pain; it is our wisdom, they say, to enjoy the pure pleasure as far as we can, and to avoid the pain which inevitably accompanies it; . . . It is not for us, through fear of pain, to reject the pleasure which our nature instinctively recognizes as congenial . . . men do not refuse to set the cooking pots on the fire because forsooth there are beggars to pester us for a share of the contents. If any one were so timid as to forsake a visible pleasure, he would indeed be foolish like a beast, as has been said by the poet: "What man, seeking his true interest, would fling away the berries of paddy, rich with the fresh white grains, because covered with husk or dust?"

They say . . . the Veda is tainted by the three faults of untruth, self-contradiction, and tautology; and again that the impostors who call themselves Vaidic pandits are mutually destructive . . . and lastly the three Vedas themselves are only the incoherent rhapsodies of knaves.

Hence it follows that there is no other hell than mundane pain produced by mundane causes; the only Supreme is the earthly monarch whose existence is proved by all the world's eyesight; and the only Liberation is the dissolution of the body. By holding the doctrine that the soul is identical with the body, such phrases as: "I am thin," "I am black," are at once intelligible.

The discussion ends with the boastful declaration of the materialist:

> Thus we fasten on our opponents, as with adamantine glue, the thunder-bolt-like fallacy of reasoning in a circle.

And all this has been said in the Sutras of Brihāspati:

> There is no heaven, no final liberation, nor any soul in another world.
> While life remains let a man live happily, let him feed on butter even though he runs into debt;
> When once the body becomes ashes, how can it ever return again?
> (*Sarvadarsana-samgrapha*, in Trubner's Oriental Series.)

Madhava concludes ironically as he began: "Hence in kindness to the mass of living beings must we fly for refuge to the doctrine of Chārvāka. Such is the pleasant consummation."

5. CO-ORDINATION OF INDIAN EGOIST DOCTRINE

I shall now attempt to make a synthesis of all the foregoing philosophical doctrines in order to ascertain, if I can, what was their practical or moral import. It may be that we are not entitled to assert that there was a school of egoist thinkers equally reputable with, and definite as the Sānkhyans, the Vedāntins, or the Buddhists; but a comparison of the various declarations I have assembled, mostly from the time of the Buddha's mission, will show that these doctrines necessarily imply one another; they are for the most part mutually consistent, and, when considered together, they make up the elements of an egoistic philosophy as thorough-going as any we have heard of before or since,

INDIAN EGOISM

I shall extract and combine the doctrines in formal propositions, theoretical and practical.

(i.) Theoretical Propositions

Atheism.
(1) No God, Creator or Cosmical director is mentioned in any of the documents, nor does there seem to be a possible place for one

Irreligion.
(2) Since there is no God, no other world and no free-will, sacrifices and offerings are "a doctrine of fools." The Vedas, and with them Vaidism, are entirely rejected.

Materialism.
(3) The five elements are the primary cause of the world.
(4) All living beings, all things, the whole world, consist of nothing but the five elements.
(5) Consciousness springs from the combination of these elements in the shape of the body.
(6) There is no soul apart from this, which, on the death of the body, is annihilated.

Determinism.
(7) There is no free-will, and consequently no moral responsibility.
(8) There is no differentiation of right and wrong, and consequently no accumulation of merit or demerit.
(9) Pleasure and pain, depravity and purity, are not within man's power; they can neither be added to nor diminished.

(ii.) Practical Propositions

Non-Moralism.
(10) Killing and mutilation of men or animals, slavery, robbery, adultery and falsehood are not morally distinguishable from generosity, self-mastery, sense-control and truthfulness.

Ethical Egoism.
- (11) "The body alone is to be worshipped, the body alone is to be served"; the full enjoyment of sensuous pleasure is the chief end of man—in fact, it is "Nirvāna."
- (12) The impulses are true guides, and are to be followed consistently, without external or volitional control.

Casuistry.
- (13) Sophistry or "eel-wriggling" is permissible in the service of the body; it is to formal logic what non-moralism is to moral control. If there are no rules for life, there can be none for thought.

6. THE REFUTATION OF EGOISM

It must be remembered that theoretical and ethical egoism appear in opposition to and in reaction against orthodoxy, not the reverse; so that while egoism will be and appear conscious of that against which it rises, orthodoxy will not explicitly, though it may implicitly, refute egoism. In a sentence, that which had constituted the main strength of orthodoxy will, on the egoistic challenge, have to be appropriately reaffirmed.

(i.) THE UPANISHADS

The declared aim of the Upanishad philosophers is to induce a *knowledge* of the Cosmical Principle, of the Psychical Principle, and a subsequent knowledge that these are identical—"I am Brahman." Any one reaching that goal is lifted beyond the possibility of desire and of immoral conduct. For him there can be no "ethics," nothing specially to be done or to leave undone. He can be neither egoistic nor altruistic. But for the mass of mankind, not so favoured, there is undoubtedly a *dharma*, a duty, so to say, within and appropriate to the general illusion. For the aspirant to liberation, conceived of as something that would happen causally (although originally likened to an awakening), there is a special *dharma* appropriate to his aims. He desires " knowledge of the ātman," to see all life as one, as declared in the teaching to which, by faith, he holds. Moral action, considered as a means of facilitating in himself the removal of all desire and the removal of the consciousness of plurality, has *a subjective value*, primarily for the actor. It has only a secondary or *objective value* for others. But as the conviction strengthens that life is one, conduct towards others must become more and more sympathetic and less outwardly egoistic, while inwardly it is more spiritually significant.

One of the earliest statements of an ethical system appears in the *Chandogya Up.* (3, 17) as composed of asceticism, liberality, right dealing, no injury to life, and truthfulness. Another passage adds self-restraint, tranquillity, hospitality and courtesy, and yet another, pity.

Now inasmuch as egoistic deeds—in the worldly sense— are done for the empirical self, the man in whom that egoity is weakening will cease to invade the lives of others. The Sannyasin and the Yogin, devotees of Upanishad ethical movements, are those who have gradually withdrawn from this world and its enchantments, in order to be fitted for their home in the other world.

The Upanishad philosophy, when met by the challenge of Indian egoism, had only to reaffirm its metaphysical conceptions and their moral consequences, or, as in the case of Madhava's epitome, to treat it with ironical contempt.

(ii.) BUDDHISM

The Buddha, as we know, differed fundamentally from the Brahmins of his day and agreed with some of the metaphysical tenets which we have identified with egoism.[1] His system was atheistic, and agnostic as regards the soul; he rejected the Vedas, sacrifices, and the whole paraphernalia of Brahminism; but he equally rejected the determinism,

[1] See Sub-Section 5.

non-moralism and egoism which I have expounded. How? It is explained by the Buddha that all suffering is dependent upon and caused by *craving*:

> Without beginning and without end is this Samsāra; unperceivable is the beginning of beings buried in blindness, who, seized of craving, are ever and again brought to new birth, and so hasten through the endless round of re-birth. And thus, Brothers, have you long time undergone suffering, undergone torment, undergone misfortune . . . long enough to turn yourselves away from all suffering, long enough to be released from it all.
> (*Samyutta Nikāya*, xiv. 1.)

This "turning away" is an effort of the will; in it the whole Buddhist ethic is comprised. Non-moralism is opposed by the most categorical distinction between conduct that is right and conduct that is wrong. The former leads away from craving and suffering, the latter perpetuates them. Egoism is refuted by love.

> Putting away the killing of living things, Gotama the recluse holds aloof from the destruction of life. He has laid the cudgel and the sword aside, and, ashamed of roughness, and full of mercy, he dwells compassionate and kind to all creatures that have life.
> (*Brahma-gala Sutta*, 8.)

And he lets his mind pervade one quarter of the world with thoughts of Love, with thoughts of Pity, with thoughts of Sympathy, with thoughts of Equanimity, and so the second, and so the third, and so the fourth. And thus the whole wide world, above, below, around, and everywhere, does he continue to pervade with heart of Love, Pity, Sympathy, and Equanimity, far-reaching, grown great, and beyond measure. Just as a mighty trumpeter makes himself heard—and that without difficulty—in all the four directions;

even so of all things that have shape or life, there is not one that he passes by or leaves aside, but regards them all with mind set free, and deep-felt pity, . . . sympathy . . . equanimity.

(*S.B.E., Tevijja Sutta*, 76–79.)

Following these emphatic statements it may be of interest to learn the Buddha's teaching as to the relative values of human welfare. The lowest aim was for a man to seek neither his own nor another's good ; a little higher aim was to seek another's good but not one's own ; better still it was to seek his own good and not that of another ; while the highest aim was to seek one's own and another's welfare. And when we understand what, in the Buddha's conception, was the nature of welfare, the above-mentioned ethical criterion becomes very clear.

Four in number are the various courses of conduct : (1) At present painful and also bringing future pain ; (2) pleasant now but bringing pain in future ; (3) at present painful but bringing future pleasure ; (4) pleasant now and also bringing pleasure in the future. . . .

What is that course of conduct which is both pleasant now and leads to pleasure in the future ?

There is a certain man who with pleasure and satisfaction abstains from taking life, shuns theft, avoids lewdness, refrains from false speech, from scandalmongering, from cruel words, from idle chatter, and he is not covetous, is not malignant, and cleaves to right views ; and by reason of his abstention from killing, from stealing, from lasciviousness, from lying, from scandalmongering, from harsh speech, from vain babbling, because of his shrinking from covetousness and from malignity, because of his cleaving to right views, he experiences pleasure and satisfaction. At the dissolution of his body after death he comes upon a happy journey to the heaven world. This is that course of conduct which is both pleasant now and leads to pleasure in the future.

(*Majjhima Nikāya*, XLVI., in *Discourses of Gotama the Buddha*, by Sīlācāra.)

We may conclude, therefore, that the Buddha's life-ideal was to obtain happiness in this life and the next, both for one's self and all other creatures. This is Positive Love, the antithesis of Egoism.

(iii.) JAINISM

The followers of Mahavira, the *jina* (conqueror) held views somewhat different from those of the Buddhists. They assumed the fact of the Soul, but not that of God. They believed in the reality of the world, in *Karma*, and consequently in free-will; they were rigorous ascetics. The link between them and the Buddhists was their tender respect for life, which they carried to extreme degrees. The aim of life is liberation of the soul, and the chief means are "comprehension and renunciation of the causes of sin."

> The living world is afflicted, miserable, difficult to instruct, and without discrimination. In this world full of pain, suffering by their different acts, see the benighted ones cause great pain! . . . He who injures these earth-bodies does not comprehend and renounce sinful acts.
>
> (*S.B.E.*, *Áchārānga Sutra*, I. 1–2.)

This is the basic ethic of the Jainas, and although it is for liberation, like the Vedānta, it is strongly altruistic as regards this life.

> He does not kill movable or immovable beings, nor has them killed by another person, nor does he consent to another's killing them. In this way a monk ceases to acquire gross Karma, controls himself and abstains from sins.
>
> (*S.B.E.*, *Kritānga Sutra*, II. 1–53.)

INDIAN EGOISM

Or else a spy in the garb of a rich merchant may borrow vast quantities of gold, . . . and allow himself to be robbed of the same at night.

(18)

Courtesan spies, under the garb of chaste women, may cause themselves to be enamoured of persons who are guilty of various crimes punishable by government. No sooner are the suspected persons seen within the abode of female spies than they shall be seized, and their property confiscated by Government. . . . Or state spies may bring about a quarrel between two guilty persons born of the same family, and administer poison to one or the other. The survivor and his party shall be accused of poisoning, and their property confiscated. . . . Or a claim may be set up against a guilty citizen of wealth for a large amount of money professed to have been placed in his custody by the claimant. . . . The king's spies may murder the claimant at night and lay the charge at the door of the citizen. Then the citizen and his party may be arrested and their property confiscated.

(19)

An outcast may be induced to enrol himself as a servant to a rich citizen. The servant may be murdered by a spy at night and the citizen accused of the crime. Consequently his property may be confiscated by the Government.

(22)

A spy, under the garb of a cook, may enrol himself as a servant to a rich citizen, and mix counterfeit coin in the money in the possession of his master, and make room for his arrest.

My extracts are a small part of a translation of the *Arthasastra* made by Pilay. A full translation of the work has lately been issued. They show how far non-moralism can be seriously carried; it is probable that many a monarch in the pursuit of his egoistic aims, or even in fancied defence of the welfare of his country, has before and since Chāndragupta's day employed just such creatures as Chānakya.

VIII : *The Buddha's Personality*

IN studying the teachings of any great man, the habit is too often exhibited of passing over the historical and intellectual conditions that surround and have preceded him, and omitting to look closely into his unique personality. These two elements, one of which is brought to him, and the other which he himself brings, go largely to the production of his teaching. His teaching, in fact, is the reaction of his personality on his environment, the flame that springs into being as flint strikes steel. The habit referred to tends to the study of a teaching in isolation, or, what is more unfortunate, in relation rather to these present times, without sufficient regard to its peculiar origins. The consequence is that the teaching, be it of Plato, Christ, Buddha or Dante, has to run the gauntlet of a sub-conscious criticism, which makes it appear artificial and extravagant. Our effort should be constantly to place ourselves in the old environment, and to appreciate the personality of the teacher whose message we desire to examine. The present Section, therefore, will exclude the teaching of the Buddha and concentrate on his personality, so as to understand what kind of man he was and therefore, at our leisure, to understand more intimately the teaching which emanated from him. It is as well to say at once that in reference to the Buddha we have to deal with two personalities ; the first is the familiar historical personality, which exhibited itself in the sixth and fifth centuries B.C., in India, while the second may be called the metaphysical personality, spoken of by the Buddha himself and enlarged, perhaps, by his admirers and interpreters from his own period down to the present day. It is right to include this second aspect in a study of his personality in general, because, although the material for its study is very hazy, yet, on the hypothesis of pre-existence and immortality, the elements contributed by the metaphysical personality cannot altogether be excluded from influencing the historical personality, and thus the teaching.

This point is of sufficient importance to allow of a digression in the direction of a famous parallel. The teaching of Jesus, emanating from the historical personality of Palestine, was certainly intelligible to the immediate hearers of the Word. But to those who came afterwards, the metaphysical or theological personality appeared very significant and largely overshadowed the historical, lending to the teaching itself new and uncertain meanings, which have exercised so great an influence. While, therefore, we must admit the legitimate claim of the metaphysical personality to our attention, we must exercise the greatest critical caution. This caution has not often been sufficiently observed by the followers of the Christ or the Buddha—with unhappy results.

1. THE BUDDHA'S BIRTH

The steadiest possible historical tradition reflected in Indian literature gives the Buddha's birth at Kapilavastu (in modern Nepal) among the Sākya clan; and, in consequence, it seems to have been assumed that Gautama himself was an Aryan, an Indian, a Hindu. But this assumption rests on another: that the Sākya clan was a member of the Indo-Aryan stock, an assumption that can easily be questioned and seriously challenged. Any thesis that would place the Buddha outside the Aryan family would not displease the greater part of the Buddhist world, but Aryans in general, and Indians in particular, would grieve to be deprived of the honour of claiming so great a teacher as one of their race. The matter, however, is of historical and psychological importance, and I propose to examine the heterodox thesis involved.

THE BUDDHA'S PERSONALITY

First, as to his birthplace: putting aside the ornate legends of the poets, and devotees, we may turn to the stone pillar which stands in the jungle at Rummindeî village in the Nepalese Tarai, a little south of the ruins of Kapilavastu. It was erected by order of the Emperor Asoka, the first and greatest Buddhist monarch, in 249 B.C., the twenty-first year of his reign, three hundred and fourteen years after the birth which it records. I venture to think that these words, to be read as clearly to-day as the day they were cut, are as deeply moving as any verse of poet!

"The King Devawanapiya-Piyadassi, when he was twenty years anointed, did the honour of coming here in person. Because the Buddha was born here, the Sākya saint, he caused a stone surrounding and screening wall to be made and a stone pillar to be set up. Because the Blessed One was born here he made the village of Lummini free of rent and entitled to the eighth share [the King's share of the harvest]."

(Hastings' *Enc. Rel. and Eth.*)

Hereafter let the poets tell their beauteous story of the birth of the child in the Lumbini garden, to which the Queen of King Suddhôdana, knowing her time had come had retired. In view of what the child became, their raptures are not inappropriate. Hiuen Tsiang, the Chinese pilgrim, records that in his day the pillar had the statue of a horse on its summit; but it has since been split by lightning, and only the bell portion of the capital remains in addition to the stump upon which the inscription is found.

2. HIS LINEAGE

We now turn back to the problem of the Buddha's lineage, and have to inquire into the stock to which the Sākya clan belonged. Anthropology, which has for many years had its eye on the races of Asia, has hardly as yet descended into such detail as we are in need of here. Yet what exact information there is goes to support the thesis that the Sākyas were not of Indo-Aryan stock, and as the point is of some importance, I give here a brief statement of the results of anthropological study, so far as it concerns the inhabitants of Northern India.

Signor V. Giuffrida-Ruggeri, Professor of Anthropology in the Royal University of Naples, in his *First Outlines of a Systematic Anthropology of Asia*, divides the peoples of Asia into two great classes—I discard the Latin terminology here —Asiatics and Indo-Europeans. The former are what we should popularly describe as Mongolians, and fall again into nine families, distinguished by physical features and index measurements. The Indo-Europeans, many times divided, extend from India to Europe. In India these two great classes meet ; and, as to any tribe or individual we are concerned with there, the question at once arises to which of these divisions do they belong ? The Sākyas in historical times occupied the high country of Nepal on the southern slopes of the Eastern Himalayas, and we have to decide whether to assign them to the Aryans of Indo-European stock who invaded India in the second millennium B.C. and onwards, or to place them with the Asiatics who could have penetrated India from the East (Assam) or even from the North through the passes of Gilgit and Chitral. If the Sākyas of the Buddha's day remained in Modern Nepal— and why should they not ?—they would have to be classed with the Mongoloids. In Nepal and Assam men with Mongoloid physiognomy still predominate.

But India was at the time of the Aryan invasion inhabited by a dark-skinned people called "Dasas" as well as by yellow-skinned people to the East. Were the Sākyas dark-skinned ? The Buddha is again and again described as "golden" in colour, which would put him either among the Indo-Europeans or, more likely, among the Mongoloids.

THE BUDDHA'S PERSONALITY

The point is a small one, though the argument is not weak. He certainly was not black. Unhappily there are no people to-day who can be defined and identified with the ancient Sākyas, so that anthropological science cannot carry the matter any further; we can, however, continue our researches in the realm of tradition, history and the Buddhist literature, where, perhaps to the general surprise, we shall find something consistent with our thesis.

3. THE ORIGIN OF THE SÂKYAS

The term Sākya is the Sanscrit form of the name of the great race known in the historical fragments of Central Asia as Sāka. According to Strabo (xi. p. 513) the Sākas occupied the frontier land along the northern borders of India. The Greek historians refer to these people as Sakei, and attribute to them qualities of quite remarkable justice and purity. On the Indian side, as represented in the Buddhist literature, the tradition of the Sākyas leads back to a famous old king Okkāka, whose children had been banished from his court at Potala on the Indus, had established themselves at Ayodhyā, anciently called Sāketa, and had finally settled on the slopes of the Himalayas further north. To complete the story, we are told that the Buddha was descended from this king, and his ancestry was carefully traced through seven generations.

If we accept the Okkāka legend, the Sākya clan passed through Aryandom without mixing with it, and, after many generations, reached complete independence. This would support our notion that they were not Aryans, nor were they Aryanized as to their political government or their religious faith. If we reject the Okkāka legend—which we may well do, for it is put into the mouth of the Buddha as part of a rather amusing wrangle with a proud young Brahmin [1]—we are left with these few facts:

[1] *Ambattha Sutta*, I. 16.

that the Sākyas were inhabitants of Southern Nepal while the Saisunâga dynasty reigned over the neighbouring Magadha, that they produced one great man in 563 B.C. and were massacred, and their town destroyed, by the King of Kosala about the year 490 B.C. Perhaps, then, it is not surprising that we cannot discover their orbito-nasal index and determine for certain whether they were *Homo-Asiaticus protomorphus* or *Homo-Indo-Europæus brachimorphus Armeno-Pamiriensis*! We can, at least, be convinced that they were not *Homo-Indo-Europæus dolichomorphus Indo-Iranus*.

There we must leave the question of the Sākya race, until our study of the personality of the Buddha from moment to moment revives it, and perhaps settles it. But a few words as to their political status will be useful here. The Sākyas were not ruled by kings, as were the majority of the Aryan states. They were republicans led by chieftains, like the Licchavis, their neighbours; they met in a general assembly in a Moot Hall, for political and social debate. Elsewhere laws were made by the kings by the advice of the Brahmins; here the laws were made by what we should call an oligarchy. Each man of the Sākyas had but one wife, chosen from within the clan, which contained 160,000 families living at Kapilavastu, Koli and the districts around. The Sākya did not observe the caste-system of the Hindus, and hence the Buddha was not making an innovation by ignoring caste, but merely carrying out the equalitarian custom of his own country. In this respect he was liberalizing the Aryans, offering them a path through life which he called the "Eightfold Aryan path," worthy of those who called themselves "noble." It would not have appealed to *them* had he called it "the Sākiyan path."

4. THE BUDDHA'S NAMES

The system of names adopted in ancient India was somewhat complicated, and in the Buddha's case it became enriched with countless additions. A man would have (1)

THE BUDDHA'S PERSONALITY

a personal name given by his parents, as are our "Christian names," such as Ananda (Bliss), Devadatta (God-given) or Siddārtha. Secondly, he might earn (2) a nickname arising out of some personal peculiarity, physical or moral. What we should call the surname was (3) the name of the *gotra*, or *gens*, such as Kassapa, Kondanna or Gōtama. Then comes (4) the clan name, such as Vajji, Malla or Sākya. Men might be addressed (5) by the mother's name, such as Sariputta, Sari's son, or by (6) their position in society— Brahmin, Mahārāja, etc. (7) Terms of respect, though not personal, were also employed, and lastly came (8) the locality name to distinguish, for instance, one Kassapa from another of the same *gotra*.

Falling into this system, we may say of the person we are considering, that his personal name was (probably) Siddārtha, his "nicknames" numerous—such as the Blessed One, the Perfect One—his *gotra* name was Gōtama, though the Sākyas probably did not adopt the Aryan custom of *gotras*. He is often called by his clan name, "the Sākiyan" or Sākyamuni, "the sage of the Sākyas." This is the universal name in China, where the *gotra* appellation Gōtama is almost unknown. It is noticeable that in the Asoka inscription the names used are Sākyamuni, Bhagavan and Buddha, the last one being specially chosen by the Master. In view of the greatness of its meaning—The Enlightened One—it can hardly be placed in the second class above mentioned, but rather in the seventh. Before his enlightenment he was known as the Samana Gōtama or the Gautamide ascetic, but afterwards as Buddha.

> "Call me not after my familiar name, for it is a rude and careless way of speaking . . . call me, therefore, Buddha."
>
> (Asvaghosa's *Life*, iii. 15, 1230.)

In the literature, the personal name Siddārtha is never used except by the later poets.

5. HIS PERSON AND CHARACTER

The Buddhist scriptures abound in particulars regarding the personal appearance of the Blessed One, some more historically based than others. The Brahmin tradition that a superman must possess bodily "marks" to the number of thirty-two was used by the compilers of the Suttas to advance a claim on behalf of their leader. He had these marks, they said. We need not press the point, but it is arguable that such claims as are contained in the recital of the "Thirty-two marks of a Superman" would have lost their force unless there had been a *prima facie* case that the Buddha possessed some or most of them. If from memory or tradition they could be contradicted there would be no point in claiming them. It is therefore of interest to endeavour to picture from these "marks" what the Buddha was like to look upon.

> He hath feet with level tread . . . with projecting heels. He is long in the fingers and toes, with soft and tender hands and feet. His ankles are like rounded shells, his legs like an antelope's. His complexion is like bronze, the colour of gold, and his skin is delicately smooth. . . . He has a frame divinely straight and his body is like a lion's. His taste is supremely acute and he has regular teeth. He has a divine voice like the Karavîka bird's. His eyes are intensely blue.
>
> (*Lakkhana Suttanta*, 2, in Rhys Davids' *Dialogues*.)

Though somewhat formal, such particulars of bodily appearance are supported by many other passages of a more casual and historical character. Here is one taken from an account of a visit by the Brahmin Sonadanda to the Blessed One. After a remonstrance from his fellow Brahmins, Sonadanda said:

> Truly, Sirs, the venerable Gōtama is well born on both sides, of pure descent through the mother and

THE BUDDHA'S PERSONALITY

the father back through seven generations, with no slur put upon him, and no reproach in respect of birth . . . he has gone forth into the religious life, giving up the great clan of his relations . . . giving up much money and gold, treasure both buried and above the ground. While he was still a young man, without a grey hair on his head, in the beauty of his early manhood, he has gone forth into the homeless life . . . though his father and mother were unwilling and wept, their cheeks being wet with tears. . . .

Truly, Sirs, the Samana Gōtama is handsome, pleasant to look upon, inspiring trust, gifted with great beauty of complexion, fair in colour, fine in presence, stately to behold . . . he hath a pleasant voice, and a pleasing delivery, he is gifted with polite address, distinct, not husky, suitable for making clear the matter in hand. . . .

Truly, Sirs, the Samana Gōtama has no passion of lust left in him, and has put away all fickleness of mind . . . he believes in Karma and in Action, he is one who puts righteousness in the forefront of his exhortations to the Brahmin race.

Truly, Sirs, the Samana Gōtama went forth from a distinguished family primeval (*adina* = primordial, aboriginal) among the Kshatriya clans . . . he bids all men welcome, is congenial, conciliatory, not supercilious, accessible to all, not backward in conversation . . . in whatsoever village or town the Samana Gōtama stays, there the non-humans do the humans no harm. . . . And so far only do I know the excellencies of the Samana Gōtama, but these are not all of them, for his excellence is beyond measure.

(*Sonādanda Sutta*, 6, in Rhys Davids' *Dialogues*.)

It is noticeable that the many excellencies possessed by the Buddha are personal to him; except his descent all is his own creation. The reference to the primeval or aboriginal family could certainly be read as implying both non-Aryan and pre-Aryan origins. The fine apologia which the Brahmin makes for the Buddha and his family was designed to overcome the existing prejudice against them. We learn the common view held by the Brahmins of the Sākyas from another account. Here a proud young Brahmin who visits the Buddha and gets a deserved humiliation, in the course of which he lets us know what he and his race think of the Sākyas.

> Rough is this Sākya breed of yours, Gōtama, and rude ; touchy is this Sākya breed of yours and violent. Menials, mere menials, they neither venerate nor value, nor esteem, nor give gifts to, nor pay honours to the Brahmins. That, Gōtama, is neither fitting nor seemly ! . . .
> Once I had to go to Kapilavatthu and went into the Sākyas' Moot Hall. Now, at that time there were a number of Sākyas, old and young, seated in the hall on grand seats, making merry and joking together, nudging one another with their fingers ; and methinks it was I myself that was the subject of their jokes, and not one of them even offered me a seat.
> (*Ambattha Sutta*, 12–13, in Rhys Davids' *Dialogues*.)

If this picture be as true as it is lively we can well believe that the dislike was mutual, and the Sākyas, though possibly Aryanized as to a good deal of their culture, were not Brahminized. Another young Brahmin, better behaved, was the victim of the most cutting exposure of Brahmin claims which the Buddha ever made. The story is told in the beautiful *Tevijja Sutta*, " On the Knowledge of the Vedas."

6. THE BUDDHA'S ENLIGHTENMENT

I cannot afford space here to tell the familiar tale of the occasion of the illumination of the Blessed One as he sat under the Bo tree at Gaya near Uruvelā, in the light of

THE BUDDHA'S PERSONALITY

the full moon of the month of May, in the thirty-fifth year of his age. In solemn and beautiful words he told of this experience many times to his disciples and hearers. Whatever was the content of that experience expressed in terms of the intellect, we may take the liberty of looking at it from the external point of view. The psychology of the great Sākiyan was not that of the Aryan Brahmins. He had sat at their feet for many years in his youth, had learned their lore, and subjected himself to their discipline; but it did not work the expected change. He could not become a Brahmin. His enlightenment was a great psychological reversion to himself, a return to the normal. It was a reversion from a colossal system of speculative dogma to *positivism*, to a certain, specific system of knowledge. That which was first in his experience he put first in his system of teaching : namely, *Suffering*. In the second place the enlightenment was a reversion from a general, hazy, and largely useless *gnosis* to *agnosticism* of a very thorough-going order. Positivism and agnosticism are co-relative. Positive knowledge is gained point by point from the mass of the unknown. Thirdly, the Buddha's illumination was a reversion from the inhuman to *humanism*. There are two extremes of *inhumanism*, both of which the Buddha rejected, as the words of the scripture declare.

> To abandon one's self to *sensuality*, to the base, the common, the vulgar, the unholy, the harmful, and also to abandon one's self to *self-mortification*, to the painful, the unholy, the harmful : both these extremes the Perfect One has rejected and found out the middle path which makes one both to see and to know, which leads to peace, to discernment, to enlightenment and Nirvāna.
> (*Vinaya Texts*, I. p. 94, in *Word of the Buddha*.)

The references to the bodily life quoted in the earlier part of this article show that, contrary to the general opinion, the middle path was not a path of suffering. Life was not scorned; its joys were raised to their purest level for layman and bikkshu alike. "Wherever in the world there is the delightful and the pleasurable, there this craving comes to disappear; there it is dissolved," says the authoritative text. This emphatic humanism is to be met with throughout the literature, although, from our Western point of view, much of it may appear like cold asceticism. Here is what a Brahmin says:

> Now, regarding that venerable Gōtama, such is the high reputation that has been noised abroad: that Blessed One is an Arahat, a fully awakened one, abounding in wisdom and goodness, happy . . . and having known the truth he makes it known to others. The truth, lovely in its origin, lovely in its progress, lovely in its consummation, doth he proclaim both in the spirit and in the letter, the higher life doth he make known.
>
> (*Ambattha Sutta*, 2, in Rhys Davids' *Dialogues*.)

We cannot forget that Confucius, the contemporary of the Buddha, was simultaneously teaching his ultra-humanistic "Doctrine of the Mean" to his own countrymen.

7. THE BUDDHA'S HUMOUR

A special article would hardly do justice to the subtle humour of the Master. The picture of the jolly Sākyas in their Moot Hall is refreshing in the panorama of Hindu religious literature, which, we may say without exaggeration, contains hardly a smile. Yet almost at once, after the solemn, terrible years are over, humour breaks out in the Pali Scriptures. The formal controversies encouraged by the Buddha and his contemporaries are distinguished by extraordinary patience—what need for haste in those expansive days?—and delicate irony. The innumerable parables and fables told and made use of by the Buddha

THE BUDDHA'S PERSONALITY

brighten and beautify the truth he is communicating, while for rollicking fun one must turn to the Jātaka Stories in which, in mock solemnity, the long-drawn-out tale is told of the five hundred previous lives of him who was to become the Buddha. Every joke strikes a blow for truth, whether it be spoken by a monkey, an elephant, or an alligator. Who can read the story of the man pierced by the poisoned arrow or the Master and the handful of leaves, or even the dramatic picture of the man crossing the river on a raft, without feeling that the point is driven home precisely when the listeners' faces are lighted up by smiles, or their bodies shaken with laughter? Many a time in tense discussion with controversialists who are about to be discomfited, the Buddha, entirely unruffled, would utter the conventional threat: "Now, if when questioned a third time you do not reply your head will split asunder!" It is a warning that it is time to give up equivocation—and it generally succeeds. For an example of sustained irony at the expense of a Brahmin—"The Very Reverend Sir Goldstick Sharptooth" as Rhys Davids calls him—I must refer the readers to the *Kūladanta Sutta*, and beg them to read the translator's learned introduction.

If humour be an expression of a peculiar psychological trait it is permissible to remark here that it is much more marked in the literature of the Chinese than of the Hindus. Many of the Suttas find humorous parallels in the discourses of Confucius and Mencius, while the Buddhist Jātakas correspond with the beautiful fun of Chwang-tze. Perhaps, after all, it was the jolly Sākyas who set all India laughing!

8. THE BUDDHA'S DIALECTIC AND RHETORIC

Logic in India had not reached a scientific stage in the Buddha's day. Though we cannot be sure as to when the Nyaya philosophy began or completed its labours, there is little sign of formal logic in the Buddhist Scriptures.

There are conventional formulæ of attack, of defence, of exposition, of exhortation, but it is hard to separate dialectic and rhetoric as used by the Buddha. The convincing instrument of the syllogism in its many forms was unknown in India. A man would sustain his case by being able to answer questions to the satisfaction of his audience, or preferably to his own. The Upanishads contain examples of eristic of this sort employed on the profound metaphysical problems of the schools.

The Buddha had several methods of teaching. He would give long expositions on some theme suggested by a passing incident. In these he would sometimes fall into a formal duologue, putting the questions himself, or inviting them from his hearers. Such discourses tend to reach a level of moving eloquence towards the end, and to be æsthetically satisfying. But in a very large number of the Suttas there is active and spontaneous debate suggestive of real intellectual strife. Brahmins, ascetics, nobles, and sometimes kings, meet with the Buddha and put before him their difficulties, or endeavour to entrap him. They never succeed. Where there is active hostility on the part of some young man, the Buddha will reprove him mildly, or, turning to his disciples, make a critical remark. In difficult cases he pulls up the interlocutor with a question, the significance of which the victim does not see, and involves him in a contradiction, something after the manner of Sokrates. The talks with Ambattha and Vasettha are masterly efforts, in which the Buddha does not so much excel in cleverness as in wisdom and goodness. It is his moral greatness that shines through both his dialectic and his rhetoric. To the Brahmin who scorns the Sākyas on account of their bad manners, he reveals the fact that this very Brahmin is descended from one of the ancient Sākyas slaves ! Many a controversialist would have left the matter there, but the Buddha, seeing his victim ridiculed by his brother Brahmins, comes to his rescue by showing what a

THE BUDDHA'S PERSONALITY

fine fellow that slave-born ancestor was. The moral aim—" handsome is as handsome does "—is kept in view right to the end. He rouses the right feelings by his demeanour, his eloquence, his friendliness. Those who come to quarrel remain to bless, uttering the formula of happy submission in the familiar words of King Ajātasattu.

> Most excellent, Lord, most excellent! Just as if a man were to set up that which has been thrown down, or were to reveal that which has been hidden away, or were to point out the right road to him who had gone astray, or were to bring a lamp into the darkness—even so has the truth been made known to me, in many a figure, by the Blessed One. And now I take refuge in the Blessed One, I take refuge in the Truth, I take refuge in the Order. May the Blessed One accept me as a disciple, as one who from this day forth, as long as life endures, has taken his refuge in them.

(*Samanna-phala Sutta*, 99, in Rhys Davids' *Dialogues*.)

9. THE BUDDHA AS A TEACHER

In spite of the backward state of experimental science in ancient India, and the difficulty of providing logical proof for any of his conceptions, the Buddha must be regarded as the greatest and most successful teacher known to history. He was neither boastful nor humble. He had an equal confidence in himself and his hearers. His secret was to rouse the intuitive faculty, which lies at a higher level than sense perception, feeling or prejudice. To the very last hour he maintained this respect for this confidence in men.

> I have beheld, Lord, how the Blessed One was in health, and I have beheld how the Blessed One had to suffer. And though at the sight of the sickness of the Blessed One my body became weak as a creeper, and the horizon became dim to me, and my faculties were no longer clear, yet, notwithstanding, I took some

little comfort from the thought that the Blessed One would not pass away from existence until, at least, he had left instructions as touching the Order.
(*S.B.E., Mahāparanirvāna Sutta.*)

Thus speaks his beloved disciple and relative, Ananda, as the Buddha reclines on his deathbed, and thus the Blessed One replies :

What, then, Ānanda ? Does the Order expect that of me ? I have preached the truth without making any distinction between exoteric and esoteric doctrine : for in respect of the truths, Ānanda, the Tathāgata has no such thing as the closed fist of a teacher, who keeps some things back. Surely, Ānanda, should there be any one who harbours the thought, " It is I who will lead the brotherhood," or, " The Order is dependent upon me," it is he who should lay down instructions in any matter concerning the Order.

Now the Tathāgata, Ānanda, thinks not that it is he who should lead the brotherhood, or that the Order is dependent upon him. Why, then, should he leave instructions in any matter concerning the Order ? I, too, O Ānanda, am now grown old, and full of years, my journey is drawing to its close, I have reached my sum of days, I am turning eighty years of age ; and just as a worn-out cart, Ānanda, can only with much additional care be made to move along, so, methinks, the body of the Tathāgata can only be kept going with much additional care. It is only, Ānanda, when the Tathāgata, ceasing to attend to any outward thing, or to experience any sensation, becomes plunged in that devout meditation of heart which is concerned with no material object—it is only then that the body of the Tathāgata is at ease.

Therefore, O Ānanda, be ye lamps unto yourselves. Be ye a refuge to yourselves. Betake yourselves to no

THE BUDDHA'S PERSONALITY

external refuge. Hold fast to the truth as a lamp. Hold fast as a refuge to the truth. Look not for refuge to any one beside yourselves. Work out your salvation with diligence.

(*S.B.E.*, *Mahāparanirvāna Sutta*.)

These were the last words of the Blessed One, the Buddha.

IX : *Buddhism and War*

IT is so generally understood that the religion of the Buddha is opposed to war, that it may be considered unnecessary to discuss the matter in any detail; but whatever be the theory held, many Buddhists, both in Japan and China, do actually take part in war; and the smaller nations, such as Tibetans, Burmese and Siamese, though very peacefully disposed, would, upon provocation, no doubt have recourse to war. The position of Buddhists is very similar to that of Christians, who, according to traditions that have never been entirely abandoned, are supposed to prefer and practise peace. At the present time there are, however, only a very small minority of professing Christians who believe that war is explicitly and implicitly forbidden by their doctrine. We are faced by several important and interesting inquiries, which may rightly engage our attention when, as now, the danger of war is preoccupying the mind of the whole world. We have to ask:

(1) What was the prevailing view regarding war held by the predecessors and contemporaries of the Buddha?

(2) In what way did he seek to modify this view?

(3) What were the moral and philosophical grounds upon which the Buddha opposed all war?

(4) What conception had the Buddha of a social order in which his followers might rightly live without war?

(5) What future did he foresee for the world as the result of the spread of his doctrine?

(6) How far has Buddhism actually affected war and peace in the World?

BUDDHISM AND WAR

The Indian social system at the time of the appearance of Gōtama has often been described. It was a firmly established civilization. The origins of many of the customs, both civil and religious, were lost for so long that elaborate myths had grown up in regard to them. India was a rich, prosperous and cultured country, divided into many great kingdoms supported by military power. This power had evolved from the time, centuries before, when the Aryan tribes invaded North-West India, led by chieftains and encouraged by priests and bards. During the long period of settlement, not only were legal and economic affairs regulated by the acute Brahmin court priest, but military affairs as well. In fact, the most precise rules of a religious and military character governed the doings of the warrior clan and their chief, the king. In those days, when armies attacked one another, they left the cultivator and his crops scrupulously untouched. In a very real sense the tribal religion of the Vaidic Period was a warlike religion. The gods of the Aryans, like those of the Greeks, were believed to partake in their contests; and gratitude and worship were poured out to them in sacrifice and praise. No question could then normally arise of antagonism between war and religion or spiritual life. We trace the divergence, which at length led to opposition, to the time when what we may call " personal religion " appeared in India. The recluse, the *yogin*, the Jain monk, or the ascetic of any kind, without in the least intending to set up a new social order, began to depart from that which was dominant; and there appeared among this class an increasing tenderness for life, which could scarcely co-exist with military activities. The ethic of *ahinsa*, non-killing, or generally non-injury, arose in most ancient times in India. Long before Buddhism, it was one of the five preliminary conditions necessary for the attainment of a higher degree of spiritual life. Non-killing, extended to animals and men, was a most important part of ancient, ascetic practice, and was, by the Jains, carried to extraordinary lengths; they would not hurt an insect, much less a man. Their practice was founded on compassion, or the ability to feel another's pain, which they took to be rooted in the nature of things:

> "As in my pain when I am knocked about or struck with a stick . . . or menaced, beaten, burned, tormented, or deprived of life; and as I feel every pain from death down to the pulling out of a hair, in the same way, be sure of this, all kinds of living beings feel the same pain and agony . . . as I, when they are ill-treated in the same way. For this reason all sorts of living things should not be beaten nor treated with violence, nor abused, nor tormented, nor deprived of life. . . ." (S.B.E., *Sutra Kritānga*, II. i. 53.)

But in Brahminism generally, where the same doctrine of non-killing appears, there is also found the doctrine of a special duty, *swadharma*, appropriate to each man. An ascetic or a householder might not kill, but a warrior must. Consequently, in a social order, consisting of many different grades of people, there were as many different *dharmas* or moral codes. If we now recall the general character of the Buddhist ethic, we can understand why it was that an Order (*Sangha*), separate from the general social order, came to be founded. The demands made upon his disciples by the Buddha were scarcely those which a person of normal association could conveniently respond to. Persons accepting and really keeping the precepts would tend to separate themselves from kith and kin—"the homeless life"—though they would not, perhaps, at first, grasp the full significance of the change they were making. But any man, whether "householder" or "homeless one," who took the first precept—"abstinence from destroying life"—and the second—"abstinence from taking what has not been given"—would be naturally cut off from the practice of war.

BUDDHISM AND WAR

In the fifth section of the Pātimokkha we read : " Not to a person with a sword in his hand, unless he is sick, will I preach the *Dhamma* ; this is a discipline which ought to be observed." We cannot yet say that this points to any special prejudice against the soldier, because the staff and the sunshade are equally prohibited. We learn also that the Buddha was questioned as to what property in brass and wood and earthenware the Order might rightly possess, and he replied : " I allow you, all kinds of brass ware, except weapons."

Members of the Order were not allowed to see an army drawn up in battle array, unless for a special reason, nor were they permitted to witness a review or any military display whatever. If these rules were broken repentance was demanded of the offender.

An instructive story is told from which we learn that the life of the Order had such attractions that even soldiers were led to seek admittance.

"Now many distinguished warriors thought : We who go to war and find our delight in fighting, do evil and produce great demerit. . . . These *Sākyaputtiya Samanas* lead indeed a virtuous, tranquil, holy life ; if we could obtain ordination with them, we should desist from evil doing, and do good.

"Then these warriors went to the *Bhikkhus* and were ordained." (*S.B.E.*, *Mahāvagga*, I. 40.)

Now, as the sequel shows, this refuge from the warring world on the part of soldiers led to serious inquiry ; Bimbisāra, the King of Magadha, pointed out to the Buddha that there were " unbelieving kings who are disinclined to the faith," and that if they were not kept at a distance by his soldiery, the members of the Order might be harassed. He begged that soldiers should not be received into the Order, and the Buddha assented with the words : " *Let no one who is in the royal service receive the ordination.*"

This was a friendly compromise with the King, an agreement not to disturb or entice his servants into a life which logically meant the downfall of military power. It was not a prohibition of soldiers as such, on account of assumed unworthiness. But we may learn from this incident that the Order was, in fact, anti-military in a sense that was recognized by the soldiers themselves, the government and the Buddha. In many similar ways the Order tended to become a privileged refuge from the world—"*I take refuge in the Order*,"—but its leader managed by tact and conciliation to maintain a friendly attitude to the state authorities. In this way, as the rigid ethic of the Buddha made headway among the people, a force was developing which would, if consistently extended, undermine the whole fabric of contemporary society, supported as it was by the twofold pillars of the Brahmins and Kshatriyas. Can we determine how far the Buddha intended that this should go? It is a difficult question, and will require further study. We may sum up the historical aspect of the matter in the following way:

When the Buddha began his mission in the midst of a highly complex society of many castes and as many *dharmas*, he undoubtedly attempted to break down the castes and to impose a uniform *dharma*;[1] not openly, perhaps, but implicitly, his teaching aimed as much at reclaiming the warrior from his war-making as the outcast from his bestial superstition. All men were to be weaned from anger, lust and ignorance, the threefold roots of suffering, and, from such beginnings, warfare, part and parcel of suffering, was to cease.

Not only the doctrine of the Buddha, but those of numerous contemporary ascetic Orders were essentially opposed to the prevailing state ethic; but so tolerant was Indian opinion that these Orders, logically subversive of existing society, were religiously patronized and protected.

As soon as we begin to examine the Buddha's *Dhamma*

[1] *Dharma* is Sanscrit; *Dhamma* is Pali, used by the Buddhists.

BUDDHISM AND WAR

on its psychological side, we perceive that, although he showed a tolerance for the military rulers equal to that which was extended to him by them, he was quite frank in his views on their warlike activities. He seems to have considered these as necessary to the life the warriors were living, but that does not prevent him from analysing them to the core. The following passage from No. XIII. of the *Majjhima Nikāya* is both a description of and a judgment on war from the Buddha's point of view.

> Again, out of desire, moved by craving, impelled thereto by craving, only because of craving, ruler contends with ruler, warrior with warrior, brahmin with brahmin, householder with householder, mother with son, son with mother, father with son, son with father, brother with brother, brother with sister, sister with brother, friend with friend. Then, quarrelling, disputing, contending, they set to with fists, clods, sticks or swords, and so come by death and deadly hurt. Such is the wretchedness of craving.
>
> Again, moved by craving, men arm themselves with sword and buckler, quiver and bow, and, each side in battle array, dash at one another; and the arrows fly, and the javelins glance, and the swords flash. And they pierce each other with arrows and with javelins, and cleave one another's heads with swords; and so come by death and deadly hurt. Or, taking sword and buckler, quiver and bow, they scale the newly-daubed ramparts, and arrows fly and javelins glance and swords flash. And they are pierced by arrow and by javelin and they are mangled in hosts, and heads are cloven with swords; and so once more they come by death and deadly hurt. Such is the wretchedness of craving, the sum of suffering which here and now comes to be by reason of craving. (*The Word of the Buddha.*)

Tracing it all to *tanhā* (craving), making no distinction

between private violence and public war, the Buddha made for himself a beginning to bring it all to an end. Such an analysis must have as its counterpart a positive doctrine. This is the renunciation of all violence and the equal extension of sympathy to every living creature. Such passages as the following, occurring often in the Scriptures, illustrate the point.

> "Putting away the killing of living things, Gōtama holds aloof from the destruction of life. He has laid the cudgel and the sword aside, and ashamed of roughness, and full of mercy, he dwells compassionate and kind to all creatures that have life."
> (*Brahma-jala Sutta*, 8, in Rhys Davids' *Dialogues*.)

> "Just as a mighty trumpeter makes himself heard ... even so of all things that have shape or life, there is not one that he passes by or leaves aside, but regards them all with mind set free, deep-felt pity ... sympathy ... equanimity."
> (*S.B.E.*, *Tevijja Sutta*, 79.)

There is not in Buddhism a trace of esoteric doctrine about war; it is everywhere implicitly, and in many passages explicitly, condemned. The fifth step in the Eightfold Path, "Right means of livelihood," authoritatively excludes the profession of soldiering, along with that of the huntsman and the slave-owner.

When in personal danger, the Buddha practises the most calm non-resistance, or else has recourse to "*iddhis*," that is, magical powers. In this connection, it is well to remember that, the very first essential laid down in the *Yoga* philosophy is non-killing; no progress can be made without such a beginning. We are assured that there is a suspension of antipathy towards the man who attains to this virtue; men, animals and birds approach him without fear, and he

BUDDHISM AND WAR

himself is secure. The Buddha again and again declares that right-mindedness relieves a man of danger. The well-known stories of the attack by Devadatta and the wild elephant led to the declaration of equal love contained in the following stanza :

> "Devadatta, who tried to murder him,
> Angulimāla, highway robber chief,
> The elephant set loose to take his life,
> And Rāhula, the Good, his only son—
> The Sage is equal-minded to them all."

Another passage reads :

"Yea, even if he should rebuke thee to thy face, should strike thee with his fists or throw clods of earth at thee, beat thee with his staff or smite thee with his sword, thus shalt thou train thyself : 'My mind shall remain unsullied, evil words shall not escape my lips, kindly and compassionate I will abide, loving of heart, not harbouring secret hate.'"

(*Majjhima Nikāya*, xxi., in *Discourses of Gōtama*.)

Before passing on to the next question, we do well to recall the psychological principles taught in Buddha's discourses. They are really very simple. There are the "three fires" of hatred, lust and delusion, out of which, in various degrees of combination, come all men's sufferings. The natural, unconverted man, goes on adding fuel to the fire by his every deed. Always deluded, ignorant of the true values of life, always wanting, craving, grasping, always at cross-purposes or in opposition to some person or another —never at rest ! These fires are the psychological roots of contention on a small or large scale. Consequently the Buddha is found dealing with things at the roots, and, conquering there, the growth dies down. It seems so simple, so true, and yet in spite of the Buddha's successful life, the fire goes on raging.

From *The Book of the Kindred Sayings* (Pali Text Society's trs.) I extract the following:

Now the King of Magadha, Ajātasattu, mustering an army of cavalry and infantry, advanced into Kāsi against the King, the Kosālan Pasenadi. And the Pasenadi, hearing of the expedition, mustered a similar army and went to meet him. So they two fought one with another, and Ajātasattu defeated the Pasenadi, who retreated to his own capital, Savatthi.

And brethren returning from their alms-round in Savatthi, came and told the Exalted One of the battle and the retreat. He said:

The King of Magadha, Ajātasattu, son of the Accomplished Princess, is a friend to, and intimate of, mixed up with, whatever is evil. The King, the Kosālan Pasenadi, is a friend to, and intimate of, mixed up with, whatever is good. But for the present the Pasenadi will pass this night in misery, a defeated man.

> Conquest engenders hate; the conquered lives
> In misery. But whoso is at peace
> And passionless, happily doth he live;
> Conquest hath he abandoned and defeat.

Now these two Kings met again in battle, as is told in what is aforesaid. But in that battle the Kosālan Pasenadi defeated Ajātasattu, and captured him alive. Then the Pasenadi thought: "Although this King injures me who was not injuring him, yet is he my nephew. What if I were to confiscate his entire army—elephants, horses, chariots and infantry—and leave him only his life? And he did so.

And brethren returning from their alms-tour in Savatthi, brought word of this to the Exalted One. Thereupon the Exalted One, understanding the matter in that hour, uttered these verses:

BUDDHISM AND WAR

A man may spoil another, just so far
As it may serve his ends, but when he's spoiled
By others he, despoiled, spoils yet again.
So long as evil's fruit is not matured,
The fool doth fancy 'now's the hour, the chance!'
But when the deed bears fruit, he fareth ill.
The slayer gets a slayer in his turn;
The conqueror gets one who conquers him;
The abuser wins abuse, the annoyer, fret.
Thus by the evolution of the deed,
A man who spoils is spoilèd in his turn.

In turning to another matter, we are entitled to wonder whether the great teacher expressed a conception of a general social order in which his people might rightly live. Though he was always teaching, and gaining disciples for the *Sangha*, we find very few references suggestive of a coming "golden age," a "utopia," a "new heaven and new earth." The explanation lies perhaps in the difficult doctrine of Nirvāna. While emphatically the Buddha wished all people to behave decently, and to follow the Path, and while he laid down the ideal of life as: "*happiness both now and hereafter for one's self and for others*," yet we are almost persuaded that his ethic was not designed to make a pleasant and happy earth, but to make for salvation, for Nirvāna. May not this be the reason why, apart from the rules of the Order, rigid to a degree, there is not in Buddhism, as there is in Brahminism, Hellenism, Taoism and Christianity, any legislation *for the world*? In a word, there is no general sociology. In Buddhism, and especially in the personal teaching of the founder, there is a striking absence of what we now call political or social reform. Again and again, in advice to Rajas and notables of good or evil disposition, the instruction is of a personal, inner character. It always points to the *Dhamma* as a refuge. The Buddha does not counsel "open diplomacy" or "arbitration" to determine the rights and wrongs of national affairs. He

MYSTICISM OF EAST AND WEST

says nothing about "self-determination," but seems to take his hearer straight to the realm of principles, and leave him to solve his practical difficulty for himself, be he king or peasant. But in spite of this, there are many glimpses afforded of the Buddha's conception of the relation of his work to society generally. In the *Samanna-phala Sutta* there occurs a notable dialogue in which is clearly and fully expressed the social effects that are conceived to follow conversion to the Master's teaching. The King Ajātasattu, after detailing the manner of livelihood of many classes of society, asks a very reasonable question; he says:

> "All these enjoy in this very world the visible fruits of their craft. They maintain themselves and their parents and children and friends in happiness and comfort . . . Can you, sir, declare to me any such immediate fruit, visible in this very world, of the life of a recluse?"

It is a fair and courteous challenge, and the Buddha, after eliciting the fact that the King has addressed the inquiry to other teachers, answers it fully. This answer is generally a recitation of the *Dhamma*, but explicitly a statement of the kind of life which, it would seem, the Buddha thought a worthy and possible one "in this very world." However, here are some of the advantages which react sometimes towards the world and its inhabitants, but always towards the recluse himself. Honour and respect will be shown to him; he is trained in mercy and kindness to all creatures, in honesty, chastity, truthfulness, and all virtues; he is kept free of all vulgarity, luxury, and of all the dangers that come in their train. He obtains confidence of heart, absence of fear; he gains control over the door of his senses, constant self-possession; he is emancipated from covetousness, ill-temper, laziness, worry and perplexity. He attains to joy and peace; he practises the four trances; obtains insight and magical powers and realizes the Four Holy Truths.

BUDDHISM AND WAR

We have to compare this "*immediate fruit visible in this very world*" with that which the man of the world was declared to attain by the practice of his normal vocation, and we have to remember that the Buddha certainly values the former more highly. But still, can we say that the world's problem is solved by the extension of the ascetic life? This doubt may be partly removed by remembering that the "life of a recluse" in the *Sangha* was not merely a *refuge* from the world. Buddhists certainly counted on a strong reflex influence exercised from within the Order *towards* the world—"a cause of welfare to men." As Nāgasena said to King Milinda:

> "The virtuous and well-conducted man is like a medicine in destroying the poison of human corruption; is like a healing herb in quieting the disease of human corruption; is like water in removing dirt and defilement of human corruption; is like the magic jewel in giving all good fortune to men; is like a ship in crossing to the further shore of the four torrents of human viciousness; is like a caravan-leader in conducting men through the wilderness of birth; is like the wind in extinguishing the heat of man's threefold fever; is like a great cloud satisfying man's longings; is like a teacher training men in the acquirement of merit; is like a skilful preceptor in pointing out to men the way to peace. . . . The longer virtuous and noble *bhikkhus* and Brahmins live, the more they avail for the welfare of the multitude, for the happiness of the multitude, for compassionating the world, for the advantage, the welfare, the happiness of gods and men."

(*Milinda-panha*, 195, 1, in Warren's *Buddhism in Translations*.)

This fine thought moves counter to some of those pessimistic passages in which we are led to look forward to æons and æons of suffering—more blood, more tears will be shed, than all the waters of four great seas. By suffering men will turn from suffering, the Buddha teaches. One by one, father, mother, son, daughter, king, citizen, slave will have had enough of it.

> "There will come a time when the great world-ocean will dry up, vanish and be no more. . . . There will come a time when the mighty earth will be devoured by fire, perish and be no more. But, brothers, verily there is no end to the suffering of beings buried in blindness, who seized by craving are ever brought again and again to renewed birth and hasten through the endless round of re-births."
>
> (*Samyutta Nikāya*, xxi. 10.)

What need then was there to legislate in particular against war? In the *Anagata Vamsa*, a document of late date and poor authority, we have what is called a "Buddhist apocalypse." It foretells the future, when every shred of the *Dhamma* will have been lost, every relic destroyed, and every sign that the Perfect One had lived and taught will have vanished from this earth. If this be true to Gōtama's doctrine, we can understand why there is no social order designed for us, no earthly paradise, no regenerated world. The "land of bliss" of the later Buddhist writers is transcendent; it is populated by those who have at one time been in the world, in *samsāra*, and have escaped from it. Thus we are strongly impressed by the fact that from the earlier point of view there is no hope held out that humanity will ever be entirely peaceful and happy. One by one the elect, the faithful, will be saved from the ever-raging storm.

In attempting an answer to our last question: "How far has Buddhism affected the actual war and peace of the world?" we are forced to leave the realm of theory and pass to history. Here we see that the Order never ceased to radiate light beyond its borders into the outside world.

BUDDHISM AND WAR

The "advantages" sought from the motive of a kind of spiritual egoism, overflowed into society, and at length captivated the admiration of no less a person than King Asoka of Magadha. With the exception of Ajātasattu—and even he is said to have repented—the contemporary rulers of India showed to the Buddha the highest respect, and no doubt after his death the attitude of the government continued to be friendly. Asoka was more than friendly; he took the three refuges, and transformed his great military kingdom into a peaceful realm. His Rock Edict cannot be too often quoted :

"His Majesty King Priyadarsin in the ninth year of his reign conquered the Kalingas. One hundred and fifty thousand persons were thence carried away captive, one hundred thousand were there slain, and many times that number perished.

"Ever since the annexation of the Kalingas, His Majesty has zealously protected the *Dhamma*, has been devoted to that law, and has proclaimed its precepts.

"His Majesty feels remorse on account of the conquest of the Kalingas, because, during the subjugation of a previously unconquered country, slaughter, death, and taking away captive of the people necessarily occur, whereat His Majesty feels profound sorrow and regret. . . . All this diffused misery is matter of regret to His Majesty. . . . The loss of even the hundredth or the thousandth part of the persons who were slain, carried away captive, or done to death in Kalinga would now be a matter of deep regret to His Majesty.

"Although a man should do him an injury, His Majesty holds that it must be patiently borne, so far as it can possibly be borne. . . . His Majesty desires for all animate beings security, control over the passions, peace of mind, and joyousness. And this is the chiefest conquest in His Majesty's opinion—the conquest by the *Dhamma*. Delight is found in the conquests made by the *Dhamma*. . . ."

(*Rock Edict*, No. xiii., in Vincent Smith's *Asoka*.)

This is the kind of thing which the *Dhamma* accomplished. Even though, theoretically, the world was to go rolling on in misery, individual Buddhists would be ready to relieve suffering, " for the advantage, the welfare, the happiness of gods and men." Is there any reason why we may not expect, when the sum of contemporary woe is visualized and calculated to the full, that a king, an emperor, a dictator, a statesman, may not feel " remorse, profound sorrow and regret " ? In the days of Açvaghosha, the great Māhayānist teacher, King Kanishka was said to have experienced a similar conversion ; and many monarchs in India and China were attracted to the peaceful *Dhamma*. We are probably warranted in saying that Buddhism went far towards forming that non-combatant temperament which is so often exemplified by Oriental nations, such as the Indians, Chinese, Siamese, and Burmese peoples.

We may now turn to that aspect of the question which I touched upon in my opening sentences. Assuming it to be proved that the teaching of the Buddha, like that of Christ, was formally opposed to all warfare, there remains for us the problem as to why war still continues. Some people find it difficult to believe that if all Buddhists and Christian priests had been faithful to their Masters' teaching, war would have continued for so long. This is a point it is impossible to settle, for the psychological and economic motives towards war are very potent, and can scarcely be turned aside by mere teaching.

The discovery that the aspirations of humanity as represented by religion are in opposition to the economic processes

BUDDHISM AND WAR

by which our life is now sustained may well seem a depressing one, but we must remember that this has for long been the fact.

Every creature is endowed with a love of life, and takes all possible means of protecting itself. The struggle that began millions of years ago on the planet, still continues in the depth of the ocean, in the forest, in the factory and city. It can be seen in a drop of water under the microscope. War hitherto has been a permanent condition of society. It never gave way; it never left the field. We must therefore regard religion, whether Buddhism or Christianity, as having invaded its sphere, knocked at its door, challenged it, and appealed to the men who were conducting it. Wherever religion has in a small way triumphed it has, as it were, only arrested the poison of the world by the antidote of positive goodwill. At times it seems about to triumph, but falls back again. The fighting states of ancient days have simply continued and perfected their Pagan methods down to the present time, and war for them has always been right—including its "atrocities." It is the last word in materialism. It is no surprise to us that there has arisen in the present century a crop of post-war philosophies which are the exact intellectual counterpart of the economic and political system by which we have for long agreed to live. Ancient India in the time of the Buddha produced precisely similar " immoralist " philosophies, to which I have referred in Section VII.

We shall probably find our minds clearer if we admit at once that religion has never conquered more than the fringe of the world. Hitherto there have been men in scores, or hundreds, or thousands, or millions, who have begged the world to be allowed to live in it; but it has always been made difficult for them, even though they have been willing to make themselves defenceless. We can but look forward to the increase in the number and influence of such men and to the removal of the causes of struggle. It is inconceivable that men who have made so many material conquests will not one day find out how not only to " conquer by the *Dhamma*," but also, by it, to supply all their needs, and to live.

X : *Krishna's Advice to Arjuna*

WITH regard to intellectual processes generally, I feel that as much importance should be laid on the manner of receiving doctrine as on its matter.

No one ought to allow himself to be spoon-fed with peptonized philosophy. We do well to remember how Plato made a marked difference between *true opinion* and *knowledge*. Philosophy, in fact, is not philosophy unless by its own force it overcomes our resistance, and captures our conviction. Merely to swallow truth is dangerous enough; how much more so is it to swallow error!

This leads me to ask on what grounds so many people have come to accept as inspired truth every jot and tittle of the *Bhagavad Gītā*. I yield to no one in my admiration for the general view of life there expressed, but I see no reason why that work should be exalted above criticism. Indians may be excused for believing that every *sloka* of it issued from a divine source, just as Christians of pre-critical days might be allowed to show similar regard for their own scriptures; but I cannot understand on what ground the Sermon on the Mount and the discourses of the Buddha, for instance, are subordinated to the rather sophistical teaching supposed to have been given by Krishna to the warrior Arjuna, to overcome his very humane scruples against war.

Before examining the poem we surely ought to inform ourselves as to its origin and position in the literary stream that flows down to us from ancient India. First came the Hymns of the *Rig-Veda*, compositions for the most part of that period when the Aryans were invading and settling in the north-western portion of the peninsula; next came the *Brāhmanas*, the priestly commentaries on the hymns; a further development is represented by the *Āranyakas*, or Forest Books, for the use of those who had retired from active participation in life and sacrificial ritual. At this point philosophy proper begins in those marvellous compositions appended to the earlier collections, of which I have given a brief account. They are known as *Upanishads*; they continued for centuries to be written by various teachers, and they enshrine, preserve and gradually strengthen the famous doctrine called Vedānta. I think it important to remark, however, that although the Vedānta of the Upanishads continued in existence, yet there were numerous departures from its high doctrine. The chief of these was the Sānkhya philosophy of Kapila, about 700 B.C. It was atheistic, and in two centuries was followed by Buddhism, 500 B.C. The Yoga philosophy, built up out of earlier material, was put into *sutra* form by Patanjali, who is believed to have lived about the second century B.C., that is, during the period when Buddhism was making the most extraordinary conquests.

1. POSITION OF THE GĪTĀ IN SANSCRIT LITERATURE

The *Bhagavad Gītā* is found enclosed in the body of the great epic, the *Mahābhārata*, a work which describes the Kuru-Panchala wars of 1250 B.C. The *Gītā* represents Sri Krishna as the Charioteer of Arjuna, teaching him what may be described as an eclectic doctrine, made up of the richest jewels of the Upanishad, Sānkhya and Yoga lore. Could this have been literally possible at a time when not even the Brāhmanas, much more the Upanishads and the philosophical *sutras* had been composed?

We do not know the exact date of the composition of the *Bhagavad Gītā*, but there can be little doubt, judging from its contents, that it made its appearance in the Buddhist period, or, to be more precise, within the century before and the century after Christ. Further, it was one of the several means taken to defend the Brahmin faith and

ADVICE TO ARJUNA

philosophy from being engulfed by the spread of Buddhism.

Now one of the reasons for believing all this is that the author of the work takes the trouble to correct a view about war which did not find expression until the Buddha's time. The Buddha's doctrine, as I show in Section IX, made war morally impossible, and is one of absolute non-resistance. And when the Buddha has occasion to speak of war between nations there is no hint of esoteric doctrine. He traces it directly to *tanhā*, craving.

India did not have long to wait before the Buddha's *Dhamma*, offered to all alike, was accepted by the warrior King Asoka of Magadha. In the ninth year of his reign he conquered the Kalingas, a hitherto independent people. The slaughter and misery were terrific, but they led to a complete change of heart and life in the monarch. His immortal words, cut on rocks for all to see, proclaimed to the world his repentance. In short, the leader of the warrior caste, Asoka, the Emperor, became a Buddhist ; he sent missionaries everywhere, and tried all he could to lay " the cudgel and the sword aside."

We can well believe that such a propaganda was distasteful to the Kshatriyas. All their past tradition of heroism, of glory, enclosed in myth and legend of a thousand fights, was to be destroyed. " Although a man should do him an injury, His Majesty holds that it should be patiently borne, so far as it can possibly be borne." Such were the words of Asoka, an echo of the Buddha's.

2. ARJUNA'S DISTRESS

I now ask my readers to turn to the *Gītā* and read Arjuna's lament, which begins with the words :

> " Krishna ! as I behold, come here to shed
> Their common blood, yon concourse of our kin,
> My members fail, my tongue dries in my mouth,
> A shudder fills my body, and my hair
> Bristles with horror."

It describes the psychology of a man who is filled with sympathy for his fellows ; it rejects triumph and ease gained by slaughter ; it declares that no victory can bring delight, or spoils a recompense for such a loss. It foresees the misery and anguish that must be bred and the guilt that will descend on those who kill. It foresees social disorder and disturbance even to the dead. It values " beggar's bread with those we love " above all rich feasts spread for the conqueror, and finally it makes a remarkable decision in favour of non-resistance :

> " If the sons of Dhritarāshtra, weapon in hand, were to kill me in battle, me being weaponless and not defending myself, that would be better for me."

While admitting that the *Gītā* appears to aim at overcoming this feeling of pity, let us reserve our examination of the way it does so till a little later. Let us first gain a conception of what the general, rather than the specific, teaching of the *Gītā* is, and see how that affects the opening argument. It is a book of "yoga," not exclusively for the warrior, but for all. It encourages men to effort in a variety of ways, and whether we will or not, we soon forget the literary artifice which determined its form and occasion. It teaches the Sānkhya view of the soul, its eternity, its indestructibility, its incorruptibility, and, most profound doctrine of all, its essential non-activity (see Section V). It teaches the yoga of meditation, the yoga of work, the yoga of knowledge, the yoga of devotion and faith. In the tenth and eleventh books the Vedānta doctrine of the unity of all life is beautifully presented, but the ethical deduction that we must therefore not destroy any form of life is *not* there drawn as it is elsewhere, perhaps for obvious reasons. The life and experience of the yogin are precisely described, "steadfastly meditating, solitary, his thoughts controlled, his passions laid away, quit of belongings." The life of the mendicant sannyasin, propertyless and charitable,

ADVICE TO ARJUNA

at the service of all, is expounded in all its spiritual attractiveness. Every discourse, as I read the *Gītā*, takes me further away from the battlefield, leads me to ignore the two waiting armies which I thought were eager for each other's blood; and often enough, when references are made to them by the teacher, the military terms appear to be allegorical. For instance:

> "Thus knowing that which is higher than the understanding, and restraining self by Self, O you of mighty arms! destroy this unmanageable enemy in the shape of desire."
>
> (iii. 43.)
>
> "Therefore, O descendant of Bhārata! destroy, with the sword of knowledge, these misgivings of yours which fill your mind and which are produced from ignorance. Engage in devotion. Arise!"
>
> (iv. 42.)

I ask my readers to consider this situation: Arjuna is supposed to have heard from the lips of a divine teacher a doctrine of the deepest metaphysical nature, the most exalted piety and the strictest ethic. We also have, so to speak, been listeners to the very best that India could at that moment produce ("and he who will study this holy dialogue of ours, will have offered me the sacrifice of knowledge"). Step by step we have been removed from the passion and turmoil of life, and have been illuminated with a fresh scale of values, by the revelation of the inner nature of the universe, "One, the self of all." When, therefore, Arjuna, true to the literary fiction of a battle on the sacred plain, declares at the end:

> "Destroyed is my delusion; by your favour, O undegraded one! I now recollect myself. I stand freed from doubts. I will do your bidding,"
>
> (xviii. 73.)

does he, and do we, forthwith seize weapons of destruction?

Do we not rather wish to remain on the high plane of life to which we have been insensibly lifted by the work of an incomparable artist ? I think we do, and I think that was the intention of the composer of the poem. In the end surely, if not at the beginning, "Kurukshetra" is seen to be no earthly battlefield.

There is another problem that meets the student of the *Bhagavad Gītā* which I would like to see solved. The teaching in regard to war is undoubtedly there, staring us in the face ; in spite of what we may think of it, it cannot be got rid of, or explained away. There are two questions we are at liberty to ask : (1) Why did the author of the poem use the artifice he does to recommend his lofty teaching ? And (2) is the teaching of the first and second discourses, by which the warrior is urged to war, philosophically and morally sound ?

We must remember the heroic character of the *Mahābhārata*, and see that any subsidiary work, of whatever nature, would have to show a similar heroic *form*, if it were to be inlaid into the main poem. It is quite certain that poets have often attempted to secure immortality for their later composed works by taking refuge within the *corpus* of an already great and accepted literature ; and many scholars are of opinion that the *Bhagavad Gītā*, the *Sanatsugātīya* and the *Anugītā* were composed and inserted in the *Mahābhārata* in this way. If so, we can understand that the author of the *Gītā* was, in a manner, compelled to choose a point in the main epic at which it would be æsthetically appropriate to insert a philosophical dialogue of some importance. The choice is an excellent one. But further, our author wishes to recommend his doctrine to the ruling caste, already, as I have argued, subject to the hostile permeation of Buddhism. While thinking, then, that he may be quite sincere in speaking to a warrior in the only manner that was psychologically possible, I advance the opinion that he wishes to do with the warrior what he

ADVICE TO ARJUNA

does with those who "study this holy dialogue of ours," namely, to lift him insensibly from the whole world which he values, perhaps too highly. There is much significance in the words in the second discourse: "Thus far I speak unto thee as from the Sānkhya—unspiritually; hear now the deeper teaching of the Yoga."

3. FOUR THESES

I think the first question has been adequately answered by the critical considerations I have offered, so that the second question, by far the more difficult, remains before us. We must examine all the passages in which Krishna seems to be urging Arjuna towards fighting, where he approves of war, explains it dogmatically or philosophically, or even when he discusses the correlative doctrines of the nature of the soul and of death. I have done this tentatively, and I divide the passages into four classes, namely:

A. Those that state the simple *military ethic* as understood by warriors at all times.
B. Those that teach a *truth*, otherwise valid, that is, as I think, *misapplied* in justifying war.
C. Those that are *dogmatic esoteric* statements about the nature of war.
D. Those that seem to rest on a philosophic basis.

I propose to select typical examples of each category, and to examine them closely and separately, though in the text they are often interwoven.

A. Military Ethic.—After the lament of Arjuna, Krishna uses these words:

(1) How comes it that this delusion . . . has overtaken you in this place of peril? Be not effeminate, O Son of Prithā! It is not worthy of you. Cast off this base weakness of heart, and arise, O terror of your foes! (II. 3.)

(2) Having regard to your own duty also, you ought not to falter, for there is nothing better for a Kshatriya than a righteous battle. . . . But if you will not fight this righteous battle, then you will have abandoned your own duty and your fame, and will incur sin. All beings, too, will tell of your everlasting infamy; and to one who has been honoured, infamy is greater than death. Masters of great chariots will think that you abstained from the battle through fear, and having been highly thought of by them, you will fall down to littleness. (II. 31–35.)

(3) Be up, obtain glory, and vanquishing your foes, enjoy a prosperous kingdom. (XI. 33.)

There can be no question that from the military point of view the compassionate doubts of Arjuna appear as effeminate weakness. It is a soldier's duty to obey his superiors, and he has to have no qualms of conscience. If he has such, they will not be understood or appreciated, but will be met by precisely the arguments above recited. Let us admit, too, that these doctrines have a validity of their own within the sphere of politico-military life. Warfare ceases to be practicable immediately the general military ethic is challenged. In war, whether for a good or an evil cause, the general welfare is served by single-eyed obedience and abandonment of personal interests. Any warrior, be he Kuru or Pandu, Greek or Persian, Roman or Goth, Frank or Hun, British or German, would use these words of the *Gītā* to overcome a doubter. The fact that the author employs the Deity to hallow such common doctrines indicates to us the power of Arjuna's compassion; but merely to put into the mouth of God what any non-commissioned officer would naturally and—in the circumstances—rightly say, is not to refute, but merely to overwhelm, the Buddhistic opposition to war, which I believe Arjuna is intended to express.

ADVICE TO ARJUNA

B. Truth Misapplied.—We come now to a more difficult matter. There were already ancient doctrines about the nature of the self (ātman) preserved in the Vedānta, Sānkhya and Yoga philosophies. In the *Gītā* these are expressed in many passages, of which I quote a few, such as the following:

(4) You grieve where no grief should be, though you speak words that sound wise. Truly wise men grieve not for the living nor for the dead. Never did I not exist, nor you, nor these rulers of men; nor will any one of us ever hereafter cease to be. As in this body, infancy and youth and old age come to the embodied self, so does the acquisition of another body; a sensible man is not deceived about that.

(II. 11–13.)

(5) Know that to be indestructible which pervades all this; the destruction of that inexhaustible principle none can bring about. These bodies appertaining to the embodied Self, which is eternal, indestructible and indefinable are declared [by the Sānkhya philosophy] to be perishable.

(II. 17–18.)

(6) Unborn, everlasting, unchangeable, and very ancient, he is not killed when the body is killed. O Son of Prithā! how can that man who knows the Self thus to be indestructible, everlasting, unborn, and imperishable, kill any one, or cause any one to be killed?

(II. 20–21.)

This last question is double-edged. The fact of the immortality of the soul is surely not a reason for the destruction of other people's bodies! Birth comes by a natural process, why not wait for natural death? As Krishna himself says, in the same discourse:

(7) But even if you think that the Self is constantly born and constantly dies, still you ought not to grieve thus. For to one that is born, death is certain; and to one that dies, birth is certain. Therefore about this unavoidable thing you ought not to grieve.

(II. 26–27.)

This is a sound argument against grieving for death, but it is not a good answer to one who, full of compassion for others, does not wish to slay them. Death by the sword is *not unavoidable*.

Now, if we regard the doctrines of the immortality of the soul and of reincarnation, as affirmed in these passages, as true, what is the logical deduction we shall draw from them? An increase of confidence and equability, while in the embodied life! A man will value the spiritual life more highly, he will perhaps be ready to lose the bodily life, if necessary, with less fear than normally. His bodily life will immediately exhibit, in his behaviour to others, the sense of his spiritual values, but he will not be warranted in despising or throwing away his own body, still less will he wish to deprive others, less wise than himself, of their bodies. For this reason I regard the military ethic—" Therefore fight "—deduced from these granted truths, as logically forced and inconsequent, and as morally false. Indeed, we have the extraordinary double *non-sequitur*, that because the body is perishable, "*therefore* engage in battle"; and because the Self is immortal, "*therefore* arise resolved to engage in battle."

The Vedas generally, and the Sānkhya philosophy in particular, elaborated an excellent ethical doctrine, known as *Karma-yoga*. To work strenuously, but not for one's own purposes, "renouncing the fruit of works," was expected to lead to two results: the welfare of one's soul, and the good of others in the world. The Sānkhya philosophy went further, and even affirmed that action was

ADVICE TO ARJUNA

not a function of the Soul (Purusha), but only of Nature (Prakriti). The author of the *Gītā* expounds these doctrines fully, and to good purpose, but in some passages, as I think, wrenches them aside to support the military ethic.

(8) As the ignorant act with attachment to action, so should a wise man act without attachment.
(III. 25.)

(9) He whose mind is deluded by egoism thinks himself the doer of the actions, which in every way are done by the qualities of Nature (the *Gunas* of *Prakriti*). But he who knows the truth . . . forms no attachments.
(III. 29.)

(10) He who is possessed of devotion, abandoning the fruit of actions, attains the highest tranquillity. He who is without devotion, and attached to the fruit of action, is tied down by reason of his acting in consequence of some desire.
(V. 12.)

4. ILLOGICAL CONCLUSIONS.

All this seems acceptable enough until we learn that the author really wishes us to deduce "therefore fight" from these doctrinal premises. Surely, *Karma-yoga* and *Karma-sannyasa-yoga* cannot be applied legitimately to war, we say: and yet this is precisely the nature of the military ethic; the ideal soldier does not direct his own actions, he does *not* fight for himself, he renounces the fruit of his action. How subtle and dangerous is the reasoning here! The author is making the profound ideas of the Sānkhya into a kind of determinism which sweeps away free-will and ethical responsibility, yet leaves the military ethic standing.

Another passage concludes this section. Krishna is speaking as Brahman, the Supreme:

(11) He who leaves this body and departs from this world remembering me in his last moments, comes into my essence. There is no doubt of that ... therefore at all times remember me, *and engage in battle*. ... He who thinks of the Supreme divine being, possessed of abstraction in the shape of continuous meditation, goes to the Supreme. ... A devotee, knowing all this, obtains all the holy fruit which is prescribed for the study of the Vedas, for sacrifices, and also for penances and gifts, and he attains to the highest and primeval seat. (VIII. 5–8.)

After reading the whole of this memorable and lofty discourse on " Union by Devotion to the One Supreme God " we feel that the words " therefore engage in battle " are either false in logic and morality, or that they are entirely allegorical. And, for the credit of the author, we should naturally choose the second alternative. The " battle " is part of the *yoga*, part of the *effort* to reach union with the Divine.

C. Esoteric Dogma.—The military ethic is supported by many statements that doubtless represent the opinion of the time, such as the following :

(12) Happy those Kshatriyas who can find such a battle, an open door to heaven. (II. 32.)

(13) 'Tis I who bid them perish ! Thou wilt but slay the slain. (XI. 33.)

(14) Whoso, for lack of knowledge, seeth himself as the sole actor, knoweth naught at all, and seeth naught. Therefore, I say, if one, holding aloof from self, with unstained mind, should slay all yonder host, being bid to slay, he doth not slay ; he is not bound thereby. (XVIII. 17.)

ADVICE TO ARJUNA

These dogmas seem terribly dangerous; they cut at the root of moral responsibility and leave to man no shred of choice.

D. *Sound Philosophy.* The doctrines brought together in the *Bhagavad Gītā* are those of the Upanishads, the Sānkhya and the Yoga, together with a great many elements of North Indian religions, not excluding Buddhism. In order to determine what view was taken about war by these systems, one would have to examine them in their pre-*Gītā* stage. I have already stated that Buddhism was entirely opposed to war, and I almost shrink from making a statement about the other three great groups from which the *Gītā* is drawn. I will say this, however: The Sānkhya Aphorisms of Kapila open with the words: "Well, the complete cessation of pain which is of three kinds is the complete end of man." They bear a remarkable resemblance to the Buddha's dictum: "One thing only, Brothers, do I teach, suffering and an end of suffering." I cannot find a single word in the hundreds of aphorisms in which war is either directly or indirectly referred to, nor are the peculiar Sānkhya doctrines (as they appear in the *Gītā*) here accompanied by the ethical deductions to which I have called attention. The same, and more, may be said of the *Yoga Sutras* of Patangali. The very first condition of yoga is *ahinsa*, non-killing, and Sutra I., 35, declares: "Abstinence from killing being confirmed, there is suspension of antipathy in the presence of him who has acquired it." The commentary adds: "When one has acquired this confirmed habit of mind, even natural antipathy is held in abeyance in his presence; needless to add that no one harms or injures him. All beings—men, animals, birds—approach him without fear and mix with him without reserve."

"Be thou yogi," says Krishna to his disciple. He cannot have forgotten the first condition of "harmlessness."

As to the *Vedānta Sutras* of Badarāyana and the immense

commentaries of Sankara and Ramānuja, I do not profess to have waded through them all ; but I can find no reference to war in the sense expounded in the *Gītā*. Krishna is only once mentioned, and the warriors not at all. The *Sutras* open with the words : " Now therefore the enquiry into Brahman, from which the origin, subsistence and dissolution of this world proceed " (I. and II.). The aim of life is to obtain the knowledge which liberates from all illusion ; when that goal is reached, they tell us, a man will be able to say, " That Brahman am I " ; he will realize his unity, nay, his identity with everything. He will see himself in his fellow-creature, " if he looks in the pupil of his eye." The old Upanishad says :

> Now that person, bright as gold, who is seen within the sun, golden altogether to the finger tips, whose eyes are like the blue lotus . . . and that person who is seen within the eye . . . the form of the one is the same as that of the other . . . the name of the one is the name of the other.
> (*S.B.E., Chand. Up.* : I. 7.)

5. NON-INJURY

Such a deep metaphysical doctrine must demand an exalted ethic. So far from regarding others as aliens or enemies, so far from being willing to harm them, the true Vedāntist will see himself in them. One is almost ashamed to draw the inevitable deduction as regards the infliction of injury and taking of life in war, but the *Gītā* at its loftiest point declares it : " He who knows himself in everything and everything in himself *will not injure the self by the self —na hinsati ātmanāh ātmānam.*"

If, then, we for the moment take our stand on the ancient and reputable philosophies that arose from the Vedas, we are bound to conclude that the *Bhagavad Gītā's* military doctrines are not directly drawn from them. They rest,

ADVICE TO ARJUNA

no doubt, on the more popular conceptions and ideals that are enclosed in the epic poetry of India, where warriors shine in as brilliant a light as Homer's or Malory's heroes.

Even though we are fascinated by the splendid deeds of ancient warriors, even though we thrill at the memory of the beautiful courage and fidelity of the men in the trenches, even though every man in his heart wished to be with those of his nation and every woman yearned to succour them—yet we must keep our judgment clear. War is a terrible thing; it is but part of that oppressive illusion out of which we long to escape; but we shall not escape until we have judged it truly.

XI : *Nirvāna*

THE study of Nirvāna has occupied the attention of scholars since the Buddhist literature first became known in the West; but it is probably true that at the present moment the general and popular notion of the meaning of the word is still vague and inaccurate.

It is difficult to speak of any special aspect of the Buddha's teaching without touching on the general nature of the whole, because the different elements are so closely bound together; but on the present occasion I shall assume such a general knowledge of the main doctrines of Buddhism as will make it unnecessary for me to do more than state them in outline, and to concentrate upon Nirvāna.

The synoptic diagram facing this page will assist the reader.

A general warning to all who study philosophy has been given by Bergson in recent years, and may be repeated here; it is, that we must distinguish between the actual unseen energy—the continuous movement of things—and the categories, divisions, or classifications into which the intellect arbitrarily separates that energy. The moral is obvious: Nirvāna, whatever it be, cannot be confined within the limits of our intellect. After all that has been said, let us admit that the precise truth may not yet have been stated.

The easiest way to approach our subject is through etymology. *Nirvāna* is derived from Sanscrit roots, which mean " outblown " or " extinguished " in relation to a flame. We must therefore inquire how it came about that this particular fire symbology was adopted by the Buddha to

NIRVĀNA

express a spiritual state. But, we may ask, What is Nirvāna? What is it that is extinguished?

The answer to this question is given in the Buddha's famous "Fire Sermon," delivered at Gayā to a large company of disciples. In a word, the whole of sentient existence is explained as "a burning." If the then current Idealism had said that there was a permanent indestructible Spiritual Reality behind the show of things; or if, on the contrary,

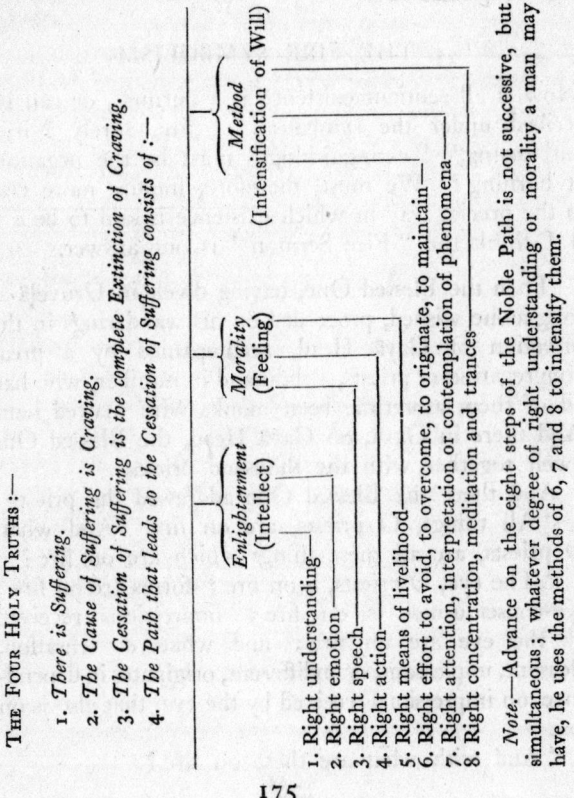

THE FOUR HOLY TRUTHS:—

1. *There is Suffering.*
2. *The Cause of Suffering is Craving.*
3. *The Cessation of Suffering is the complete Extinction of Craving.*
4. *The Path that leads to the Cessation of Suffering consists of:—*

Enlightenment (Intellect)
1. Right understanding
2. Right emotion

Morality (Feeling)
3. Right speech
4. Right action
5. Right means of livelihood

Method (Intensification of Will)
6. Right effort to avoid, to overcome, to originate, to maintain
7. Right attention, interpretation or contemplation of phenomena
8. Right concentration, meditation and trances

Note.—Advance on the eight steps of the Noble Path is not successive, but simultaneous; whatever degree of right understanding or morality a man may have, he uses the methods of 6, 7 and 8 to intensify them.

Materialism of that day had declared that all phenomena have material causes, the Buddhist formula replied in these terms :—*Everything burns*; everything is a flamelike *in-force*, a form of energy, clamant, affirmatory, in a state of perpetual change and combustion ; it is a fire kept alight by fuel being continually added to it. While the Buddha was preaching his " Fire Sermon " in India, Herakleitos at Ephesus was uttering his famous formula *panta rei*, " all flows " ; nothing is permanent. He, too, reduced all things to primal fire.

1. THE FIRE SYMBOLISM

Now if all sentient existence is a burning, or can be so described under the symbolism of fire, surely Nirvāna, " outblowing," " extinguishing," must be the negation of that burning ? We must, therefore, inquire more closely into the precise way in which existence is said to be a fire, and I think the " Fire Sermon " is our answer.

> Then the Blessed One, having dwelt in Uruvelā as long as he wished, proceeded on his wanderings in the direction of Gayā Head, accompanied by a great congregation of priests, a thousand in number, who had all of them aforetime been monks with matted hair. And there in Gayā, on Gayā Head, the Blessed One dwelt together with the thousand priests.
>
> And there the Blessed One addressed the priests :
> " All things, O priests, are on fire. And what, O priests, are all these things which are on fire ?
> " The eye, O priests, is on fire ; forms are on fire ; eye-consciousness is on fire ; impressions received by the eye are on fire ; and whatever sensation, pleasant, unpleasant, or indifferent, originates in dependence on impressions received by the eye, that also is on fire.
> " And with what are these on fire ?

NIRVĀNA

"With the fire of passion, say I, with the fire of hatred, with the fire of infatuation; with birth, old age, death, sorrow, lamentation, misery, grief, and despair are they on fire.

"The ear is on fire; sounds are on fire; . . . the nose is on fire; odours are on fire; . . . the tongue is on fire; tastes are on fire; . . . the body is on fire; . . . things tangible are on fire; . . . the mind is on fire; . . . ideas are on fire; mind-consciousness is on fire; impressions received by the mind are on fire; and whatever sensation, pleasant, unpleasant, or indifferent, originates in dependence on impressions received by the mind, that also is on fire.

"And with what are these on fire?

"With the fire of passion, say I; with the fire of hatred, with the fire of infatuation; with birth, old age, death, sorrow, lamentation, misery, grief, and despair, are they on fire.

"Perceiving this, O priests, the learned and noble disciple conceives an aversion. And in conceiving this aversion, he becomes divested of passion, and by the absence of passion he becomes free, and when he is free he becomes aware that he is free; and he knows that rebirth is exhausted, that he has lived the holy life, that he has done what it behoved him to do, and that he is no more for this world."

[*Mahā-vagga*, 1, 21. Warren's translation.)

The word Nirvāna is not used here, but the idea that stands behind it is emphasized: "he becomes divested of passion, and by the absence of passion he becomes free (i.e. Mōksha), and when he is free he is aware that he is free."

Observe, it is not stated that life is a burning, and *death* is its extinction; rather life and death are a fire; out of fire comes misery and suffering. Nirvāna is the dying down of the flames, the assuagement of the misery. Already there is a close analysis of the consciousness into various forms—the eye, the touch, the mind, etc.—and a tentative analysis of the passions.

A passage from the Jātakas takes us a step further.

" '. . . Wherein does Nirvāna consist?' To him whose mind was already averse to passion, the answer came: 'When the fire of lust is extinct, that is Nirvāna; when the fires of hatred and infatuation are extinct, that is Nirvāna; when pride, false belief and all other passions and torments are extinct, that is Nirvāna. She has taught me a good lesson. Certainly Nirvāna is what I am looking for.'"

(*Introduction to the Jātakas*, i. 58. Warren's translation.)

It must be noted that the passage from the Jātakas refers specifically to at least five fires, and leads us to believe that there are many others; but as the doctrine became more definite and formal, we find that the fires were reduced to three in number, namely (1) that which refers to all degrees of craving or attachment—lust, infatuation and greed (Lobha); (2) that which refers to all degrees of antipathy—hatred, anger, vexation or repugnance (Dosa); and (3) that which refers to all degrees of ignorance—delusion, dulness and stupidity (Moha or Avidya).

The first and second fires relate to the emotions, and cover the whole scale of one's attitude and *feelings* towards other beings, while the third fire relates to all *ideas* that are in any way removed from the truth.

Having shown the nature of the fires which in Nirvāna are supposed to be "blown out," we may now turn to passages in the scriptures where such states of consciousness are directly referred to, without the fire symbol, or under some other symbol.

NIRVĀNA

" . . . excited by greed (Lobha), brothers, furious with anger (Dosa), blinded by delusion (Moha), with mind overwhelmed, with mind enslaved, men reflect upon their own misfortune, men reflect upon the misfortune of others, men experience mental suffering and anguish. If, however, greed and anger and delusion are done away, men reflect neither upon their own misfortune, nor upon the misfortune of others, men experience no mental suffering and anguish. Thus, brothers, is Nirvāna visible in this life, and not merely in the future; inviting, attractive, accessible to the wise disciple."
(*Anguttara Nikāya*, III. 53, in *Word of Buddha*.)

In this passage the symbol " fire " has been replaced by others—" excited," " furious," " blinded," " overwhelmed," " enslaved "—but their antithesis " done away " is expressed by Nirvāna, the opposite of " fire."

2. FUEL AND THE FIRE

If we adhere to the fire symbolism, we may amplify a remark made in the opening, as to the way in which fuel is added to the flame. The Buddhist doctrine of Karma (or Deeds) may be reduced to a sentence : *Deeds of a certain kind add fuel and keep the furnace raging ; the cessation of those deeds and the performance of others facilitate the extinction of the fire, or let it die out.* Thus bad Karma makes for fire, good Karma makes for Nirvāna. I quote a passage to illustrate this :

"(1) Lust is thus defined : passion, infatuation, fawning, compliance, delighting in, longing, languishing, devouring, greed, generation, cleaving to, craving, wanting, cupidity ; craving for forms, sounds, odours, tastes, tangible things, property, children, life, intemperance, agitation, longing for the agreeable, lawless lust, hungering for, envying, imploring, thirst for sensual indulgence.

"Good Karma will be made by the diminution of these mental states.

"(2) Hatred is thus defined : annoyance that springs from the thought 'he has done, is doing, or will do me harm,' or 'he has done harm to some one dear or precious to me, or he has conferred benefit on some one I dislike,' or when annoyance springs groundlessly, because it rains too much, or does not rain, or the sun is hot, or not hot enough, or because one cannot sweep away the dead leaves, or because one cannot put on one's robe because of the wind, or because one has fallen over a tree stump. All such vexation of spirit, repugnance, resentment, hostility, ill-temper, irritation, indignation, hatred, irascibility, getting upset, derangement, opposition, hostility, churlishness, abruptness, disgust.

"Good Karma will be made by the absence of these states.

"(3) Ignorance is briefly defined as the lack of knowledge about the four great truths—that is to say, about the existence of pain and sorrow, ignorance as to the cause of pain and sorrow, ignorance as to the means of extinguishing pain and sorrow, and ignorance about the path that leads towards the extinction of pain and sorrow. It is also lack of insight, understanding, wakefulness, penetration, comprehension, sounding, comparing, contemplation, perspicacity; impurity, childishness, stupidity, obtuseness—in short, avidya.

"The removal of any of these mental states will be a step towards vidya, and the making of good karma."

(Mrs. Rhys Davids' *Dhamma-Sangani*, abridged.)

The whole Buddhist ethic, therefore, is designed to put

NIRVĀNA

out these fires, or more correctly speaking, *to let them go out*.

It is perhaps not necessary to fortify the position taken up by further quotations, yet before passing to another phase of the subject a few more passages may be usefully stated. Here the fire symbol disappears and Nirvāna is defined in terms of psychology.

"These wise people, meditative, steady, always possessed of strong powers, attain to Nirvāna, the highest happiness." *(S.B.E., Dhammapada, 23.)*

"A Bhikshu who delights in reflection, who looks with fear on thoughtlessness, cannot fall away—he is close upon Nirvāna." *(Ibid., 32.)*

"One is the road that leads to wealth, another the road that leads to Nirvāna." *(Ibid., 75.)*

"Those who are free from worldly desires attain to Nirvāna." *(Ibid., 126.)*

"If, like a shattered gong when struck, thou utter not, then thou hast reached Nirvāna; contentment is known to thee." *(Ibid., 134.)*

"Health is the greatest gift, contentedness the best riches, trust the best of relationships, Nirvāna the highest happiness." *(Ibid., 204.)*

"Those who are ever watchful, who study day and night, who strive after Nirvāna—their passions will come to an end." *(Ibid., 226.)*

"The getting rid of the "conditions," the destruction of desire, the absence of passion, quietude of heart, Nirvāna!" *(Mahā-vagga, I. 5, 4.)*

"I have gained coolness by the extinction of all passion and have attained Nirvāna."
(*Ibid.*, I. 6, 8.)

"He who has overcome doubt is without pain, delights in Nirvāna, is free from greed, a leader of the world of men and Devas—such a one the Buddhas call 'victorious on the path.'" (*Kunda Sutta*, 4.)

> "To him who gives such virtue be increased;
> In him who curbs himself no anger can arise;
> The righteous man casts off all sinfulness,
> And, by the rooting out of lust and bitterness
> And all delusion, doth to Nirvāna reach."
> (*S.B.E., Mahāparanibbāna Sutta*, IV. 58.)

3. THE FORMULA OF RELEASE

A well-known formula recurs in the Scriptures as follows:

"And ere long he attained to that supreme goal Nirvāna, the highest life—for the sake of which men go out from all and every household gain and comfort, to become homeless wanderers; yea, that supreme goal did he himself, and while yet in this visible world bring himself to the knowledge of, and continue to realise and see face to face. And he became conscious that birth was at an end, that the higher life had been fulfilled, that all that should be done had been accomplished, and that after this present life there would be none beyond it."
(*Ibid.*, V. 68.)

So far we have established the nature of what may be called the *Moral Nirvāna*. It is undoubtedly for the amelioration of this life; but we are still faced with intellectual problems concerning it. It is clear that this

NIRVĀNA

moral, terrestrial Nirvāna must have a more than moral and earthly significance. It may well be asked, what happens to the Arhat or Nirvāni, who in this life has attained to it, as he approaches his death ? For others, who have not attained Nirvāna, there is still the heaving ocean of Samsāra, there is still *Time*—as Nāgasena says to King Milinda :

" . . . there are conditions of heart which are now producing their effect, or still have in them the inherent possibility of producing effect, or which otherwise will lead to reindividualization. Where there are beings, who when dead, will be reborn, there time is. Where there are beings who are altogether set free (who having attained to Nirvāna in their present life have come to the end of that life), there time is not, because of their having been quite set free."

(*S.B.E.*, *Milinda-panha*, II. 2, 9.)

4. NIRVĀNA AND THE FARTHER NIRVĀNA

We must therefore distinguish betwixt Nirvāna as heretofore described, and Paranirvāna, its consequences after death.

Nāgasena explains the matter thus :

" All foolish individuals, O King, take pleasure in the senses and in the objects of sense, find delight in them, continue to cleave to them. . . . But the wise, O King, neither takes pleasure in those things, nor continues cleaving to them. And inasmuch as he does not, in him Craving (Tanhā) ceases, and by the cessation of Craving Grasping (Upādāna) ceases, and by the cessation of Grasping Becoming (Bhava) ceases, and when Becoming has ceased, Birth ceases, and with its cessation old age, death, grief, lamentation, pain, sorrow, and despair cease to exist. Thus has the cessation brought about the end of all that aggregation of pain." (*Ibid.*, III. 4, 6.)

Thus it is that cessation is farther Nirvāna. Cessation, that is, of becoming, of birth, and of all its consequences. This is obviously much more than the moral Nirvāna.

Having gone thus far in tracing the Moral Nirvāna, and the Metaphysical Paranirvāna, can we be surprised that this latter becomes, in the literature, the more objectively real? We soon find the Buddhists speaking of Nirvāna as existing "of itself," discussing its origin, as if it formed a part of the cosmos. In the *Milinda Panho*, and elsewhere, there is sufficient proof of this development, in spite of efforts made to oppose it.

> "The Blessed One gave hundreds of reasons for entering on the way to the realization of Nirvāna. But he never told us of a cause out of which Nirvāna could be said to be produced. . . .
> "Nirvāna is unproducible, and no cause for its origin has been declared. . . .
> "It is uncompounded, not made of anything. Of Nirvāna it cannot be said that it has been produced, or not been produced, or that it can be produced, that it is past, present, or future, that it is perceptible to the eye, or the ear, or the nose or the tongue, or of the sense of touch." (*Ibid.*, IV. 7, 13–16.)

On the contrary, the idea of *cause* is associated with that which prevents the Nirvāna which, so to speak, is waiting to supervene when the chain of causation—craving, suffering, rebirth—is exhausted. Since Nirvāna is said to be not only the goal of any given life, but of life itself considered as a chain of embodiments, and also of life in the aggregate for all sentient beings, it is almost inevitable that Buddhists should invest that goal with a greater degree of *Reality* than any other form of existence. If the Terrestrial

NIRVĀNA

Nirvāna for me is the highest, the best of Time's Experiences, how can the more exalted Parinirvāna be less real?

It is clear that many critics, both ancient and modern, have regarded Nirvāna as Annihilation. I quote an answer said to have been given by the Buddha on this very topic.

"However, Brothers, through the complete fading out of delusion, through the arising of Wisdom, through the annihilation of craving (Tanhā), no future birth lies any more before ; for the actions (Kamma) of men, Brothers, that are not due to greed, anger, or delusion, which do not spring from greed, anger, or delusion, which are not brought about by them, which have not their origin in them, inasmuch as greed, hate, and anger have disappeared, have been abandoned and rooted out ; such actions, like a palm tree torn out of the soil, are cut off, and do not lead to any further entry into existence.

"In this respect, Brothers, verily one may rightly say to me, 'The ascetic Gōtama teaches Negation, the ascetic Gōtama teaches Annihilation,' for certainly, Brothers, I teach Annihilation—the Annihilation namely, of Greed, the Annihilation of Anger, the Annihilation of Delusion, as well as the Annihilation of the manifold evil, unwholesome conditions of the mind."

(*Majjhima Nikāya* and *Anguttara Nikāya II* and *III*.)

This passage may be regarded as an escape from an intellectual dilemma by a refusal to satisfy curiosity—characteristic of many of the Buddha's answers to questions about the after-life. We have, however, among others, the following remarkable declaration on *The Unchangeable* :

"Verily, Brothers, there is a condition, where there is neither the Solid (Pathavi), nor the Fluid (Āpo), neither Heat (Tejo) nor Motion (Vāya), neither this world nor any other world, neither sun nor moon.

"This, Brothers, I call neither arising nor passing away, neither standing still nor being born, nor dying. There is neither substance nor development, nor any basis. This is the End of Suffering.

"There is, Brothers, an unborn, an unoriginated, that has not become, that has not been formed. If, Brothers, there were not this unborn, this unoriginated, that has not become, that has not been formed, escape from the world of the born, the originated, the become, the formed, would not be possible.

"But since, Brothers, there is an unborn, an unoriginated, that has not become, that has not been formed, therefore is escape possible from the world of the born, the originated, the become, the formed."

(*Udana*, viii. 3, in *Word of the Buddha*.)

5. MAHĀYANA DEVELOPMENTS

There is no difficulty in understanding the tendency, seen in later Buddhist writings, to increase the reality of this "Unchangeable," to objectify it, to symbolize it under all kinds of beautiful imagery. It is "the other shore," "the land of bliss," "the untrodden country," "the place where having gone one does not grieve," "the immortal peace," "salvation," "the imperishable," "eternally perfect state," "the perfect world."

It is difficult to say whether this persistent claim of reality for Nirvāna is due to logical necessity or whether it be founded on a kind of *desire*. Do we feel that Parānirvāna *ought* to be a state of which there is to be some such experience, or is it that we wish it to be so? Are we reluctant to let go and plunge into nothingness?

One may here make a general distinction between the two great schools of Buddhism. The earlier, the Hinayāna,

NIRVĀNA

directs most of its attention to what I have called the Terrestrial Nirvāna ; *The Questions of King Milinda* begin the speculative discussion of the subject, but in the Māhayāna texts we hear more about the ultimate Nirvāna and its remoteness. The higher worlds are mapped out with surprising and picturesque detail.

Intermediate realms of happy intellectual activity are drawn for us, and we learn how the great saints, for the sake of all sentient beings, renounce or postpone, again and again, the Nirvāna which is theirs by merit. This is a very significant modification of the doctrine.

From the *Saddharma Pundarika* (A.D. 200) I take a few quotations :

"[The Buddha] instantly announced his complete Nirvāna to the world, including the Gods, Māras and Brahmas, to all creatures saying : 'To-day, O monks, this very night in the middle watch, will the Tathāgata, by entering the element of Absolute Nirvāna, become wholly extinct.'" (*S.B.E.*, I., 56.)

"That very night, in the middle watch, he met complete extinction, like a lamp when the cause of its burning is exhausted." (I., 84.)

"Many years have I preached and pointed to the stage of Nirvāna, the end of wretchedness and mundane existence." (II., 126.)

"It is only by knowing all laws that the immortal Nirvāna is reached." (V., 63.)

"There is no Real Nirvāna without all-knowingness ; try to reach this." (V., 74.)

work from which I have quoted seeks to put a different construction on the early teaching that Nirvāna could be reached in this life. There are not two Nirvānas, much less three, it says. That which was *thought* to be Nirvāna on the attainment of saintship (Arhat) was an "able device of the Perfect One" to encourage and, as it were, give temporary rest and refreshment to those who, tired of making a long journey, were in a mind to go back.

> "We were contented with a little of Nirvāna; we required nothing higher, nor even cared for it. But the Friend of the world has taught us better: '*This* is no blessed Rest at all; the full knowledge of the highest men, *that* is blessed Rest, that is supreme beatitude.'"
>
> (VIII., 43–44.)

In the same work we hear, for the first time, the doctrine of the Eternal Buddha. "I was not completely extinct at the time; it was but a device of mine, repeatedly am I born in the world of the living"—all statements to the contrary notwithstanding!

6. THE LOGICAL STRENGTH OF THE DOCTRINE

I cannot pursue our theme any further into the mazes of the Māhayāna literature, where Nirvāna seems to undergo subtle yet significant changes, and will now draw this study to a close with a few general observations.

(1) In this life, the diminution of willing is the prelude to contemplation, so that the entire laying down of the will would presumably raise contemplation to its maximum height. This may be the Nirvāna of which we have diluted foretastes here on earth. As the race lays down its will, it exchanges multiplicity and separateness for unity and union, towards which it is led, not by reason, but by Nirvānic instinct or intuition. Although no one can return thence to tell us of it, perhaps, in the language of one of the Suttas, he may "see Nirvāna" on the horizon of Being, and point it out to us.

NIRVĀNA

(2) Every change is a transmutation of elements. Emotionally, the Terrestrial Nirvāna consists in the diminution of egoism and the consequent increase of love ; or, in the alternative, the increase of love and the consequent diminution of egoism. It is therefore inconceivable that the goal of life, its pinnacle, can in any sense be the annihilation of that, the increase of which has led to it. Nirvāna must therefore be Love's consummation.

(3) We are not obliged to assume that the attainment of Nirvāna in its terrestrial and cosmical aspects, is the return to a *pre-established* harmony. May it not be regarded as itself the *establishment* of harmony ? Not the return to a long lost home, but the discovery of a hitherto " untrodden country " ?

(4) In order to be in touch with a living tradition, I conclude with a quotation from an address delivered by the Bhikkhu Ānanda Metteyya a few years ago.

" Imagine to yourself an infinitude of space, and suppose that that space is itself, not consciousness as we know it—which is differentiated—but the very underlying substrate, the essential ultimate of what we know as consciousness. That done, suppose that somewhere in that infinite spatial conscious substrate there comes into existence, no matter how, a cube of some alien material. Now—although of course the infinitude of the space itself will in no wise be diminished by this cube—as regards the cube itself, we may consider the six walls of it as limiting that space. As we have endowed our space with the very underlying substrate of consciousness, what will follow ? Obviously that where the top, the bottom, the four sides of our cube define or limit the spatial consciousness, there will arise a consciousness such as we know it : a differentiated consciousness of the order of our own perceptions. Then suppose the top, bottom, and sides of the cube are annihilated, there will then be an end to the limitation imposed. That is the simile of the Buddhist idea of Nirvāna. When, by the destruction of the self-illusion, the Five Groups that constitute our being no longer cohere—for it is the self-illusion that holds them all together—then, where was but differentiated and hence suffering consciousness, the Illimitable, the Element of Nirvāna, will reign supreme. It is only by such similitudes, all of them negative, that we can gain any idea of that Beyond of Life ; but it is the teaching of the Buddha—a teaching endorsed by all the Holy Ones who have followed the Pathway He declared to us—that all can be It ! "

XII : *Nietzsche's Critique of Buddhism*

1. NIETZSCHE'S FORERUNNERS

IN his *Genealogy of Morals* Nietzsche declares as follows :

"Let us speak out this new demand : we need a *critique* of moral values, *the value of these values* is for the first time to be called in question. . . ."

"No one has, up to the present, exhibited the faintest doubt or hesitation in judging the 'good man' to be of a higher value than the 'evil man,' of a higher value with regard to specifically human progress, utility and prosperity generally, not forgetting the future."

It may be that Nietzsche was thus expressing himself in reference to his own times ; otherwise the words are so exaggerated as to be entirely untrue if a view is taken over the history of philosophy generally. At any rate, if the "evil man" had not been valued "with regard specifically to human progress" above the "good man" he had certainly been valued highly, by many thinkers of antiquity, for his own sake. The Taoists of China devalued "the Superior Man" of Confucius as unnatural and disorderly, while Yang-chu, the egoist, exalted the "villains" of his country to the highest posts of honour and ridiculed the sages and altruists. In India there were, at the time of the Buddha, and long after, several minor schools of hedonists, non-moralists, materialists, and others, who made quite as emphatic a challenge to moral values as Nietzsche's, though, of course, in the circumstances, not so complete. I have quoted many specimens of this kind of teaching in Section

VII. Nietzsche was fully acquainted with the Code of Manu, the Brahmin law book, which he admired on account of its exaltation of aristocratic castes by means that were utterly devoid of what is generally known as morality; and even if the work of Chānākya, the Minister to Chāndragupta—the document, *par excellence*, of political non-moralism in the East—had not fallen into his hands, there is little excuse for his claim to be the first to suspect that the bad man was better than the good man. In Plato's time, and before it—Theognis is a case in point—aristocratic thinkers had expressed themselves quite clearly in scorn of "goodness," from what we might describe as an eugenic point of view. The discussions of Kallikles in the *Gorgias* and Thrasumachos in the *Republic* prove this beyond question (see Section XV). But although in the realm of speculative and moral philosophy of the ancients there is enough to refute Nietzsche's claim to priority, there is abundant evidence from the page of political history to show that non-moralism was *practised* as widely then as it is to-day.

2. EGOISM AND ALTRUISM

As I am about to enter upon a discussion of Nietzsche's *critique* of Buddhism, and as Buddhism may be considered an excellent type of what Nietzsche calls "moral valuation," I wish to attempt an explanation of the significance of this remarkable *recurring* challenge to morality of which Nietzsche (who actually formulated a doctrine of Eternal Recurrence) does not seem to have been aware.

I observe a general law relating to the appearance of moral systems in the world, a law under which Nietzsche's own doctrine naturally falls. It may be stated briefly in the following terms: (1) The Nature-Will supplies to every creature egoistic impulses towards self-preservation and gratification. (2) Upon these impulses is based an incipient scheme of purely egoistic values. (3) Necessity reveals

CRITIQUE OF BUDDHISM

to the individual its dependence, partial or complete, on others, and from this perception are derived the social impulses. (4) As the sensibility of individuals intensifies, impulses of another kind are liberated, namely, altruistic impulses towards securing the welfare of other creatures. (5) As the social and altruistic impulses combine and strengthen, the earlier egoistic values are gradually modified. (6) This modification of egoistic values at length becomes *articulate*, conscious and powerful at the hands, say, of such men as the Buddha, Kung-fu-tze, Sokrates or Christ. They attempt a transvaluation of existing egoistic values on a comprehensive scale. They are the *initiators of new values*, in the proper sense of the words. They aim at organizing life on the basis of new principles which they clearly perceive. But their transvaluation seems to go beyond the faith of men in altruism; it is, therefore, challenged by (7) an *articulate revival of egoistic values*, formerly held without question. It leads, I think, to the formulation of *egoistic philosophies* such as that of Nietzsche, who speaks emphatically for the will in Nature, the will to life and power. I do not shrink from describing it as intellectual atavism.

3. NIETZSCHE'S ATTACK ON RELIGION

For our present purposes all works written by Nietzsche before his *Dawn of Day* may be disregarded, for it was with this work that he began his characteristic " campaign against Morality." It must be remembered what Nietzsche's campaign involved and upon what it was founded. Schopenhauer had already propounded a philosophy of the will-to-life which at first captivated the younger philosopher. The primary form of all Will is will-to-life [1]; he traced all evil to this affirmation. Nietzsche, however, conceived

[1] Craving for individual existence, sensual craving, and craving for happiness (or as Buddhism has it, *Bhava-tanhā*, *Kāma-tanhā* and *Vibhava-tanhā*.

of life itself as will-to-power. Life, he said, was essentially struggle, attack, appropriation, and consequently was itself the criterion by which all things were to be measured. Wheresoever there was more power, there was more life; and conversely. In his view, all that was designed to "tame" life was the only evil. It was with regard to Christianity, and for these reasons, that he used the terrible words:

> "I denounce Christianity as the one great curse, as the one Corruption, as the great instinct of revenge for which no means are too poisonous, treacherous and small. . . . I denounce it as the one undying disgrace of humanity."

We shall find that Buddhism is treated with greater respect, although it is included in a general condemnation on account of "its negative attitude towards life." Nietzsche says:

> "There have been more thoughtful and more destructively thoughtful times than ours: times like those in which Buddha appeared, for instance, in which people, after centuries of sectarian quarrels, had so sunk deeply into the abyss of philosophical dogma as from time to time European people have done in regard to the fine points of religious dogma."
> (*Will-to-Power*, Aph. 31.)

We must here understand that thought itself is viewed by Nietzsche as destructive to life; the thought in question was, of course, that vast web of discussion about *Karma, Samsāra, Ātman*, etc.,[1] as well as the myriad rules of the Brahmin priesthood. In such times the Buddha appeared, says Nietzsche, and founded his religion. On the way in which religions in general are set up in the world, the

[1] The significance of deeds; transmigration; the Self.

CRITIQUE OF BUDDHISM

philosopher expresses himself with admirable lucidity. For convenience of criticism I have separated the selected passages into three :

> (*a*) The real inventions of the founders of religion are, on the one hand, to establish a definite mode of life and everyday custom, which operates as a disciplining of the will, and at the same time does away with *ennui* ; and on the other hand, to give to that very mode of life an *interpretation*, by virtue of which it appears illumined with highest value ; so that henceforth it becomes a good for which people struggle, and, under certain circumstances, lay down their lives. . . .
>
> (*b*) The import, the originality of a founder of a religion, discloses itself usually in the fact that he *sees* the mode of life, *selects* it, and *divines* for the first time the purposes for which it can be used.
>
> (*c*) The founder of a religion possesses psychological infallibility in the knowledge of a definite, average type of souls, who have not yet *recognised* themselves as akin. It is he who brings them together : the founding of a religion, therefore, always becomes a long ceremony of recognition.
>
> (*The Joyful Wisdom*, Aph. 353.)

These interesting generalizations may perhaps be allowed to pass without present challenge when it is noted that they refer to the procedure of historical "founders" of religions within given visible civilizations—such as, for instance, the founding of Islam in Arabia and of Buddhism in India during the sixth century B.C. But what needs to be said in reply to Nietzsche is that *Religion* is not "founded" in the way that *religions* are ; it is not in the hands or within the power of half-a-dozen of the great initiators ; it is a process as deep, if not deeper, than the life process itself. What the historical founders sometimes do is to establish disciplines to facilitate its progress, and to formulate philosophies about it. If, therefore, Nietzsche seems to say that *religions* are dangerous to life, I merely offer the counter-proposition, which I cannot argue here, that *Religion* is the redemption of life. (*See* Section I.)

4. NIETZSCHE'S VIEW OF THE ORIGIN OF BUDDHISM

Having learned the philosopher's general view, my readers will be prepared to hear his specific references to Buddhism. It was all founded on laziness, we are told.

" Buddha found the same type of man—he found it, in fact, dispersed among all the classes and social ranks of a people who were good and kind (and above all inoffensive), owing to indolence, and who likewise, owing to indolence, lived abstemiously, almost without requirements. He understood that such a type of man, with all its deadweight, had inevitably to glide into a belief which promises *to avoid* the return of earthly ill—(that is to say, all labour and activity) —this ' understanding ' was his genius."
(*The Joyful Wisdom*, Aph. 353.)

This indolence in its turn was traced by Nietzsche to physical conditions, as the following passages will show:

" The two physiological facts upon which it [Buddhism] rests and upon which it bestows its attention are : in the first place, an excessive irritability of feeling which manifests itself as a refined susceptibility to pain, *and also* as super-spiritualization, an all toolengthy sojourn amid concepts and logical procedures under which the personal instinct has suffered in favour of the ' impersonal.' . . .

" Thanks to these physiological conditions, a state of depression set in which Buddha sought to combat by means of hygiene. Against it, he prescribed life in the open, a life of travel ; moderation and careful choice of food ; caution in regard to all intoxicating liquor, and also in regard to all the passions which tend to create bile and to heat the blood. . . . He understands goodness—being good—as promoting health."

(*The Antichrist*, Aph. 20.)

"The pre-requisites for Buddhism are a very mild climate, great gentleness and liberality in the customs of the people, and *no* militarism. The movement must also originate among the higher and even learned classes. Cheerfulness, peace and absence of desire are the highest inspirations."

(*The Antichrist*, Aph. 21.)

"Buddhism is a religion for *senile* men, for races which have become kind, gentle, over-spiritual and which feel pain too easily (Europe is not nearly ripe for it yet) ; it calls them back to peace and cheerfulness, to a regimen for the intellect, to a certain hardening of the body. . . . Buddhism is a religion for the close and exhaustion of civilization. . . . Buddhism is a hundred times colder, more truthful, more objective [than Christianity]. It no longer requires to *justify* pain and its susceptibility to suffering by the interpretation of sin—it simply says what it thinks, 'I suffer.'"

(*The Antichrist*, Aph. 22–23.)

It is verily surprising to hear such a declaration as this last one. It is true that the word "sin" is not used, but, as everybody knows, the doctrine of *Karma* (or the significance of deeds) was the very marrow of the Buddha's system. Nietzsche ought to have remembered that if the first Holy Truth seemed to him to affirm simply " I suffer," [1] yet the second purports to trace the suffering to its roots in desire and deeds, *tanhā* and *karma*, which are the roots of what is, in Christianity, called *sin*.

To the physical causes and pre-requisites of Buddhism must also be added the " great error in diet." Pessimists, says Nietzsche, are victims of the mistakes of their forefathers regarding food.

> " When a profound dislike of existence gets the upper hand, the after-effect of a great error *in diet* of which a people has been long guilty comes to light. The spread of Buddhism (*not* its origin) is thus to a considerable extent dependent on the excessive and almost exclusive rice fare of the Indians and the universal enervation that results therefrom."
> (*The Joyful Wisdom*, Aph. 173.)

We may now summarize Nietzsche's explanation of the rise of Buddhism :

(1) The climate, rice food, indolence and susceptibility to pain.

(2) Kindness and gentleness, cheerfulness and the absence of desire, and no militarism.

(3) The Buddha's " genius " in understanding what kind of social order could be made out of all these elements.

There is, however, a curious inversion of causes and effects in this theory, for, leaving environment and heredity aside, Buddhism surely tended to *generate* the moral qualities —kindness and so forth—which Nietzsche regards as its pre-requisites ; and as to " no militarism," it is well known that in India, at any rate, Buddhism was its pre-requisite. I do not see how Nietzsche is to explain away Asoka, in whose case the logical chain is : Militarism, The *Dhamma*,

---

[1] It is not so phrased in the Pitakas, but generally, " there is suffering."

CRITIQUE OF BUDDHISM

Repentance, Anti-militarism. How could the fourth link be the pro-requisite of the second?

5. NIETZSCHE'S CLASSIFICATION OF RELIGIONS

Nietzsche discriminated between religions that were affirmative of life and those that were negative; also as to their origination in certain social strata. He classes Buddhism, according to its type, by the side of other faiths in the following manner:

(1) An Affirmative Aryan religion, the product of the ruling classes, is Brahminism (The Laws of Manu).

(2) Affirmative Semitic religions, the product of the ruling classes, are Early Judaism and Islam (Old Testament and Koran).

(3) A Negative Semitic religion, the product of the oppressed classes, is Christianity (New Testament).

(4) A Negative Aryan religion, the product of the ruling classes, is Buddhism.

Nietzsche further says:

> "It is quite in the nature of things that we have no Aryan religion which is the product of the oppressed classes; for that would have been a contradiction—a race of masters is either paramount or 'goes to the dogs.'"
>
> (*Will-to-Power*, Aph. 145.)

The statement is historically correct, no doubt, with regard to India: the Vedic cults were the products of the chiefs of the clans and their attendant bards; the Upanishad philosophy was at first taught by the Kshatriya caste and not by Brahmins; Jainism was founded by Mahavira, a member of the Royal family of Kōsala; the Buddha was the son of a chief of the Sākyas. Nevertheless, I see no point in the reference to rule in the case of the last three religions just mentioned. I cannot recall in what I have read of the Upanishad philosophy or Jainism or Buddhism any references to their *advantages* to the ruling classes, such as we find in the Code of Manu. In any case, the fact that a religion has emanated from the *rulers* is a mere coincidence; it emanated from the wise, the intelligent, the learned. In the modern world the distinction is artificial in the extreme—the King of England is the head of the Church, the Sultan of Turkey till 1922, the Khalif of Islam. These may well use the offices of religion for the purposes of government, irrespective of the social source of the faith, or its negative or positive character. In the case of Buddhism, however, there is a further point of interest which deserves to be mentioned. The race that had conquered the natives of India called itself Aryan, i.e., "noble," and was everywhere supreme. Not without good reason did the Buddha call his system the Eightfold *Aryan* Path; for it was, he thought, a path suitable to Aryans, one which any man of dignity and good-will might reasonably be invited to take; the appeal to "young men of good family" is a constant refrain in the Suttas. It was certainly not *confined* to Aryans, nor was it recommended as a means of increasing the Aryan rule. Nietzsche's inference falls to the ground.

In this question of rule and religion I think Nietzsche deserves some strong counter-criticism, for he is too prone to attribute much to "cuteness" which more reasonably should be regarded as the outcome of sincerity. He pretends to be able to penetrate into men's minds and tell us from what ulterior motives they proceeded—the Christians out of resentment, the Buddha by a sly stroke of genius, and so forth. He is perpetually uncovering conspiracies of which the conspirators themselves are innocently ignorant. In reference to resentment, I may mention in passing that whereas suffering is often used as a motive for resentment, giving rise to what Nietzsche calls "resentment-morality," in Buddhism this is not the case. He speaks of triumph over resentment as its greatest accomplishment, and with

CRITIQUE OF BUDDHISM

approval quotes what he calls "the touching refrain" of the whole of Buddhism : *not through hostility doth hostility end.* The refrain should have been completed by the words : *but by love.* I think we have the right here to ask why it was that Nietzsche, in explaining the phenomena of Buddhism, put so much down to climate, diet and indolence ; whereas the "triumph over resentment" is surely due to the will of man, and from it flow those many qualities of kindness and peacefulness which have been otherwise explained. As against Nietzsche's "House-that-Jack-built" chain of causation I here place a passage which in spite of its formality is of more convincing power :

"If a dyer should take some cloth that is pure and clean, and dip it in some one colour or another, the result will be a good pure tint—and why ? Even because the cloth was clean. In the self-same way, a good outcome may be expected from a mind that is pure.

"And what are impurities of the mind ?

"Covetousness and vicious craving, ill-will, anger, enmity, dissimulation, jealousy, mean grasping, deceit, cunning, obstinacy, clamorousness, conceit, arrogance, vainglory, heedlessness—all these are impurities of the mind.

"Now when a man has perceived that these are impurities of the mind, he sets about to rid himself of them . . . and he abandons self-regarding ends, empties himself of them, frees himself from them, renounces them and rejects them. And so he wins to comprehension of the Teaching, and the joy that comes of it. From this lofty enthusiasm is born. The bodily frame becomes quieted, and he is at ease. Whoso is at ease attains collectedness and calmness of mind.

"His heart overflowing with Loving-Kindness, Compassion, Sympathetic Gladness, and Even-mindedness, he abides, raying them forth towards one quarter of space, then towards the second and the third, then towards the fourth, above and below, thus all around. Everywhere, into all places the wide world over, his heart overflowing, streams forth, ample, expanded, limitless, free from enmity and all ill-will."

(*Majjhima Nikāya*, VII., in *Discourses of Gōtama*.)

6. "PESSIMISM" A MALADY OF THE WILL

I think Nietzsche is on firmer ground when he comes to the metaphysical and psychological aspects of Buddhism, upon which he has some striking sayings. In calling the movement an older and stronger manifestation of pessimism than the modern type, he breaks out as follows:

"The whole attitude of 'man *versus* the world,' man as a world-denying principle, man as the standard of value of things, as judge of the world, who in the end puts existence itself into the scales and finds it too light—the monstrous impertinence of this attitude has dawned on us as such and has disgusted us."

(*The Joyful Wisdom*, Aph. 346.)

These are strong words; what do Buddhists say in reply to them?

I do not at this moment undertake fully to meet this charge, which is one that cannot be lightly dismissed, even though it is made dogmatically with little argumentative support; but I think there are two ways by which it might be met. The first is a consideration of whether Buddhism really "puts existence itself into the scales and finds it too light," and, if so, whether this judgment of the world is a true one. I should be inclined to argue that what the Buddha put into the scales and found too light was *avidya*, i.e., an unilluminated vision of the world. From such one might well turn aside, accepting and justifying the term "pessimism." But further, in view of the enlightenment declared to be possible, and the evident design of a discipline to favour its attainment, the movement should more correctly be called "an older and more scientific manifestation of *optimism* than the modern type." But the use of the terms "optimism" and "pessimism" as epithets cannot be fruitful unless we determine from what it is the pessimist turns away, and in what it is the optimist places his hopes. The crux of the matter is : which has the truth ?

Yet another suggestion is put forward by Nietzsche to account for the spread of Buddhism ; it is due, he says, to a malady of the will :

". . . The less a person knows how to command, the more urgent is his desire for one who commands —who commands sternly—a god, a prince, a caste, a physician, a confessor, a dogma. From whence perhaps it could be inferred . . . that Buddhism . . . might have had its rise and especially its rapid extension in an extraordinary *malady of the will.* And in truth this has been so. This religion lighted on a longing, monstrously exaggerated by malady of the will, for an imperative, a "Thou shalt," a longing going the length of despair."

(*The Joyful Wisdom*, Aph. 286.)

The formula "Thus, Brothers, and well must ye exercise yourselves," is the Buddha's imperative ; but when we remember how full and rich is the content of the word *thus*, we cannot allow Nietzsche's accusation the weight he claims for it.

I can only hint at the line by which these criticisms about the malady of the will may be met ; namely, that the theory of the Will in Buddhism should be thoroughly studied. It has always struck me, however, that, *given certain aims*, the will is to be continually strengthened. The Eightfold Path is "willing" all the time, qualified by "rightness" (e.g., *right* intention, *right* effort), not qualified by weakness, as Nietzsche affirms. Far from falling back on others, the

Buddhist disciple was taught to be "a refuge unto himself." To be "conscious, strenuous, mindful" is the reiterated formula of Buddhist discipline. But even if we grant to Nietzsche historical accuracy here, and admit that Buddhism "lighted upon the longing" in question, we ask: Did it pander to that malady of the will by giving it what it longed for? Though Nietzsche infers so much, he does not clearly say so, nor does he offer the slightest particle of proof.

When Nietzsche had defined life as "essentially struggle, attack, appropriation" carried forward by the will-to-power, he had made a decision which gives to the word *will* the restricted though definite meaning suggested by Schopenhauer. If, however, a man should turn from such a life and such a will, aiming at a life of a "certain *quality* of refinement and sublimity," he does not lay down the will-to-live, but lays down *the will-to-live by struggle, attack and appropriation*. Will, for him, becomes an energy, not for life, but for a certain quality of life, as the means of enriching life, of raising it—and not only for himself—to planes of feeling and perception hitherto unknown to him. I quote a passage by way of illustration:

"The disciple begets in himself *the will not to permit* to arise evil unwholesome things, and summoning all his strength, he struggles and strives and incites his mind . . . and so watching the senses he becomes master of them. . . . He begets in himself *the will to overcome evil . . . the will to develop wholesome things . . . the will to maintain wholesome things.*"
(*Anguttara Nikāya*, IV. 13, 14.)

7. BUDDHISM AND THE SOCIAL ORDER

I will close this study by a brief review of Nietzsche's estimate of the social significance of religion. Here we shall meet his subjective preferences masquerading as causes of certain phenomena. Life is will-to-power; religion also is one of the means of gaining power for those who

CRITIQUE OF BUDDHISM

foster it in others; it is useful to the rulers, the aristocrats. The Brahmins secured by their religious importance the power of nominating kings for the people, while their sentiments prompted them to keep apart and outside as men with a higher, super-regal mission. Nietzsche says:

> "And finally, to ordinary men, to the majority of the people, who exist for service and general utility, and are only so far entitled to exist, religion gave invaluable contentedness with their lot and condition—peace of heart, ennoblement of obedience, additional social happiness and sympathy, something of justification of all the commonplaces, all the meanness, all the semi-animal poverty of their souls. Religion sheds sunshine over such perpetually harassed men, and makes even their own aspect endurable to them. . . . There is perhaps nothing so admirable in Buddhism as its art of teaching the lowest to elevate themselves by piety to a seemingly higher order of things, and thereby to retain their satisfaction with the actual world in which they find it difficult enough to live—this very difficulty being necessary."
>
> (*Beyond Good and Evil*, Aph. 61.)

While it must be admitted that rulers have always turned to account the religious aspirations of the people—Buddhist rulers, perhaps, as well as others—Religion itself is not accountable for this misuse. Again, Nietzsche would seem to leave no room for sincerity—all is clever scheming and deceit, with a view to rulers fulfilling the purposes of life—that is, gaining power. I cannot remember, in any of the Buddhist literature that I have read, a passage remotely suggestive of the truth of Nietzsche's statement, which would appear to represent the Buddha as an appendage, a useful man of "genius" who made it possible by his clever devices for the ruling race to save itself from "going to the dogs."

Then, again, Nietzsche seems to want "to eat his cake and have it." Not satisfied with the excellent work which, according to his reading of the facts, Buddhism performed for the ruling classes by providing a universal popular soporific for indolent rice-eaters, he turns upon the religion the force of his adverse judgment.

> "However highly we may esteem this indulgent and preservative care, [Buddhism] is among the principal causes which have kept the type 'man' on a lower level—have preserved too much of *that which should have perished*."
>
> (*Beyond Good and Evil*, Aph. 61.)

A statement such as this cannot either be proved or refuted; it is a generalization which needs a great amount of data upon which to rest, but, in reality, is supported by little but the preferences of its writer. I have, I believe, refuted, or at least challenged, all the logical arguments that lead up to it, as the final adverse judgment of Nietzsche, and I now briefly summarize these arguments and remind my readers of the way in which each has been dealt with.

In Part 1 Nietzsche's claim to be the first "immoralist" is shown to be invalid; in Part 2 a theory is advanced which explains his significance in the general scheme of human philosophy. In Parts 3 and 4 his views of the motives of "founders" of religions, and of the Buddha in particular, are shown to be coloured by his prejudices and not supported by the facts. In Part 5, while accepting Nietzsche's classification of Buddhism, his extended inference that it was founded in the interests of Aryan rulers is denied.

Coming to Part 6, I have shown that "pessimism" as applied to Buddhism is a loose term lacking precision and, from an ultimate point of view, entirely inaccurate; also that the Nietzschean view of Buddhism as a sop to weakness of will is, as the discipline itself shows, incorrect when

CRITIQUE OF BUDDHISM

once is understood the kind of will-direction which the Buddha counselled. Finally, in this Part 7, I have called for proof of the allegation that the Buddha was by motive or in fact an appendage to the ruling caste, and thus a means of depressing the people and lowering the type. Perhaps, therefore, my readers will feel that the Aphorism 61 quoted above has been, by anticipation, sufficiently undermined, and, in view of its closing words, may now be left alone. But I claim that the passage I am about to cite from Nietzsche himself is an almost total refutation of his own harsh judgment which I have been examining.

8. A FAVOURABLE VIEW

I reserve for the last what is the most sympathetic estimate of Buddhism by Nietzsche. It occurs in a passage where he is comparing it, and very favourably, with Christianity, but I need only quote the relevant parts:

"Buddhism is the expression of a *fine evening*, perfectly sweet and mild—it is a sort of gratitude towards all that lies hidden, including that which it entirely lacks, viz., bitterness, disillusionment, and resentment. Finally, it possesses lofty intellectual love; it has got over all the subtlety of philosophical contradiction, and is even resting after it, though it is precisely from this source that it derives its intellectual glory and its glow as of a sunset (it originated in the higher classes). . . .

"Moreover, it is the cultured and very intellectual classes who find blessedness in Buddhism: a race wearied and besotted by centuries of intellectual quarrels and not *beneath all culture*. . . . In the Buddhistic ideal there is essentially an emancipation from good and evil: a very subtle suggestion of a Beyond to all morality is thought out in its teaching, and this Beyond is supposed to be compatible with

perfection—the condition being that even good actions are only needed *pro tem.* merely as a means—that is to say, in order to be free from *all* action."
(*Will-to-Power*, Aph. 154–5.)

It will be pleasant now to close with a few words taken from one of the discourses of the Buddha in which he appears to express that "subtle suggestion" referred to by Nietzsche, but in a different sense :

" Under the similitude of a raft do I lay my teaching before you, designed for escape, O disciples, not designed for retention. . . .

" And what ought a man to do if he would act rightly as regards the raft [with which he has crossed a river] ? Thus ought the man to consider : ' Truly this raft has been very serviceable to me ! Supported by this raft, and exerting hands and feet, I am crossed in safety to this further shore. How now if I lay this raft upon the bank or leave it to sink in the water, and so proceed on my journey ! '

" In like manner do I lay my teaching before you under the similitude of a raft ; meant for escape, not for retention. Understanding the similitude of a raft, O disciples, ye must leave righteousness behind, how much more unrighteousness ! "
(*Majjhima Nikāya*, XXII., in *Discourses of Gōtama the Buddha.*)

XIII : *A View of Karma*

1. THE ORIGIN OF THE WORD *KARMA*

THE Sanscrit word *karman* from the very beginning simply meant "work," "deeds" or "actions." From this are derived many applications and compound words such as *kritakarman*, "one who has done his duty," *krūrakarman*, "a cruel deed," *grihakarman*, "domestic work," *dushkarman*, "a bad action," and so on. Naturally also the word was used to refer to ritual and sacrificial actions, such as *antyakarman*, "a funeral rite," *toyakarman*, "a religious ceremony," etc. In this way it came to be used in such forms as *karmakanda*, the "work part" of the Vedas in contradistinction to *jnānakanda*, the "knowledge part." The word was thus one of the commonest and simplest in the language, devoid of all profound or doctrinal implications; but in process of time it came to mean, for those who used it in relation to religion, the due performance of religious duties; and by those who used it more widely as the practice of deeds which have a moral value. *Hinakarman* means the neglecting of religious acts. Although the word *karma* is an Indian word, its meaning, so far, is not peculiarly or exclusively Indian. On the contrary, it would be easy to show that, *mutatis mutandis*, all nations have used the equivalent of *karma* both in religion and ethics. I would go further, and say that all peoples who have been capable of discriminating between good and evil deeds have formulated somewhat similar doctrines to those we find expressed in the earlier forms of the Indian religion. Men were said to be rewarded for their piety by earthly prosperity. The texts of the Shu King, the Rig-Veda, the Iliad, and the Old Testament, are full of illustrations too numerous and too familiar to mention. Not only so, but all ancient religions, and the Vaidic religion no less than the others, looked forward to some definite reward or some indefinite retribution in the after life as the result of good or evil deeds. Such ideas, though naïve and founded on a very slender basis of facts and observation, were "vividly moral." They expressed the natural, if unphilosophical, view that man *ought* to benefit by his good deeds and to suffer for his delinquencies. With all our modernity it is hard to believe that he *ought not*. This general view of the significance of deeds in relation to the destiny of man or mankind is, I maintain, all but universal, and if it be untrue it is not the Hindus alone who must bear the discredit.

2. THE SIGNIFICANCE OF DEEDS

In all ancient religions and in some of their modern forms this view of reward and retribution passes through well-marked phases. The primitives looked for the return of good or evil in this present life in obvious and well-understood forms : cattle, good harvests, posterity, strength, longevity, power and good reputation. Their ritual acts and their moral conduct were designed accordingly. With the strengthening of the belief in survival after death, the heavenly life was, quite naturally, pictured as a continuance, in greater assurance and security, of the earthly happiness already experienced. The third phase, developed especially by the Jews and the Greeks, was the result of a much closer observation of life and a deeper experience of human suffering. It became clear that good men whose deeds—whose *karma*, to use the Indian word here—might have been expected to earn for them some degree of earthly happiness were nevertheless denied it. The spectacle of "the wicked" prospering and "the righteous" suffering even unto death became so familiar to the Jews from the prophetical period to their national extinction that it was impossible to harbour the

A VIEW OF KARMA

old ideas in their crude form. It was this which gave rise to an intense desire for an after life where the delayed reward might be experienced; and the doctrine of the resurrection was the first notable result of this hope in Persian, Jewish and Christian religions.

The most remarkable intellectual and moral reaction to undeserved suffering endured by the righteous was that spirit of resignation displayed in the presence of life's tragedy. In Jewish literature the highest example is the Book of Job; in Greek, the writings, as well as the lives of the Stoics. Without formulating a theory akin to karma they seemed to conclude that man is better than the world, or, at another angle, that some few men are better than mankind. Such a view needs serious examination; but not here.

3. THE DOCTRINE OF KARMA IN BRAHMINISM

Having indicated the general use of the word *karma* in the non-technical sense, I now propose to concentrate upon its use as a technical term in Indian philosophy, and I may remark that I can find no hint or reference to it in the Rig-Veda or their commentaries, the Brāhmanas.[1]

When the word *karma* assumes a technical form in the Indian literature it does so with surprising suddenness; and still more surprising is the fact that another doctrine, that of transmigration, appears simultaneously and in the most intimate association with it. The older non-technical view of deeds as deserving from the heavenly powers some reward or punishment in this or an after life became transformed into, or replaced by, a newer view which set forth the process or machinery by which this retribution was administered.

4. THE FIVE FIRES AND THE TWO WAYS

But this change did not occur without some preparation, the nature of which we may learn from the myths known

[1] Macdonell and Kieth's *Vedic Index* contains no article on Karma or Karman, a very significant fact.

as "The Two Ways" and "The Five Fires." Both are found in the earliest Upanishads. The former relates how very pious men, who have performed all the necessary sacrifices, leave the world at death by the *Devayāna* or path of the Gods which leads to the Sun. Some less favourable destiny is allowed for those whose piety has not been so excellent; they take, at death, the *Pitriyāna* or path of the Fathers which leads them to the Moon. They do not remain there for ever but, as a measure of privation of blessedness on account of their not having excelled in virtue, they have to return to the earth for another life. This, I venture to think, is the turning-point in Vaidic life-valuation. Hitherto, as the Rig-Veda shows, men embraced earthly life with the greatest ardour, but now a new life on earth is not represented as a new blessing, but as a lesser blessing than had been possible to those who take the Way of the Gods. It is also the oldest text in Indian sacred literature in which rebirth is affirmed, and also the oldest text in which complete release is shown to be dependent upon virtuous deeds. "Those who proceed on that path do not return to the life of man, yea, they do not return." (*Chand.: Up.:* iv. 15, 6.)

The myth of "The Five Fires" is more complicated, and, for our subject, equally important. At death "those who know this" go up in the flames of the funeral pyre to heaven and by a long process of five permutations or "sacrifices" they descend again to earthly birth. Here, too, the kind of life to which they descend depends upon their deeds. As in the myth of "The Two Ways," so in this one is found the germinal form of a doctrine of reward or retribution by means of rebirth in this world. The meaning of the doctrine, reduced to its shortest formula, may be expressed in the words of the Upanishad :

> Those whose conduct has been good will quickly attain some good birth . . . but those whose conduct

A VIEW OF KARMA

has been evil will quickly attain to an evil birth.
(*S.B.E., Chand. : Up. :* v. 10, 1.)

Still more important is the declaration of Yājnavalkya (*Brihad. : Up. :* iii. 2, 13), which seems to have been made by him with the full knowledge of the philosophical content of the two myths. In answer to a direct question as to "where is that person" when the elements composing his body have been dispersed at death, he supplies the amazing response, in effect, *that the person is in his deeds.* It was too difficult, too incredible a view to be discussed in public; evidently it had not long been formulated, and was now being tentatively communicated to that Brahmin world. Yājnavalkya says:

> "Take my hand, my friend; we two alone shall know of this; let this question of ours not be discussed in public." Then these two went out and argued, and what they said was Karman, what they praised was Karman, namely, that a man becomes good by good deeds, and bad by bad deeds.

A second passage of an equally authoritative character may be quoted:

> Now as a man is like this or like that, according as he acts and according as he behaves, so will he be—a man of good acts will become good, a man of bad acts bad. He becomes pure by pure deeds, bad by bad deeds.
> (*S.B.E., Brihad. : Up. :* iv. 4, 5.)

I cannot help wishing that critics would try their powers on these two short sentences which, to my mind, are the fundamental statement of the law of *karma*, as formulated by the ancient thinkers of India. A man becomes what he does. Can this doctrine be refuted? If it be true it is the most important and the most neglected truth in the world.

At this point we may note the important fact, so often overlooked, that karma is the primary doctrine, while reincarnation is a secondary doctrine supplied as an explanatory myth.

5. THE DOCTRINE IN BUDDHISM

Buddhism had what, in some respects, was the advantage and in other respects the disadvantage of having India prepared for its message. In any case, at the time of the Buddha, the greater part of northern India had become familiar with the double doctrine of karma-reincarnation. We cannot suppose, however, that everybody believed it or there would have been no reason for the Buddha to devote his great powers to enforcing the doctrine.

There must have been a great amount of simple Vaidism of the older type in India in 500 B.C. in spite of the teachings of the Upanishad philosophers. The various schools dependent upon the Vedas were slowly separating and specializing, each producing sutras and commentaries. There were some who believed in no God, but in Soul; others who believed in neither and yet were regarded as religious; others openly irreligious and immoralist, and of course the vast majority were merely worldly.

Every Indian philosophy had some conception of bringing to an end the unhappy side of human life and of reaching, sooner or later, to Liberation or Release, *Mōksha*. The idea that Release was taught by the Upanishads in opposition to Karma is only partially correct, with certain qualifications. The greater number of texts show that Release in various forms was simply the culmination of a struggle against evil tendencies, and was realizable in this life. *Mōksha* of the Sānkhyans, *Kaivalya* of the Yogins, and *Nirvāna* of the Buddhists, were not other-worldly states or places but, as advertised by their various exponents, states attainable here below. Once attained they led, at death, to "never returning." They were the new form of *Devayāna*. It would be much more true to say that the doctrines of Karma and Release, working together, were intended to, and did as a matter of fact, combine to oppose the claims and burdens of sacrificial ritual. For Buddhism they abolished such things altogether. The relation between Karma and Release in the Vedānta philosophy is another matter which must be separately explained hereafter.

The Buddha's teaching ignored the God (Brahman) at the head of the Universe and the permanent Ego or soul (Ātman) at the centre of the human personality. But it maintained a firm hold on karma and rebirth. The metaphysical difficulties which seem to be involved in this decision must not detain us here; we merely have to appreciate what the Buddha taught, in a popular and impressive way. His powerful ethic was propounded for the good of mankind, and he had to point out the advantages of the religious life, which he said was "lovely." His gaze was continually forward. But being India's greatest storyteller he had to turn backwards in order to draw upon the immense stores of the past—history, Brahmin mythology, folklore, the conversations and conduct of elephants, monkeys and alligators—which he set forth with wonderful art in a subtle and humorous, yet earnest, manner. This constant reference to the past was not to satisfy idle curiosity or even for philosophic speculation; it was for edification, for the sake of the future. He had to show that life is not full of accidents and aberrations, but that it exhibits the operations of law in relation to human conduct, as to physical processes. He sought to give scientific precision to the idea of retribution according to deeds by means of rebirth. This he stated over and over again, in dogmatic form, with tremendous force.

> Nor in the air, nor in the ocean's depths, nor in the mountain caves, nor anywhere in all the worlds, find'st

thou a place where thou art freed from evil deeds. There will come a time, Brothers, when the great world-ocean will dry up, vanish and be no more. There will come a time when the mighty earth will be devoured by fire, perish and be no more. But, Brothers, verily there is no end to the Suffering of beings buried in blindness who, seized by Craving, are ever brought again and again to renewed birth and hasten through the endless round of rebirths.
(*Samyutta Nikāya*, xxi. 10, in *Word of the Buddha*.)

But with this there was not the hopeless pessimism, the eternal unprogressive round of lives which some critics represent to us. On the contrary, the statement of the problem by the Buddha and his followers in such terrible words was for the sake of its attempted solution. One sentence out of hundreds like it, will suffice to show this to be the case.

O that a man who seeks his own welfare might pull out this arrow—this arrow of lamentation, of pain and sorrow. For whether the world is eternal, or the world is temporal, or the world is finite, or the world is infinite, *certainly* there is sorrow, lamentation, grief and despair, the cessation of which, attainable even in this present life, I make known unto you.
(*Majjhima Nikāya*, 63, in *Word of the Buddha*.)

I will conclude the matter of karma in Buddhism by three quotations which I venture to think put the case very powerfully. The first is in answer to the doubt as to the utility of the religious life. It is to overcome the *otherwise inevitable* operation of the law of karma, says the Buddha.

If any one says that a man *must* reap according to his deeds, in that case there is no use for a religious life, nor is any opportunity afforded for the entire extinction of misery. But if any one says that the reward a man reaps accords with his deeds, in that case there *is* a use for a religious life, and opportunity is afforded for the entire extinction of misery.

We may have the case of an individual who does some slight deed of wickedness which brings him to hell; or, again, we may have the case of another individual who does the same slight deed of wickedness, and expiates it in the present life, though it may be in a way which appears to him not slight, but grievous.

It is as if a man were to put a lump of salt into a small cup of water. Would now that small amount of water in this cup be savoured and undrinkable by the lump of salt? . . . But if a man were to throw a lump of salt into the river Ganges, would now the river Ganges be savoured and undrinkable by the lump of salt?

(*Anguttara Nikāya*, iii. 99, Warren's translation.)

Again, in the following passage, the religious life, that is to say the life of moral effort, is represented as the soil in which our normal deeds will not fructify with evil results either in this life or a future one. It is otherwise if these deeds are done in a surrounding condition of covetousness, hatred or infatuation.

There are three conditions under which deeds are produced. And what are the three? Covetousness, hatred and infatuation are conditions under which deeds are produced.

It is like seed that is uninjured, undecayed, unharmed by wind or heat, and is sound, and advantageously sown in a fertile field on well-prepared soil: if then rain falls in due season, then will that seed attain to growth, increase, and development. In exactly the same way, when a man's deeds are performed through covetousness, hatred or infatuation, wherever his per-

MYSTICISM OF EAST AND WEST

sonality may be, there those deeds ripen, and wherever they ripen, there he experiences the fruition of those deeds, be it in the present life, or in some subsequent one.

In the converse way, when a man's deeds are performed without covetousness, hatred or infatuation, then, inasmuch as covetousness, hatred or infatuation are gone, these deeds are abandoned, uprooted, pulled out of the ground like a palmyra-tree, and become non-existent and not liable to spring up again in the future.

(*Anguttara Nikāya*, iii. 33, Warren's translation.)

The third passage is of exceptional interest because it shows the ethical fervour of the Buddha in answering an apparently trivial question similar to those we hear too often to-day. A Queen named Mallikā is the interrogator; she says:

Reverend Sir, what is the reason, and what is the cause, when a woman is ugly, of a bad figure, and horrible to look at, and indigent, poor, needy and low in the social scale? What is the reason and what is the cause when a woman is ugly, of a bad figure, and horrible to look at, and rich, wealthy, affluent and high in the social scale? What is the reason, and what is the cause when a woman is beautiful, attractive, pleasing and possessed of surpassing loveliness, and indigent, poor, needy and low in the social scale? What is the reason, and what is the cause, when a woman is beautiful, attractive, pleasing and possessed of surpassing loveliness, and rich, wealthy, affluent and high in the social scale?

The Buddha offers an answer which is too long to print here, the substance of which may be guessed from the Queen's reply:

A VIEW OF KARMA

Since now, Reverend Sir, in a former existence I was irascible and violent, and at every little thing said against me felt spiteful, angry, enraged, and sulky, and manifested anger, hatred, and heart-burning, therefore am I now ugly, of a bad figure, and horrible to look at. . . .

Now, in the royal family, Reverend Sir, there are maidens of the warrior caste, of the Brahmin caste, and of the householder caste, and I bear rule over them. From this day forth I will not be irascible nor violent, and, though much be said against me, I will not feel spiteful, angry, enraged, or sulky, nor manifest anger, hatred, and heart-burning : I will give alms of food, drink, building-sites, carriages, garlands, scents, ointments, bedding, dwelling houses, and lamps ; and I will not be of an envious disposition nor feel envy at the gains, honour, reverence, respect, homage, and worship that shall come to others, nor be furious and envious thereat.

(*Anguttara Nikāya*, iv. 197, Warren's translation.)

6. KARMA IN JAINISM

The doctrines of the Jains were taught by Mahavira, a contemporary of the Buddha. Like the Sānkhyans, the Jains rejected a belief in God, affirmed the Soul, its transmigration and its accumulation of karma. They held to a view that every evil act admits into the soul a portion of atomic matter which goes to build up a karmic body. Man's deeds have objective consequences which are visible to those around him ; they also have subjective consequences which, though invisible, result in the construction of an inner karmic body which accompanies the soul on its migrations, but which, by asceticism, can be gradually exorcised. This primitive and possibly mistaken view was at the same time vividly moral. It gave a materialistic form to the difficult Upanishad conception that a man becomes what he does. The Jains simply showed the machinery of this process, otherwise hard to understand. They also had the merit of expressing it in a very elaborate and logical manner, so much so that their system has been called "spiritual mathematics." The intrusion of karmic matter in response to karmic thoughts, words and deeds of different kinds and intensities created a complex very much like that which the modern psycho-analysts describe to us—a dynamic unconscious, full of explosive impulses. The Jainist analysis of this karmic body was as follows: The soul is bound or weighted down by karmic matter of eight kinds, four of which obscure the soul's essential nature, and are called "Destructive Karma"; other four which do not obscure the essential nature are called "Undestructive Karma." The eight taken together are (1) knowledge-obscuring, (2) faith-obscuring, (3) infatuating, (4) obstructive, (5) bodies, sensations, forms, (6) life-duration, (7) family, (8) the cycle of pleasure-pain. These eight karmas are again subdivided into one-hundred-and-forty-eight categories, most of which are of common knowledge to any psychologist or moralist.

To any one who is in search of an ethical criterion I would recommend that of the Jains—if it be not too simple for this sophistical age. Indians speak of *hinsa* and *ahinsa*, injury and non-injury, which we are capable of practising to any degree. As is well known the fundamental ethic of the Jains is non-injury which, in their logical way, they carry too far for illogical people. There are two reasons why we should not injure any sentient creature, they say; the first is rather like the golden rule: we know that other beings like ourselves are capable of suffering and pain: and secondly, because injury to others causes the soul to receive a fresh invasion of the deadly karmic poison which corrupts and weighs it down. I will quote the Jain ethical criteria here.

A VIEW OF KARMA

The living world is afflicted, miserable, difficult to instruct, and without discrimination. In this world full of pain, suffering by their different acts, see the benighted ones causing great pain ! . . . He who injures these earthbodies does not comprehend and renounce sinful acts.
(*S.B.E., Akārānga Sutra*, I. i. 2.)

The venerable one has declared that the cause of sins are the six classes of living beings. . . . As in my pain when I am knocked or struck with a stick . . . or menaced, beaten, burned, tormented or deprived of life, and as I feel every pain and agony, from death down to the pulling out of an hair, in the same way, be sure of this, all kinds of living beings feel the same pain and agony as I . . . when they are ill-treated. For this reason all sorts of living things should not be beaten, nor treated with violence, nor abused, nor tormented, nor deprived of life. . . .

This constant, permanent, eternal, true Law has been taught by wise men who comprehend all things.
(*Ibid.*, 48–49.)

He does not kill movable or immovable beings, nor has them killed by another person, nor does he consent to another's killing them. In this way he ceases to acquire gross karma, controls himself and abstains from sins. (*S.B.E., Kritānga Sutra*, II. i. 53.)

Too naïve to deserve attention perhaps ? We can put it into modern terms, in which it appears rational enough. *Our deeds have both objective and subjective consequences for good or evil. Therefore we should choose the good and avoid the evil.*

7. KARMA IN THE VEDĀNTA PHILOSOPHY

The Vedānta was the Alpha and Omega of Indian philosophy, opening with the wonderful intuitive declarations of the early Upanishads, and closing more than a thousand years later with the commentaries of Sankara. For this reason I have reserved it to the last; also because its treatment of karma is unique. As is well known, the Vedānta philosophers expound their doctrine in two ways: the "lower knowledge" and the "higher knowledge." The former is similar in character and content to the other Vaidic systems in that it concedes reality to the universe; allows a transcendent god, Ishvara; teaches a strict ethic, transmigration and karma. The lower knowledge accommodates itself to normal, empirical experience and belief of the many. The higher knowledge, however, explains that the lower knowledge, though true so far as the normal mind can appreciate truth, is insufficient when man reaches a higher form of consciousness to which the higher knowledge conducts him, but which it cannot of itself bestow. The intellectual processes of the higher knowledge are directed to expounding the unity of all life and the identity of the Ātman, or innermost self of man with the Brahman or innermost self of the universe. These intellectual processes provide the *conception* of the ultimate truth but cannot give the *perception*, the vision itself. Brahmavidya or the awaking of Brahman-Ātman within, demonstrates beyond all doubt the final truth. This "knowledge of the Self," more than knowledge, is a matter of grace, as Western theology would say. It is a mystical experience which is explained as well as it can be by the dialectic of the higher knowledge. It is the peculiar and special form of Release or Liberation taught by the Vedāntins, and part of its content, at least, is to show that the lower knowledge is no longer useful or true. The realization of identity with Brahman, formerly contradicted so forcibly by empirical experience, disposes of the lower knowledge altogether, wipes it out of memory. And with it accumulated karma departs.

According to Vaidic philosophy generally, eventual release

A VIEW OF KARMA

was possible as the result of the struggle against karma. The Vedānta release was of a different character; for it did not terminate a *real* transmigration or break a *real* bond of karma, but an apparent one : it did not *bring about* a union of man and God but it *established in mystical consciousness* the fact of their eternal identity. All the apparatus of life with its samsāra, its suffering, its bondage, its karma, and its release turned out to be illusion.

8. SUMMARY OF CONCLUSIONS

From the preceding paragraph it is obvious that all discussions regarding the truth of the doctrine of karma-reincarnation, all discussions as to the precise process by which men earn the reward of their deeds, belong to the cycle of the " lower knowledge." Time, space, life, history are all included therein. I propose therefore to leave the " higher knowledge " apart for the moment and endeavour to draw some conclusions on the theme as hitherto debated here below.

The first decision we have to make is one of great importance. Do we consider the universe a cosmos or a chaos ? Does it exhibit order in various degrees in its many provinces ? If we answer this last question in the affirmative we are not obliged to profess an encyclopædic knowledge of how that order is maintained on other planes than human life; but we are compelled, I think, to assume that human life is subject to law and is guided by moral law. There are, I know, two ways of regarding the moral law; one as superior to man, to which he is called to subordinate himself, and the other as invented by man for his own convenience. But if the universe be amoral and man alone moral—a perfectly conceivable position—it is hard to see how karma could operate in the sense generally understood by popular tradition. Yet we may take another view, namely, that the universe is a complex of metaphysical, physical, psychical and moral processes whose co-ordination is so thorough and so deep that the phenomena of human morality, as we experience them, are necessary and natural: in brief, that man is moral because the universe is moral and expressive of a moral law.

From this decision we can pass to another one, namely, that man's deeds must have some significance in regard to the universe, or at least in regard to that part of it which is human life. Every deed is either permissible or not; it conforms to or adds to harmony; it either tends towards chaos or it enriches the existent ordination of the world. Perhaps the smaller the circle in which the deed is done the more significant it is. As the Buddha said: a lump of salt in a cup of water will make it taste salt, but in the river Ganges it will have no effect. Thus we may admit a relativity in the moral value of deeds that belong to different cycles while at the same time we affirm an absolute value in relation to their particular cycle. All deeds, sub-conscious or conscious, are deeds of the will which, while it is limited or determined in regard to the kind of deeds it can or cannot perform, is free and responsible regarding those it can perform.

We may now come to the discussion of the theory of karma expressed in several ways: (1) the simple idea of man punishing his fellow for doing those things which are contrary to the moral canon of the day or civilization; (2) the punishment of man in this life by gods or spirits who have the power to bring him retribution; (3) immunity for deeds done in this life but the punishment beyond the grave by the ministers of spiritual beings; (4) the theory of pre-existence and an after life as proposed by the Greek philosophers and the theory of samsāra, or a chain of successive births as taught by the Indian philosophers.

Admittedly we do not know for certain whether souls reincarnate or not; we know that many believe it and others believe that they know it. For the purpose of a study of karma we must regard it as a hypothesis. It is

A VIEW OF KARMA

this fourth type of karma, taught by Hindus, Buddhists, Jains and Theosophists in various forms, with the nature of which we are concerned.

9. THE KARMA OF EXPERIENCE

I draw attention to the well-known fact that deeds of any kind when oft repeated, quite apart from their moral value—which may be negligible—have a tendency to become habitual. Athletes generally, such as cricketers, boxers, fencers, and racers, find that after steady discipline they become what they do. The sub-conscious bodily processes seem to be performed automatically and a series of actions and reactions is set up. Any one who is not an athlete, but merely an observer of his own experience, will notice how his thoughts, words and deeds, even those of an indifferent character, are, by constant repetition, rendered habitual and after a time inescapable. Still more so is it in reference to repeated deeds that have a positive or negative moral value. Every one capable of retrospection and introspection must be able to discern in the vista of his own past life his own critical acts. He can trace with fair accuracy the line of causation in his general experience, mark the years' achievements and failures and observe their consequences; perceive the significance of his own deeds in relation to his immediate position and destiny. His character has been moulded by his dominant deeds; his fate or his fortune are the outgrowth of his character. Even his circumstances, within certain limits, he can connect with his temperament, his character, and the accumulated impetus of his deeds. It is a remarkable fact that, without knowing anything about " karma," people have always been found who know intuitively the connection between their deeds and their bodily life or circumstances. Religious experience is full of the " karma of experience " in the sense in which I am now dealing with it.

There are deeds : deeds have *objective* effects upon those who come within their orbit. Our life is one long complaint of what others are doing to us and saying of us—at home, in society, in industry, in politics, and by word and pen. Yet deeds have also a *subjective* effect which is more serious than that which is inflicted upon us from without. The subjective effect of his deeds upon the actor is the ground, the soil of his further deeds, which arise appropriately from it. The Buddha's words on " fruitful and barren karma " quoted earlier are surely irrefutable.

10. KARMA IN NATURE AND HUMANITY

The belief that we become what we do can be illustrated more forcibly when we turn to observe sub-human animate nature. It may not have occurred to critics that the story of evolution, as revealed by Darwin and his successors with increasing detail down to this day, may equally be regarded as a demonstration that in nature " life becomes what it does." The deeds of the lowest forms of life, visualized through the microscope, are in essence very like those of the higher forms. Constant self-affirmation in ways open to each species and to each individual is their general character, and tends at last to fix in each species definite traits which are inherited by later generations. This is their karma which, without knowing it, they enjoy or endure. Antipathy, ferocity, lust, gluttony, fear, stealth, gentleness, friendliness and affection are written on the faces and forms of the animals. They are the product of these various qualities of the will. The human race, which belongs to Nature, inherits this karma of animal will, specializes it in different ethnic families, in one direction or another. Human history, from one point of view, is nothing but a record of the Karma of Humanity, working itself out according to the good or evil of our racial, national and personal deeds.

A VIEW OF KARMA

11. THE ETHICAL CRITERION

Herbert Spencer defined human conduct, apart from the large volume of unconscious action, as "the adjustment of acts to ends"; Schopenhauer divided man's deeds into two main classes whose ends are egoistic and altruistic respectively. In varying degrees these two motives are found embedded in all our deeds. Egoistic self-affirmation extends to the greatest depths of cruelty and malice, and is formative of bad karma for ourselves and the race to which we belong and for which, in part, we act. Altruistic deeds which extend to loving-kindness and self-renunciation are formative of good karma. It may be difficult for man to escape altogether from the karma of his nation, or the karma of the human race, and still more difficult to disentangle himself from the deeper karma of Nature, but he need not, by his individual contribution, intensify the misery of life by merely following the evil tendency that is bequeathed to him. He can help to bring it to an end. This is the meaning of the Buddha's words, quoted before, as to the function of the religious life.

These thoughts give us a criterion of moral action by which to try all deeds and to know whether or not they are such as tend towards Release. Schopenhauer has said that "the whole of Nature looks to man for salvation." But, as yet, man has not saved himself!

12. KARMA AND THE CREATIVE WILL

If the law of karma operates in man, it must do so within the cycle of laws of a wider sweep; and I cannot do more here than convey to thinkers on this profound subject the hint that the work of Schopenhauer, Darwin and Bergson contain the material for a sound philosophic synthesis on the subject of karma. The first deals more clearly than any modern with the nature of the will and its manifestations; the second, with the help of his followers, assembles the data from Nature; and the third provides the luminous idea of a *creative* and consequently a volitional evolution. The door of the future, he says, is always open. Having created we can recreate ourselves!

But one must go back to the old Upanishads to find compressed into short formulæ what seems to be the truth in regard to the will, our deeds and our destiny.

> Man is altogether formed of desire; according as his desire is, so is his will; according as his will is, so are his deeds; according as are his deeds, so does it befall him.
>
> (*Brihad.: Up.: iv. 4, 5.*)

> Truly of will is man formed; according as his will is in this world after its likeness is born the man when he has departed hence; therefore a man should strive after good will.
>
> (*Chand.: Up.: iii. 14.*)

> Then this my body ends in ashes. Om! Will, remember, remember thy deeds! Will, remember, remember thy deeds!
>
> (*Brihad.: Up.: v. 15, 3.*)

13. THREE HYPOTHESES FOR KARMA

The rest of the argument may be simple and brief. If by analysis of our innermost experience we can discern, even in one life, the operations of a law of deeds and their objective and subjective reactions which Hindus, Buddhists, Jains and Theosophists call *Karma*; and if added to that we can discern in biological and human history the operations of the same kind of law embracing masses of animals and men, then our chief speculative difficulties are passed.

(1) On the hypothesis of immortality, even as professed by Christians, the residuum of our deeds has to be carried over into the after life, producing appropriate suffering or

A VIEW OF KARMA

felicity. Otherwise those deeds are of no significance whatever; and as Bernard Shaw's Donna Anna would say, "we might have been so much wickeder."

(2) On the hypothesis of reincarnation the same residuum of deeds of the creative will has to be carried over from one life to another; if not, again, these deeds have no significance, and we have wasted our time in discriminating, valuing and devaluing them.

(3) On the hypothesis of the Vedānta higher knowledge there is but one sole reality, the Brahman-Ātman, with which we are identical. But having fallen into illusion we have the experience of a separated life which is not terminated at death. We remain in the illusion until we have exhausted it, until we have learned the full significance of our deeds, and remoulded them so that a return to the identity-consciousness is possible: for works are a means to knowledge, and knowledge the means to liberation. Thus karma-reincarnation is alike the machinery of the illusion and of the escapement from it. The beautiful words of the Vedānta text explain the idea:

> As a goldsmith, taking a piece of gold, turns it into another, newer and more beautiful shape, so does this Self, after having thrown off this body, and dispelled all ignorance, make unto himself another newer and more beautiful shape . . . That Self, indeed, is Brahman.
> (*S.B.E.*, *Brihad.*: *Up.*: iv. 4, 4.)

Whichever of the three hypotheses we adopt we can join to the conception of Karma as a doctrine of Deeds, their significance and their subjective and objective reactions. This study is intended to go no further than to establish the essential principle on the basis of reasonableness rather than on authority.

14. THE HIGHEST WORD

I wish I could induce in my readers and possible critics the feeling that this doctrine of karma, in its highest form, is vitally moral and intensely practical. We have often been regaled with details of the supposed method of the working of this mysterious law which, while they were intended to convince and to edify, have alienated and shocked us. The case has been overproved by an abundance of "evidence" which became lighter and more trivial the more it was added to. Belief has been made too easy and conviction too difficult. I feel, however, that the truth that lies within the many theories and presentations of karma is almost too sacred to understand as one understands worldly things. We need, as it were, to take the hand of Yājnavalkya and retire into the realm of the spiritual intuition and there hear the highest word and perceive the brightest and most helpful truth. This cannot be stated in the terms of science, but it can be, and has been attempted in the language of poetry.

* * * * *

He who looks into the pupil of his brother's eye, sees himself; he who sees the Self in all and all in the Self—he will not injure the Self by the Self.

XIV : *The Key to Pythagoras*

OF all the pre-Sokratic philosophers Pythagoras is the most obscure ; and this, besides the fact that he left no writings, is due partly to the multiplicity of his interests, and mostly, I should venture to say, to the misinterpretation of his supposed " theory of numbers," a theory which has fascinated many thinkers from the earliest days until now. Taken by himself Pythagoras cannot easily be understood, but if studied relatively to those other physicists who before and after him were speculating on the ultimate substance of Nature, he offers less difficulty.

1. THE FIRST PRINCIPLE OF NATURE

We must regard him as one of a chain of scientific investigators to whom was put a simple question : What is *arche*, or first principle of things out of which *phusis*, or the panorama of Nature, is made ?

The first scientist, in order of time, who replied to his own query was Thales of Miletos. Water is that substance, said he ; the second thinker was Anaximandros, who said *to apeiron*, " the boundless," " the infinite," " the unlimited," was the *arche* out of which Nature was made. We must understand this to mean, in the first place, that he rejected Thales' decision ; for instead of choosing *one* of the objective, existing substances known to men, he decided to posit a substance which was prior to all known differentiated substances. If he had spoken more precisely he would have said that the world was made out of " undifferentiated substance," to which he could not give a better name than The Unlimited. The next answer, that of Anaximenes, is reactionary ; he goes back to *one* of the known substances, namely, *aer*, i.e., mist or vapour. But he was advancing on Thales; for obviously water, even in those days, was known to be a condensation of mist, though mist was not, without experiment, known to be a rarefaction of water.

2. LIVING MATTER

It is important to remember that the nature of these inquiries does not warrant us in thinking of the early scientists as "materialists"; though they are commonly classed as "physicists," this is because of their interest in *phusis*, or Nature. But from the first it is clear that the "matter" of Nature they seek to define is not dead but intensely alive; it is *hylozoon*. "All things are full of gods," said Thales, the first of the hylozoists, and yet he added "water is the material cause of all things."

If now we regard Pythagoras primarily and simply as a hylozoist, having put to him the same cosmogonic problem as that put to Thales, Anaximandros and Anaximenes, we may get some light. He rejected Thales and Anaximenes in their choice of the primacy of water and *aer*, and, as I maintain, fell back upon *to apeiron* of Anaximandros. But now, having accepted that decision, he raises a *new* problem, namely: *how* was the world made out of boundless substance? The answer must obviously be of a different character; it will not refer to a substance but to a *force*, a *process*, a *method* of operation which works upon substance. And, say the pundits—Aristotle included—Pythagoras decided upon "Numbers." But, having lost the true tradition as to the *question* to which "numbers" was said to be the answer, they were almost bound to misunderstand the answer when it came: and perhaps with good reason.

3. A LAW OF MOTION

Pythagoras, as I have said, left no writings as his contemporary scientists have done, and perhaps this crucial word,

THE KEY TO PYTHAGORAS

transmitted orally, soon came to be misunderstood. I shall analyse it shortly, and hope to show that Pythagoras was the first of the physical philosophers to propound a Law of Motion to account for the creation of the cosmos. Herakleitos, who professed to despise Pythagoras, in reality followed him very closely. As to the much-sought-for " substance " he decided in favour of fire. In a certain sense this was reactionary, like Anaximenes' *aer*, for the choice fell upon *one* out of many substances, differentiated objectively, whereas both Anaximandros and Pythagoras had agreed to go behind them all to *apeiron*, the undifferentiated *arche* or first principle of the world. But, like Pythagoras, he shows that merely to know the substance was not enough; there must be a process, a motion. This idea was expressed by Herakleitos in his famous formula *panta rei*, " all flows," which must be extended as meaning that all things flow " down " from their original fiery condition through liquids to solids, and " up "again through liquids to primal fire. But there is, as we shall see later, great significance in the word " flows " ; it is the key-word of Pythagoras. Herakleitos added a new and fundamental idea of " The One." *All things are One*, he said. Parmenides, following him, accepted the doctrine of The One and elaborated it in his own way, but rejected the theories of motion—of Herakleitos explicitly and of Pythagoras implicitly. He adheres to Permanency as a sovereign truth and thus interrupts and stops for a time the long philosophical conversation which had continued since Thales began to speak.

The foregoing remarks are intended to show how completely Pythagoras belongs to the cosmologists who preceded and who followed him. It is as a cosmologist that we must understand him first, as a man who believed himself to have discovered the process by which, out of chaos, there comes a cosmos, an orderly world. And thus we come back to his " Numbers."

4. THE "NUMBER" FAMILY OF WORDS

As we are now about to attempt to grasp the meaning of the key-word of Pythagoras I must ask my readers to have patience during the philological discussion which follows.

According to the steady tradition the word used by Pythagoras to define the *arche* of the world was *arithmos*. Number; I have shown already that this is a mistaken view. The *arche* for Pythagoras was *apeiron*, the Boundless, unlimited, proto-matter; his second decision, then, relates to the process or law of motion which transforms *apeiron* into *peras*, or the limited objective forms we know. Let us, then, examine *arithmos* and see what sense we can get out of it. It belongs to a family of words as follow:

1. *arithmeo*, to count, to enumerate.
2. *arithmetis*, enumeration.
3. *arithmetikos*, one who enumerates.
4. *arithmetos*, counted.
5. *arithmos*, number, quantity, multitude.

Can we feel any intelligible meaning steal into our minds as we contemplate these words? Personally, I cannot. The act of counting relates to things already in existence; one who counts, does not thus make things, and the abstract principle of number has no creative power. The later Pythagoreans, still struggling with their Master's unintelligible dogma, appear to have said that "things were *like* numbers rather than that they actually *were* numbers." According to Aristotle, the Pythagoreans held that the elements of number were the elements of things, and, therefore, that things were numbers, but such a statement conveys no concept to our minds. I could fill pages with discussion of the Odd and Even, the "number" of a horse, or a man or a soul, all of which are mentioned in the various commentaries, but the mere multiplication of nonsense by itself does not make sense. Our aim should

THE KEY TO PYTHAGORAS

be to start with sense—and this, I think, is possible by following a thread that leads us out of the commentator's labyrinth.

5. THE "RHYTHM" FAMILY OF WORDS

If we were dealing with the English word "numbers" we could at once put our hand on the guiding thread by remembering that the word has another significance than that of abstract enumeration. Says Longfellow:

> Tell me not in mournful numbers
> Life is but an empty dream;

and he gives a clue leading in another direction. It is possible that even in Greek we can follow it up. There is a second family of words to which we now turn.

1. *reo*, to flow, to stream forth, to run; this is the verb employed by Herakleitos in his famous dictum *panta rei*, "all flows."
2. *ruthmizo*, to reduce to time and measure; to form, to modulate and arrange in due proportion.
3. *erruthmezomen*, to put in symmetrical order, to arrange.
4. *ruthmikos*, formed, according to due proportion, rhythmical.
5. *ruthmos*
    (a) primary significance: rhythm, measured movement.
    (b) in dancing: modulated movement, gait or step.
    (c) in marching: marking time with the feet.
    (d) in music: the movement or time.
    (e) in poetry: rhythm, as distinct from the metre.
    (f) in prose: harmonious flow or cadence.
    (g) in objects: shape, form or fashion; also proportion or adaptation to their purpose.
    (h) in psychology: disposition of mind, moderated temper, equanimity.
6. *eurythmos*, comformable to orderly movement.

7. *eurythmia*, perfect harmony, due adjustment of parts, regulation of the respective position of things.

8. *numerus*, the Latin equivalent of *ruthmos* (5 e, above), signifying rhythm in poetry, and hence the English :

9. *number*, that which is distributed, e.g., sounds distributed into harmonies, metre, verse, especially as in the plural : " numbers."

6. RHYTHM IS OPERATION, MOVEMENT

I suggest that we now turn away from the " numbers that are things, and things that are numbers " and devote our attention to the second family of words, and of these, especially the fifth in its varied significance. We at once get the impression of an *operation* as distinct from an *object*. Rhythm is the imposition of special forms on the formless ; it is the measurement of that which flows ; it is the substitution of the symmetric for the erratic ; it is the reduction of chaos to cosmos, of discord to harmony ; it is the *distribution* of the " unlimited " into " limited " forms ; the passage from *apeiron* to *peras* ; it is the cosmological process from the One to the Many. After all, the Herakleitean formula *panta rei* may contain, rather than contradict, the Pythagorean idea of *rhythmical* movement ; it is not mere wild flux.

If we reflect that Pythagoras is stated distinctly to have left no writings and to have given oral instruction which was not to be divulged, it is quite easy to see how the word *arithmos* might have displaced the word *ruthmos* in the literary tradition. But, if we do not care to entertain such a hypothesis, we are not left without a solution, for it is clear that the first family of words is *derived* from the second, logically, if not philologically. When Rhythm has done its work upon the Unlimited and has produced the Limited, then—and not till then—there are both Things and Numbers simultaneously. And, happily, we are able to save the reputation of Aristotle by admitting that, looked at in this way, numbers are things and things are

THE KEY TO PYTHAGORAS

numbers! The older family of words has reduced the younger family to relative intelligibility, and we are thereby enlightened. In this way many of the obscurities and riddles of the commentators' tradition about Pythagoras and his school may be cleared up, and I shall illustrate this by a single case. "Modern geometers," says Mr. Burnet, "regard points, lines and surfaces as limits; but, as we have seen, the Pythagoreans thought they were a 'Harmony' or compound of the Limit and the Unlimited." And so they are: the Limit is form imposed on the Unlimited, which is matter; and the points, lines and surfaces are the "numbers" of position and extension which are produced by the peculiar motion of the rhythm operating upon the *arche*, or first principle of Nature. I do not pretend that all the puzzles of Pythagorean tradition would yield solutions so readily as this one, but many of them would do so if we cared to take the necessary trouble.

7. THE RHYTHM OF SOUND

We may now cast a glance upon Pythagoras as an observer and scientist, and try to divine how it was that he was led to frame his great cosmological generalization. His year of "flourishing" is given as 532 B.C., when Polykrates became tyrant of Samos. He left the island and settled in Kroton in Southern Italy, where he founded a scientific school and a religious community; that he intended his science and religion to have social and political results—as Plato did generations later—may be taken as certain, but I cannot go into that matter now. The phenomena of sound greatly interested Pythagoras; taken alone, isolated from all other phenomena, they exhibit a general law which the philosopher was in process of discovering. Music in particular results from the imposition of form on sound in general, of "limit" on the "unlimited." The mechanics of music in regard, for instance, to the lyre, consist in the imposition of seven different degrees of tension or strain on seven strings of equal length. The *results* of this tension are seven different musical tones. In the case of the pipe or flute, the mechanics of music consist in the placing of wind outlets at particular positions in the barrel of the instrument; the result, here, is the production of as many different tones as there are outlets. It is, then, the imposition of "form," or limit, on the general "matter" of sound. Both the flute and the lyre are illustrations of *ruthmos*—not merely movement, but "measured movement"; both illustrate the "distribution" of sound into its parts, into tonic intervals. But there is a still finer *ruthmos* in each tone itself—namely, the vibration of the string of the lyre, and the vibration of the air escaping from the pipe. Both these rhythms, when established, are capable of being numbered or counted, and Pythagoras was the first, we have reason to believe, to discover the numerical ratio for the notes of the scale; since his day the numerical ratio of the vibrations have also been discovered. I will only add, before passing to the next topic, that I think on the basis of the conception outlined in this paragraph many of the supposed "mysteries of numbers" in relation to music as discussed by the Pythagoreans might be turned out of bathos into sense. The single idea I wish to convey here is that Rhythm was discovered by Pythagoras to be the creative process of sound in general and music in particular. *Ruthmos* creates objective sounds, and consequently also the *arithmos*, or number of them. Thus only things are numbers.

8. THE RHYTHM OF THE BODY

We may now pass to another order of things, which, according to tradition, occupied the attention of Pythagoras. By intuition, observation and deduction from musical phenomena, the philosopher applied the same ideas to the body. The art of medicine once practised empirically, was considered scientifically as a remedial art, as a means of restoring conditions already belonging to the body.

THE KEY TO PYTHAGORAS

Health, in fact, was the natural attunement or *harmonia* of the body. But the body itself, like every other object possessing "limit," was the result of the creative process of *ruthmos*; and different bodies—such as horse or man—each had a different *ruthmos*. Further, each body, like each note as we now know, was based on an inner *ruthmos* or health of its own,—to preserve which was the art of medicine. Creation and healing, therefore, were not so distinct from each other as might commonly be supposed, for the man who knew the principles of the one would be guided in the operations of the other. Thus recreation is really re-creation. This explains the close relation between cosmology and medicine in the ancient days, and the fact that Empedokles and Pythagoras were both "medicine men" or supposed wonder-workers. We can be sure that Pythagoras believed himself to observe the law of rhythm in the body; in its symmetrical form, in its respiration, in its periodic sleeping and waking, nourishment, etc., and that he had the ideal of *eurythmia* or perfect harmony and due adjustment of the parts thereof. The Pythagorean use of the word *isonomie* as the basis of health is very significant, for it means "equal distribution" of the elements of the body, a "sharing equally" and a resultant balance or poise which gives beauty and strength. It may be well to mention here the modern rediscovery of the presence of rhythm in the body and the mind, as demonstrated by Professor Dalcroze in the Eurythmic dances. In certain circles we talk much of the "powers latent in man," and it is right to be reminded that among these powers is rhythm, or the modulated movement in gait or step which can then be measured and expressed by arithmetical numbers.

9. THE RHYTHM OF THE SOUL

Pythagoras must also have made research into the *ruthmos* of the soul, and this may have given rise to the later doctrine met with and refuted by Plato, that the soul is the attunement of the body. In his own way Aristotle adopted it by his view that the soul is the *entelecheia*, the completion or perfection of the body. In any case we can see how closely related were science and religion in the hands of Pythagoras. His special teaching of a psychological nature must have pointed out the natural *ruthmos* of the mind, and his remedial instruction must have been directed to its restoration as moderated temper, equanimity and serenity. We can at once understand the meaning of those fragmentary hints which come down to us about the Pythagorean Brotherhood and its discipline of silence; its practice of mathematics in order to attain to *mathesis* or reminiscence of all that which lies hidden in the unconscious mind. Here as elsewhere *ruthmos* is the key-word that is likely to open what doors are still locked—not " numbers " ! They will not help us until we understand the creative force which originates the things to which numbers are applied.

10. THE RHYTHM OF SOCIETY

The philosopher betook himself to one of the distant Hellenic colonies because, as we have learned, the tyranny of the ruler was uncongenial to him. His scientific, medical and religious disciplines were doubtless co-ordinated into one system for a definite end. We do not know, in set terms, what this end was, but many indications go to show that it was to lead men, or a certain class of men, to a life of infinite significance. Just as at the Olympic games some men come to trade, some to compete for the prize, and some to look on, so Pythagoras is said to have divided men into three classes, lovers of gain, lovers of honour, and lovers of wisdom. The categories need not be questioned at this moment, but we do well to remember that Pythagoras was one of the first of the Greek philosophers to teach the doctrine of transmigration of souls. His school, therefore, was for both worlds. The political endeavour of his Order was to introduce *isonomie* into Hellenic society, to enjoy

THE KEY TO PYTHAGORAS

an equality in rights and privileges, in other words to establish order, or on the medical analogy, to re-establish social health by the elimination of all forms of social disease. But undoubtedly Pythagoras and his school looked beyond the horizon of the grave to another phase of existence on this earth, where, perchance, those who had formerly loved gain would now love honour instead, and the lovers of wisdom also will be multiplied.

Tradition has it that Pythagoras adhered to the aristocratic party, and was overthrown by the democrats, but there is no warrant for this belief. The probability is that like all those who endeavour to introduce rhythm into the Social Order, he was misunderstood and mistrusted by both aristocrats and democrats.

11. THE RHYTHM OF THE COSMOS

Pythagoras, as we know, applied himself to astronomy or the knowledge of the movements of the heavenly bodies. I need not here repeat the various discoveries attributed to him in detail, some of them in advance of the ideas of their predecessors. What is certain, however, is that he must have looked for *ruthmos* in the heavens, just as he looked for it in the body, in mathematics, and in music. The traditional phrase "the harmony of the spheres" indicates a belief that the heavenly bodies occupy positions established according to numerical ratio; if so, this is another illustration of the operation of rhythm, which Pythagoras, once having discovered, must have seen everywhere.

It is somewhat remarkable that none of the traditional fragments of Pythagoreanism indicate the place occupied in the cosmos by an artificer, or creator. We may take it for granted, however, that the philosopher himself was deeply imbued with mystical feeling and theological thought, and probably, if we had his whole mind, we should learn from him that the various orders of rhythm seen in the world are but radiations from the central wheel of life.

My present effort is now concluded; it has been to arrange the materials of the Pythagorean fragments in such an order that they yield, of themselves, certain synthetic ideas—namely, that the first principle of the material universe was an undifferentiated *hylozoon* or vitalized matter; that the creative process is rhythmical motion operating upon the matter and bestowing upon it its multiple forms; that the maintenance of symmetrical and harmonious form depends upon the maintenance of the original specific rhythm appropriate to each form. That the co-ordination of different rhythms leads to the maximum degree of order and harmony in the cosmos and human society. That the Divine mind is the designer of the Cosmos in all its forms and consequently in its unity.

XV : *Sokrates the Moral Innovator*

A STUDY IN GREEK EGOISM

1. INTRODUCTION

THE word "egoism" is used primarily to denote a fundamental impulse exhibited in every living creature, but especially as it appears in mankind. The Principle of Individuation, having differentiated each being from the rest of living beings, has given it an impetus towards self-preservation : this branches out into numerous directions, producing consequences of the utmost complexity. It is permissible, therefore, to group together under the term "egoism" all the subconscious and conscious motives and activities of a self-regarding nature, and to distinguish them from those altruistic motives which consider the welfare of others alone—if such there be. For the present I do not attempt to put a value on the fore-mentioned egoistic impulse, but to turn my readers' attention to the secondary use of the word "egoism," namely, as it denotes a philosophical view of life, set up throughout the ages and expressed in modern times with great clearness by Nietzsche and his school. I have referred to the subject already in Sections III, VII and XII.

From what has been said above, it will readily be understood that all thinkers must have been compelled to make egoism, in some of its forms, a subject of study, either as "the will," "the desires," "ambition," "the passions" or "the spirits." It is important to remember, however, that long before such positive and formal thinking, men had been unconsciously acting from egoistic impulses, and we may suppose that radical tendency, so long as it exists, will continue to stimulate thinking in the direction of egoist philosophies.

There is a general impression that the egoist philosophies which have appeared of late are new, and that they represent an invasion of the sphere already held without question by moral philosophies of an opposite tendency. A boast is made on behalf of such writers as Stirner and Nietzsche that they have established "a new system of values" as against those proposed by moral philosophies of a Christian type. This, however, is not quite correct: the facts are that the deeply-rooted impulses of egoism were first in the field, and had produced in human thought a certain scheme of values; it was Sokratism, Platonism, Christianity, Buddhism and the like which attempted to make transvaluations, which have been partially accepted by mankind; while modern egoistic philosophies must be regarded as the very old impulses reappearing from time to time in articulate form. In a word, they are conscious revivals of the hitherto unconscious.

It is not surprising that egoistic impulses and valuations based on them do not allow themselves to be easily swept away. The compromise, for it can never be more than that, a *modus vivendi*, is as yet incomplete. In the following pages I have collected from the Greek classics all that I can conveniently find representative of ancient egoistic philosophy, and my effort has been a twofold one: first, to illustrate the way in which such a philosophy came into existence, and second, to demonstrate the significance of Sokrates as the first initiator of a scale of moral values which culminated in Christian Ethic. When we realize what he battled against, we can understand the reason of his noble martyrdom.

2. THEOGNIS

It is hard in these grey days to transpose ourselves in imagination to times and lands illumined by the earlier Greek civilization, but when in some degree the feat has been achieved,

SOKRATES THE INNOVATOR

we are faced by a picture of glory, beauty and violence. In the pages of ancient myth, Homeric song, Athenian drama or the histories of Herodotus and Thucydides, there is a constant illustration of life as the play of the egoistic motive under the most varied conditions. We can there see that the struggle for existence, realized so intensely and without disguise, produced in all the early States similar social phenomena—ruling military castes and a general body of inferior citizens and slaves. Egoism appears not only as a natural and universal impulse, but as an aristocratic cult, a system of ideas and practice evolved by experience from caste necessities. It was inevitable that the impulse behind this cult should in time come to be the subject of reflection by some of those more vitally interested in the maintenance of caste advantages ; therefore we are not surprised to learn that the elements of the egoist philosophy are first stated by an aristocrat and a poet, rather than by a dispassionate philosopher. Theodore Gomperz writes : " In the second half of the sixth century we find the Megarian aristocrat Theognis longing to ' drink the black blood ' of his adversaries, with the same unbridled passion as had characterised the Homeric hero praying that he might ' devour his enemy raw.' "—(*Greek Thinkers*, II. 4.)

Theognis was a member of the nobility controlling the State of Megara : his life covers a period of ninety years between 570 B.C. and 480 B.C. His verse comes to us in numerous fragments, and reflects the fluctuating fortunes of himself, his party, his democratic enemies, his false friends and his State. The aristocratic philosophy accepts the traditional worship of Zeus and his Olympian Company, together with the special cult of Apollo, the protector of the City of Megara. In times of prosperity it amounts to an easy epicureanism—wine and song flow freely at the banquets of the favoured ones ; in danger there are vows of mutual loyalty among boon companions, and in desperation, threats of terrible revenge. Ostracism and exile bring despondency and fatalism, old age and poverty bring bitterness of spirit, while restoration to home and a depleted treasury yields a fruitful crop of maxims in couplets about Providence and Fate.

But the peculiarity of the philosophic reflections of Theognis is their limited point of view. Of humanity in general he knows nothing; of other States—until his own fortunes became dependent upon them—he cares little. But as a member of the nobility, he looks out on the world as the sphere in which his caste is to disport itself, and this determines his scheme of values. "The good" are the aristocrats, the clean, the beautiful, the active, the happy; and "evil" is all that would rob them of their wealth and felicity. On the other hand, "the bad" are the plebeians; "the base," "the commonalty," those who are exploited, those who serve. Virtue is only looked for in "the good"—consequently it can only be related to that which administers to the preservation, enrichment and upliftment of the caste. Even the State exists for the caste.

The following fragment from Theognis, written at a time when the fortunes of his party were depressed, illustrates the aristocratic conception of the status of "the people":

> Our commonwealth preserves its former frame,
> Our common people are no more the same:
> They that in skins and hides were rudely dressed,
> Nor dreamed of law, nor sought to be redressed
> By rules of right, but in the days of old
> Flocked to the town, like cattle to the fold,
> Are now the dominant class and we, the rest,
> (Their betters nominally, once the best)
> Degenerate, debased, timid, and mean:
> Who can endure to witness such a scene?
> Their easy courtesies, the ready smile,
> Prompt to deride, to flatter, and beguile;
> Their utter disregard of right or wrong,
> Of truth or honour: out of such a throng

SOKRATES THE INNOVATOR

> Never imagine you can choose a just
> Or steady friend, or faithful in his trust.
>
> (Lines 53 to 68 Frere's Translation.)

The democratic "utter disregard of right or wrong" relates, of course, to the aristocratic system of morals, while popular dreamers of law and rules of right represent a newer scheme of values that clashes with that accepted by Theognis and his friends. It is obvious that at that time no common ground had been discovered, no mutual and necessary relationship discerned, on which a common morality could be based. This task was reserved for later philosophy.

There must, of course, have been many who, in their day, thought and spoke like Theognis, and he, far from being regarded here as unique or specially remarkable, is one whose reflections, fortunately preserved to us, are typical of a point of view which is very significant for ethics. It was Nietzsche who "discovered" Theognis in this respect, and who, on a very slender basis of an ancient example, built up for himself his own aristocratic and egoistic philosophy.

It was not only in the circles of aristocratic rulers that this one-sided view of ethical values was taken and expressed. As the fragments of Theognis show, and as Nietzsche demonstrates from them, the democratic party in Megara, when victorious, took a precisely similar view to that of the aristocrats, by simply turning their scheme of values upside down. They themselves were the "good" and their opponents the "wicked." Neither side had been able to think of a universal ethical scheme, which included both classes by subordinating them to its canon.

3. THE SOPHISTS

Beyond this there were some who perceived that the relativity of ethical conceptions amounted in practice to the denial of a moral criterion, and who went as far as they could in their teaching to relieve men of the troublesome burden of moral ideas. In part this was the work of the "Sophists," about whom much learned discussion has taken place where Hellenists do congregate. The Sophists from the Athenian or metropolitan point of view, were all foreigners, yet they professed, and in many respects on good grounds, to impart a superior culture which, taken together, amounted to a general illumination. Though not a school of thought, they were a class of educators in Rhetoric, Poesy, Politics and the minor arts. That they did not teach morals we have the testimony of Gorgias to prove—one of their greatest representatives. Between them, these Sophist teachers and disciples have a good deal to say of interest to our present study. Protagoras of Abdera, Gorgias of Leontinoi and Prodikos of Ceos were the most notable of the influential body of men who appeared in Athens in the fifth century, providing the budding philosophers of that time with many tough problems upon which to sharpen their intellects. Professor Blackie, in an interesting essay on these men, attempts to reduce them to a system with the following result:

1. General information and alert intelligence without a philosophical basis or a scientific method of verification.

2. The art of public speaking considered as a means of moving masses of ignorant men with a view to political advancement, but not necessarily connected with pure motives or lofty purpose.

3. The exercise of a dexterous logic, that aimed at the ingenious, the striking and the plausible, rather than the judicious, the solid and the true.

4. A theory of metaphysics which, by confounding knowledge with sensation, made wisdom consist rather in the expert use of present opportunity than in moulding of materials according to an intellectual principle.

5. A theory of morals (in conformity therewith) which, by basing right on convention, deprived our sensuous feelings and animal passions of the imperial control of reason, and substituted for the eternal instinct of justice, arbitrary enactments whose ultimate sanction is the intelligent selfishness of the individual.

(Horæ Hellenicæ.)

4. METAPHYSICAL NIHILISM

The aphorism of Protagoras "that man is the measure of all things" proved a very formidable obstacle to moralists like Sokrates and Plato who were searching for ethical universals by which man himself might be measured. Consistent with the view of Protagoras, which—whether he intended it or not—abolished the moral criterion, but much more profound, is the "metaphysical nihilism" of Gorgias. Gorgias of Leontinoi in Sicily visited Athens in 427 B.C. He was a thorough-going nihilist. Devoted to the teaching of rhetoric, he was dramatically exposed by Sokrates in masterly fashion as wanting in ultimate moral conviction; but the nature of his philosophy could scarcely permit him to have any. He had long given up the gods and all belief in science; for him there was no certitude or truth at all. In his book *On Nature or the Non-existent* he had sought to prove (1) that there is nothing; (2) that even if there is anything, we cannot know it, or communicate anything about it. In the ethical sphere the counterpart to this doctrine was that there is no natural distinction between right and wrong, and there were not lacking politicians in Athens who welcomed this as a measure of some relief. Efficiency and success in any direction, by means of the arts taught by Gorgias, were sufficient rewards for his pupils. Expediency replaced justice, and we shall see shortly how far his doctrines were carried in the moral sphere by Kallikles, one of his chief admirers.

5. ATHENS *versus* MELOS

The Megarian doctrine that the "right" resides alone with those who have power, though typically an aristocratic one, was shared by democratic Athens; indeed, the case of the Athenian attack on Melos shows that the possession of power is the essential factor in determining where the right lies—not the quality or descent of those who exercise it. It is therefore appropriate to glance at this tragic occurrence. The island of Melos was a Spartan colony, but had not joined in the war against Athens, nor had it entered the Confederacy of Delos, of which Athens was the head. In 416 B.C. the Athenians called upon the Melians to join their empire; after a dignified refusal they laid siege to the city, massacred every man, and took the women and children into captivity. For our purposes the incident is useful because of the dramatic dialogue, preserved by Thucydides, in which the Athenian envoys advance the doctrine that justice does not exist between unequals—otherwise, that might gives right. The following are some of the most telling passages in the argument advanced by the Athenian spokesman :

> Since you know as well as we do that "right," as the world goes, is only in question between equals in power, while the strong do what they can and the weak suffer what they must. . . . Of the gods we believe, and of man we know, that by a necessary law of their nature they rule wherever they can. And it is not as if we were the first to make this law, or to act upon it when made : we found it existing before us, and shall leave it to exist for ever after us ; all we do is to make use of it, knowing that you and everybody else, having the power as we have, would do the same as we do.
>
> (*Peloponnesian War*, Ch. XVII.)

SOKRATES THE INNOVATOR

The essential points of this address are that the law of Nature is more ancient and widely observed than the so-called law of Right, which only need be invoked between those who are of equal strength. Inasmuch as no two forces are ever exactly equal, the practical result is that the moral law need never be observed. In fact it had not at that time (416 B.C.) seriously made its appearance. This we may learn from the case of Kallikles, a citizen of democratic Athens, friend and disciple of Gorgias, the Rhetor and Sophist.

6. KALLIKLES

In the hands of Plato (429 B.C.–347 B.C.), by birth an aristocrat who lived under democracies, tyrannies and oligarchies, and who had the stimulus of Sokrates' friendship, the theme already made familiar by Theognis receives more adequate treatment. Egoistic philosophy in its aristocratic form, had become more widely articulate, even although aristocratic governments were losing their power to the growing democracies fostered by the Athenian Republic. Indeed, I venture to think that the philosophic aspect of egoism, as distinct from its natural aspect, was forced into light as a protest, as an intellectual justification and defence against the growing advances of the popular movement : and further, when the democracies exercised power devoid of moral sanction, they, like the aristocrats, fell back upon an egoistic philosophy. This explains how Kallikles, a democrat, uses the same arguments as Theognis.

The pre-Sokratic philosophers did not, in the main, devote themselves to moral problems, but to physical and metaphysical speculations ; it was Sokrates (with Plato as a listener) who concentrated his mind on moral problems. He sought, by an interminable series of questions, to find ethical universals that lay behind the varying and often contradictory concrete ethical conceptions of his day : just as the physicists had sought for the material basis of reality, so he tried to replace a cosmic *phusis* by a logical one. Inevitably he came into contact with the egoistic philosophers of the Sophistic schools ; and it is to one of these encounters that we owe the Platonic dialogue, the *Gorgias*. Herein Gorgias, Polus and Kallikles, men of like bias, converse with Sokrates on rhetoric and its purpose, but are driven by him backwards in search of ultimate moral criteria. With Sokrates " the good " could not mean a class, aristocratic or popular ; his thinking is unrelated to Megara, Athens or Corinth. The worm of his thought is eating its way into ancient and established ideas with irritating persistency, and the philosophy of egoism, when forced to become articulate, is not spared. Kallikles is represented by Plato as having witnessed the discomfiture of Gorgias and Polus, and he feels instinctively that the values current throughout Hellas are being challenged by Sokrates. He estimates truly the nature of the new Sokratic values, and their danger to his own, for which he makes a gallant fight, as the following words show :

K. " Tell me, Chaerephon, does Sokrates say these things seriously or is he joking ? "
C. " He appears to me, Kallikles, to speak most seriously—but there is nothing like asking him himself."
K. " Tell me, Sokrates, whether we must now believe that you are speaking seriously or joking, for if you are speaking seriously, and if what you are saying is true, is not our human life altogether upside down, and are not our actions contrary to what they ought to be ? "

I call attention to the fact that Kallikles' evident surprise proves what has already been urged, that Sokratism seemed altogether strange and unrelated to practical life when its quiet challenge was first issued. Egoists could scarcely believe their ears ; they had not, as we have to-day, twenty-four centuries of cognate ideas to prepare them for Sokrates' proposals. The discourse of Kallikles must be read in the light of this fact.

Sokrates answers in a speech opening with words very characteristic of Plato, and deeply significant in view of the ultimate argument to be made against egoism in general:

> "If there were not a certain community of feeling among mankind, but each of us had a peculiar feeling different from others, that were not shared by the rest of his species, it would not be easy for us to make known our impressions to one another. . . ."

7. THE CONFLICT OF NATURE AND LAW

Kallikles replies in terms that must now engage our attention, for they set forth the doctrine of egoism more clearly than Theognis had been able to do, and I may say here that, before long, Kallikles will be found developing what may be called a doctrine of individual egoism.

> You seem, Sokrates, to be nothing but a mob-orator! . . . I do not congratulate Polus, who has conceded to you that "to commit injustice is more base than to suffer it"; for into this admission he has been entangled by you, because he was ashamed to say what he really felt. . . . Nature and Law are, for the most part, contrary to one another; and when Polus spoke of suffering injustice as being more base than inflicting it, he meant, of course, according to Nature. For by Nature everything is more base which is the worse, such as to suffer injustice, whereas by Law it is said to be more base to commit it.

This first distinction of Kallikles is sound; it recognizes two voices: that of Nature, which dictates quite clearly an ethic of her own, and that of Law, which is evidently a modification, or even a denial, of the ethic of Nature.

He therefore proceeds to give Sokrates his own opinion of the rival claims of Nature and Law, deciding, as might have been expected, in favour of the former.

> I think those who make the Law are the weak and the many; they therefore make laws with a view to their own advantage, and with the same view they bestow praise and blame; they terrify such as are stronger, and say it is base and unjust to obtain a superiority, and that to endeavour to acquire more than others is to commit injustice. . . . But Nature evinces, on the contrary, that it is just that the better should have more than the worse, and the powerful more than the weaker. And it is evident that this is so, both in animals and whole cities and races of men. . . . For I think they do these things according to Natural Justice, yes, by Zeus, according to the Law of Nature: not perhaps according to the Law which we have framed; for, taking the best and strongest amongst us from their youth, like lions, we tame them by incantations and juggleries, telling them it is right to preserve equality, and that this is the beautiful and the just.

Obviously Kallikles is finding the principles of a system of egoistic thought—which shall withstand the deadly attack of Sokratism, founded on a basis more subtle and hidden—on "a certain community of feeling among mankind." He continues confidently:

> If there should be found a man with sufficient natural power, having shaken off all the trammels, and broken through and abandoned, and trampled underfoot written ordinances, quackeries, incantations and Laws contrary to Nature—then Natural Justice would shine forth. . . .
>
> (Jowett's Translation of *Gorgias*.)

SOKRATES THE INNOVATOR

8. THE ANSWER TO EGOISM

I am not at present concerned with the counter-philosophy by which egoism is said to be refuted, but my readers may wish to know the principles of Sokrates' attack—for such it is—on its strongly entrenched position; therefore I give the briefest outline: (i.) Behind all is an intense conviction that he has the truth—" my statement is always the same, that I know not how these things are, but that of all the persons with whom I have ever conversed, no one who says otherwise can avoid being ridiculous." (ii.) Secondly, the conviction that the welfare of the soul is dependent upon its deeds in the body; it must acquire a certain power and art of self-government, so as neither to injure others or be liable to injury from others. (iii.) Thirdly, that the Universe is a Kosmos, an Order " that heaven and earth, gods and men are held together by communion, friendship, order and justice . . . it has escaped your notice that geometrical equality rules among gods and men; you neglect geometry; you think that every one should strive to get *more* than the others." Here Sokrates reduces the egoist principles to a sentence, and in view of the declared *geometry* (one might almost say *economy*) of the Kosmos, demonstrates, as he believes, their absurdity. (iv.) Finally, the philosophic, as distinct from the interested point of view, enables Sokrates to discuss these problems in a detached way: " Each person seems to me for the most part to be a friend to each," as the ancient sages say, "a certain passion common to all men "—phrases like these show that Sokrates is not bound down to local and political conditions when seeking for the principles of his philosophy. What is clear is that he is initiating an entirely new view against the unconscious egoism of his day, and forcing the latter to articulate itself, through this typical Athenian citizen, Kallikles.

9. ETHICAL NIHILISM OF THRASUMACHOS

Thrasumachos, to whom we now turn, was already a famous teacher of rhetoric at the time that Gorgias came to Athens, and it is clear from his discourse that he had gone much further than Kallikles. He exhibits an utter scorn of all moral criteria; his ethical nihilism is the exact counterpart of Gorgias' metaphysical nihilism; it might well have been its consequence; but that we do not know.

In the *Republic*, Book I., in a casual way, some one mentions the uneasy feeling of a man who is aware that he has done an injustice, and wishes to make restitution: upon this, after a tentative definition of justice has been abandoned, Polemarchos proposes and is led on to support the following propositions:

(i.)

(*a*) Justice is to give every one what is his due.

(*b*) Friends ought to do their friends some good and no ill.

(*c*) But to an enemy there is due what is fitting, that is, some evil.

(*d*) Justice, then, is an art of dispensing to persons what is fitting and due; good offices to friends, and injuries to enemies.

(*e*) In actions, Justice will best be expressed by fighting in alliance with friends against enemies.

(*f*) In time of peace, therefore, Justice became a kind of thieving for the profit of friends and the hurting of enemies.

Here Sokrates, instead of pressing on toward a *reductio ad absurdum*, introduces a new point, namely, the uncertainty as to whether our friends are good and our enemies evil. He sees the impossibility of allowing Justice to be dependent upon the accident of friendship. He proposes:

(ii.)

Justice will profit the just and injure the unjust; this will sometimes imply that it will be just to hurt our friends if they are evil, and benefit our enemies if they are really good.

But as Justice has been made independent of the accident of friendship, so it must be separated from the idea of "injury." Will the just man injure anybody at all—his evil friend or his evil enemy? The argument goes to prove that people are made worse by injury, and that it is precisely the unjust man who is injurious. How then can the just man take the same course? The conclusion of Sokrates after all is this:

(iii.)

Neither is it the part of a just man to injure either friend or any other . . . for it nowhere appears to us that any just man hurts any one.

Sokrates, pleased at having got thus far, quietly remarks to his hearers that the aforementioned view, that justice consists in profiting our friends and hurting our enemies, must have been the saying of Xerxes "or some other rich man who thought himself able to do a great deal." This is more than Thrasumachos can stand.

We are convinced that, although we are but reading a Platonic dialogue, the protest of Thrasumachos is historically and philosophically genuine. The Sokratic morality, as it advanced in clearness, must have forced the egoistic impulse to become intellectually articulate. In Thrasumachos it has "its back to the wall."

It will be unnecessary to follow the long argument in detail, or the mode of refutation adopted by Sokrates. The salient words of the ultra-egoist will now be sufficiently clear, as we quote them with little comment. Thrasumachos declares:

(iv.)

(*a*) I say that what is just is nothing else but the advantage of the more powerful.

(*b*) Do you not know that with reference to states, whether tyrannically, democratically or aristocratically governed . . . the governing part of each is the more powerful ? And every government makes laws for its own advantage . . . and when they have made them they give out that to be just for the governed which is advantageous to themselves ; and they punish the transgressor of this as one acting contrary to both law and justice.

(*c*) Governors of states are liable to err, but when they attempt to make laws they make some of them right and some of them not right. To make them right is to make them advantageous to themselves. . . . And what they enact is to be observed by the governed, and this is what is just.

(*d*) You think that shepherds and neatherds ought to consider " the good of the sheep," to fatten them and to minister to them, having their eye on something apart from their master's good ; and in the same way you fancy that those who govern cities are somehow otherwise affected towards the governed than one is toward sheep, that they are attentive day and night to " the good of the people," to somewhat else than how they shall be gainers themselves.

(*e*) The governed do what is for the governor's advantage, he being more powerful, and, ministering to him, promote his happiness, but by no means their own.

SOKRATES THE INNOVATOR

At this point Thrasumachos becomes aware that he is using words in a different sense to Sokrates, and for the sake of making a clearer issue, he adopts the Sokratic terms. He therefore abandons his use of the word "Justice," defining the thing *he* values, and is willing to speak of the thing Sokrates values as "Justice." We have from him then a detailed catalogue of the disadvantages of the Sokratic "Justice" and the advantage of the Sokratic "Injustice." Nothing could be clearer:

(f) On all occasions the "just man" gets less than the "unjust." In co-partnership you never find, on the dissolving of the company, the "just man" gets more than the unjust, but less; in civil affairs the "just man" pays more taxes, the other less; when there is anything to be gained, the one gains nothing, the other a great deal; in any public magistracy less befalls the "just man" in that his domestic affairs are in a worse situation through his neglect; he gains nothing from the public because he is "just." But all these things are quite otherwise with the "unjust," such an one, I mean, who has it greatly in his power to become rich. Consider him, then, how much more it is for his private advantage to be unjust than "just," and you will easily understand it if you come to the most finished Injustice such as renders the unjust man most happy; that is, autocratic rule. . . . For when any one, besides these thefts of the substance of his citizens, shall steal and enslave the citizens themselves, he is called happy and blest. . . . For such as revile "wickedness" revile it not because they are afraid of doing but afraid of suffering unjust things. And then, Sokrates, "Injustice" as you call it, when in sufficient measure, is both more powerful and more free, and hath more absolute command than "Justice."

Sokrates seems to realize that there is something fundamental in the sentiments that divide him and his opponent; it is not a matter of words, but of ultimate values.

> Sok. "Convince us then, blest Thrasumachos, that we imagine wrong when we value 'Justice' more than 'Injustice.'"
>
> Thras. "But how shall I convince you? Shall I enter into your soul and put my reasoning within you?"
>
> Sok. "God forbid you should do that!"

Sokrates may well reply: "Your meaning is now more determined, and it is no longer easy for one to find what to say against it." "Might not you say," asks Sokrates, "that a state was unjust that attempted to enslave other states unjustly, and did enslave them, and had many states in slavery under itself?" "Why not?" replies Thrasumachos. "The best state will chiefly do this, and as such is the most completely unjust."

10. THE FINAL VALUES

I may here add a passage from the *Crito*, in which the conception of justice mentioned above (iii.) seems to have been carried to the extreme degree of non-injury, almost to non-resistance. But as the *Crito* preceded the *Republic* by many years, we are warranted in thinking it to be the first statement of Sokrates' strong conviction on the subject, before he had had time to support it by the extended argument that appears in the *Republic*. He says to Krito:

(v.)

> Can we begin our deliberations from this point that it is never right, either to do an injury or to return an injury, or when one has been evil entreated to revenge oneself by doing evil in return? For so it appears to me long since and now.

SOKRATES THE INNOVATOR

We can be sure that if Sokrates had added this further definition to those already laid down in the conversation with Polemarchos, the protest that follows would have been even more violent. It would have turned the whole moral world of that day upside down and inside out.

11. SOKRATES THE RATIONALIST

Sokrates was not always able—as, indeed, none of us are—to give *proof* of the rightness of his moral judgments. His contemporaries, as we have seen, realized that he was "always saying the same kind of thing," but yet was not satisfying them as to the rightness of those views of his which appeared to them to turn the world upside down. The sage resorted to several means in order to bring to the minds of others some measure of the convictions of which he was possessed; the first of these was rational argument, in which he was more competent than most men of his time. The Sokratic dialectic, as reported by Plato, is often most penetrating, and quite valid according to modern canons of logic; sometimes, however, it is more subtle, resembling the sophistic displays of the professional disputer, whose *eristic*, or verbal contention, overthrew without being able to convince his antagonist. Sokrates uses this lighter kind in lighter moods, but not when he is in grim earnest. When, however, his dialectic (of both kinds) leaves his interlocutors unimpressed, he has resort to legendary tale or poetic story (*mythos*), which is intended to lift the hearers beyond mere reasoning and produce in them a transcendental feeling of the essential rightness of the position which he is for the time attempting to make good. But the myth, like dialectic, may also fail; in these moments Sokrates falls back upon his own inner convictions, which he explains in terms that may be called mystical. Sokrates' bed-rock of morality, upon which all his conduct is based, is *in himself*; yet, further, *through* him it rests in God. For this reason it may be worth our while to see what one of the greatest of the ancient moralists had to say about the " voice " which guided him when in doubt.

12. SOKRATES THE MYSTIC

From Homer to Plato the word *daimon* was used to denote either a *god* or a spiritual being inferior to a god; it was a name given to the souls of men of the golden age who formed a connecting link between gods and men; consequently, its meaning applies to such beings in their dealings with men, and not otherwise. It is noteworthy that neither Sokrates nor his friends ever claim that he was privileged to receive guidance from such an attendant *daimon* or genius; this notion was commonly adopted by his accusers, by later Greek writers, and by certain of the Christian fathers, after many centuries. His " old accusers " —Aristophanes, the comic dramatist, and those who accepted his caricature—had for more than twenty years fastened on Sokrates the charge of impiety, while the official indictment as recorded by Xenophon reads thus :

> Sokrates offends against the laws in not paying respect to those gods whom the city respects, and in introducing new deities ; he also offends against the laws in corrupting the youth.

The charge of introducing new deities rested on a misunderstanding or misrepresentation of the teaching which Sokrates gave about divine guidance, for the word used in all the authoritative texts is not *daimon* but *to daimonion*, which means " the divine agency." In this sense, Xenophon, who has a great deal to say about the inspiration and guidance of Sokrates, always uses the word *daimonion*, and not simply *daimon* ; thus he frees Sokrates from the charge of introducing " new deities." The more important passages are as follows :

> It was a common subject of talk that Sokrates used to say that the divinity instructed him. . . . He,

SOKRATES THE INNOVATOR

however, introduced nothing newer than those who practise divination. ... He spoke as he thought, for he said that it was the divinity which was his monitor. He also told many of his friends to do certain things, and not to do others, intimating that the divinity had forewarned him; and advantage attended those who obeyed his suggestions, but repentance those who disregarded them.

(*Memorabilia*, I. i. 2–5.)

Euthydemus. The gods certainly appear to exercise the greatest care for man in every way. ... They seem to show you, Sokrates, more favour than other men, since they indicate to you, without being asked, what you ought to do, and what not to do.

Sokrates. And that I speak the truth you yourself also well know, if you do not expect to see the bodily forms of the gods, but will be content as you behold their works to worship and honour them. Reflect, too, that the gods themselves give us this intimation. ... The soul of man, moreover, which partakes of the divine nature, if anything in man does, rules, it is evident, within us, but is itself unseen.

(IV. iii. 12–14.)

... he said that the *daimonion* admonished him what he ought to do and what he ought not to do.

(IV. viii. 1.)

... when I was proceeding, a while ago, to study my defence to the judges, the *daimonion* testified disapprobation.

(IV. viii. 5–6.)

Those who knew what sort of man Sokrates was continue to regret him above all other men even to this present day ... so wise that he never erred in distinguishing better from worse, needing no counsel from others, but being sufficient in himself to discriminate between them.

(IV. viii. 11.)

... for he thought that the gods paid regard to men, not in the way in which some people suppose, who imagine that the gods know some things and do not know others, but he considered that the gods know all things, both what is done, what is said, and what is meditated in silence, and are present everywhere, and give signs to men concerning everything human.

(I. i. 19.)

Thus we see that Xenophon tells us nothing about the nature of Sokrates' *daimonion*, except that it was the instrument through which divine intimations reached him without solicitation on his part. In ordinary divination men seek for a "sign," but in the case of Sokrates it was given spontaneously, and was also called by him a "voice," and an "oracle," as recorded by Plato in *The Apology*:

You have often heard me speak in times past of an oracle or sign which comes to me, and is the divinity which Meletos [the prosecutor] ridicules in the indictment. This sign I have had ever since I was a child. The sign is a voice which comes to me and always forbids me doing something which I am going to do, but never commands me to do anything. . . .

(*The Apology*, 31, c–d.)

Again, in his closing discourse, Sokrates says to the minority judges who have voted for his acquittal :

O my judges—for you I may truly call judges—I should like to tell you of a wonderful circumstance. Hitherto the familiar oracle within me has constantly been in the habit of opposing me even about trifles, if I was going to make a slip or error in any matter ;

... but now the oracle has made no sign of opposition.... What do I take to be the explanation of this? I regard this as a great proof that what has happened to me is good, and that those of us who think that death is an evil are in error. For the customary sign would have opposed me had I been going to evil and not to good.

(Ibid., 40, a–b.)

There remains another passage in *The Republic* to which reference should be made before we endeavour to estimate aright this "voice" of Sokrates. The sage is speaking about philosophy in relation to politics, and explains his own withdrawal from public life:

My own case of the internal sign is indeed hardly worth mentioning, as very rarely, if ever, has such a monitor been vouchsafed to any one else. Those who belong to this small class have tasted how sweet and blessed a possession philosophy is, and have also seen and been satisfied of the madness of the multitude. . . .

(The Republic, VI. 496, c.)

13. "THE VOICE" IS CONSCIENCE

Apart, then, from Sokrates' own view as to the meaning of the divine agency, and of Xenophon's and Plato's accounts of it, what do we take it to be? The statement that the "voice" never *approved* but only *disapproved* of his intended actions must not be taken too literally, for when his intention and his guidance harmonized he would be conscious only of the former; when they were at variance he would be conscious of both. We may therefore conclude that the *daimonion*—"the sign," "the voice," "the oracle"—though believed by Sokrates to be peculiar to himself, or at least very rare, was only so because he was careful to keep himself open to moral and intellectual inspiration. It was his substitute for the divination which other men practised;

he made and kept himself the medium for divine guidance; rather than have recourse to external and irrational expedients, he found a guide within himself. His mental acts, so far as he could follow, understand, and explain them, were human, but beyond his ken they were divine, dependent upon an immediate inspiration.

We shall surely not be wrong in supposing that Sokrates was a man of very sensitive "conscience"; rather than mark him off as one of a class apart, we must claim him and his wonderful attainments as essentially human and normal. Conscience with him reached a higher level than the average man's—so high a level, indeed, that he thought it supernatural. That is but a call or encouragement to others to follow his example.

XVI : *Neo-Platonism*

1. RELIGION COMBINED WITH PHILOSOPHY

ALTHOUGH Sokrates never professed to be a philosopher in the classical sense of the term, and was not one in the modern sense, yet it is a fact that all the Greek philosophy which preceded him was focussed in his great personality and passed through him on its way to his many successors. He was a kind of archway under which passed the three processions of thought which are commonly, and rightly, called Pre-Sokratic philosophy. The first was a scientific research which began in Miletos with Thales (640–550 B.C.) and terminated with Demokritos (470–390 B.C.); the second was mystical and philosophical dogma initiated by Xenophanes of Elea (556–460 B.C.) and carried on in different ways by Pythagoras, Parmenides, Herakleitos, Kratylos and Empedokles of Agrigentium (490–430 B.C.). The third procession was of a different character, representing at first, the normal, worldly, practical utilitarianism of the day, and culminating in a reaction against both scientific and philosophic dogma; it was the scepticism of the Sophists, whose greatest figures were Protagoras, Gorgias and Prodikos, contemporaries of Sokrates, who began his own philosophical career as a practical agnostic but ended it as a convinced believer.

The tragic times compelled Sokrates and his numerous disciples to impart a predominantly ethical quality to all philosophy immediately issuing from them in four new processions : Plato specialized on political morality (Academics), Eukleides on the discipline of thought (Megarics), Antisthenes on the control of the desires (Cynics), and Aristippos on the attainment of happiness (Cyreniacs). After two or three generations a new grouping of schools was discovered. Aristotle broke away from the Platonic school and established a movement of extraordinary steadiness—the philosophy of "development" in biology, sociology, ethics and politics (Peripatetics). Platonism continued its majestic course : the schools of Eukleides and Antisthenes combined to form the Stoics ; while Epicurus gave a permanent and rational turn to the hedonism of Aristippos. With occasional minor revivals of Pre-Sokratic systems these four streams flowed on uninterruptedly to the Christian era, and, crossing the line that our imagination and the sense of time has marked there, went on—we might almost say—to the present day ; for the fact is the occidental genius continues to reveal itself in four of its chief temperaments—the dogmatic mystical (Platonic), the practical empirical (Aristotelian), the pessimistic apathetic (Stoic) and æsthetic, rationalistic, pleasure-seeking (Epicureanism).

2. GRÆCO-JUDAISM

We now start from a point early in the second century B.C. when the conceptions of all philosophers were the common property of those who chose to adopt them ; in other words, all philosophy was eclectic in its character, no longer adhering rigidly to older ideas of the founders. It was this fact which made possible the development called conveniently, though perhaps inaccurately, "Neo-Platonism."

The extension of the Greek Empire by Alexander and his successors to Asia Minor, Mesopotamia, Persia, India and Egypt had carried Greek thought and culture everywhere. Generally it found a welcome and "hellenized" a new world. One instance of remarkable resistance was that of the Palestinian Jews whose tale is told in Section XVII, "Between the Testaments." It was other-

NEO-PLATONISM

wise with the Jews of Egypt, who, under a milder sway, absorbed all that they might of Greek philosophy.

For the study of Neo-Platonism it is desirable to know all that can be known of the early Jewish thought of Egypt, but unfortunately there is not much to hand. The second book of the Maccabees gives the text of a letter written from Palestine as follows :

> They that are in Jerusalem and they that are in Judea and the senate and Judas, unto Aristobulus, King Ptolemy's teacher, who is also of the stock of the anointed priests, and unto the Jews that are in Egypt, send greeting and health . . . (I. 10.)

This king is Ptolemy VII, who ruled in Egypt from 182 to 146 B.C., and the letter was despatched in the year 124 B.C. Aristobulus had therefore been many years in Alexandria and had dedicated to the king a work on the Pentateuch in which he tried to show that the doctrines of the Aristotelian school (of which he was an adherent) were derived from the Old Testament. We have but a few fragments of this work. Again, Philo, the learned Jew of Alexandria (B.C. 20–50 A.D.) had likewise studied and assimilated the Greek wisdom, attaching himself to the school of Plato ; and we have his voluminous works as a testimony to the extent of his approach to Hellenic ideas. Græco-Judaism is one of the three main streams tributary to the broad river of Neo-Platonism. The second was an Alexandrian combination of the revived Pythagorean and Platonic systems led by Eudoxas, Thrasillus (A.D. 36), Plutarch (A.D. 125), and Maximius of Apamea (A.D. 132–180). It was this last-named leader who effected a synthesis of Græco-Judaism with his own Pythagorean-Platonic school. Lastly, there was Christianity, which, when it reached Alexandria, fell into two groups : the Catholic, or universalist gnosis and the dualist gnosis led by Basilides and Valentinius. To this latter kind Ammonius Sakkas (A.D.

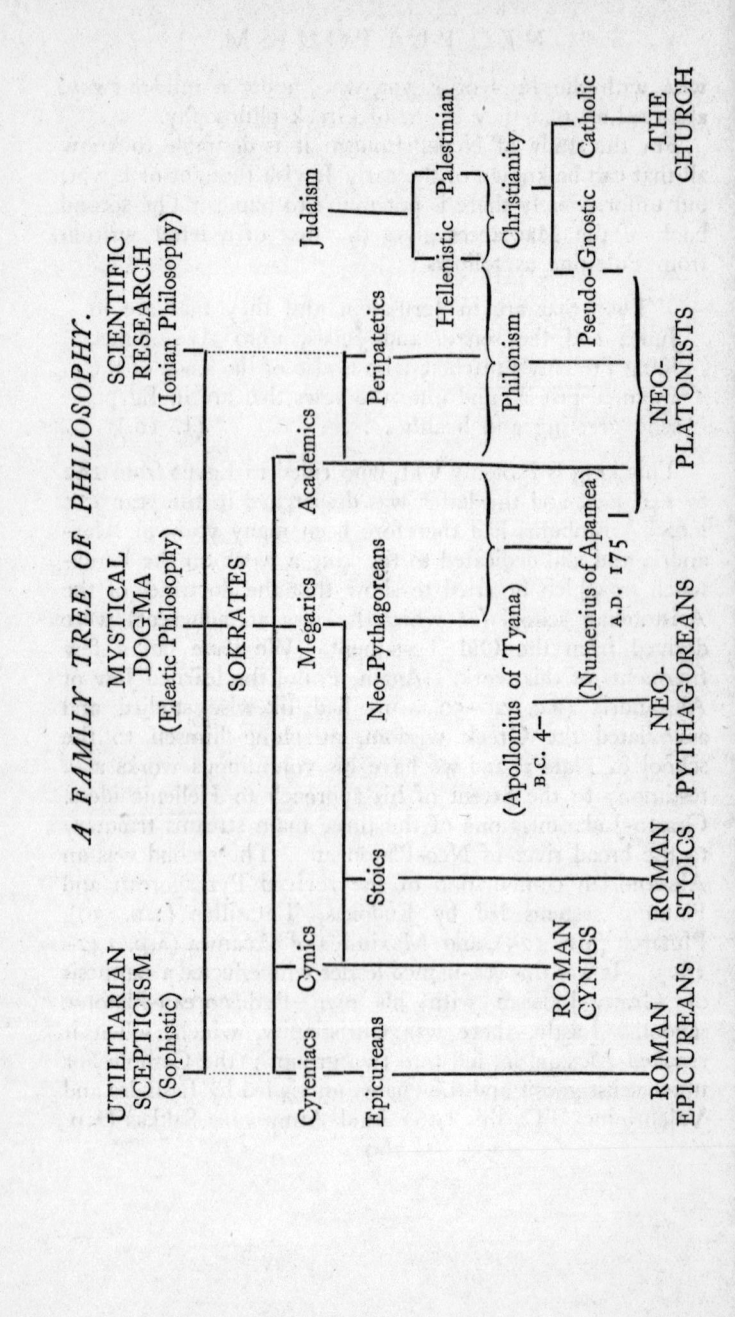

A FAMILY TREE OF PHILOSOPHY.

	UTILITARIAN SCEPTICISM (Sophistic)	MYSTICAL DOGMA (Eleatic Philosophy)	SCIENTIFIC RESEARCH (Ionian Philosophy)
		SOKRATES	
	Cyreniacs — Cynics — Stoics	Megarics — Academics	Peripatetics
	Epicureans	Neo-Pythagoreans	Hellenistic — Judaism — Palestinian
		(Apollonius of Tyana) B.C. 4—	Philonism — Christianity
		(Numenius of Apamea) A.D. 175	Pseudo-Gnostic — Catholic
		NEO-PYTHAGOREANS	NEO-PLATONISTS — THE CHURCH
ROMAN EPICUREANS	ROMAN CYNICS	ROMAN STOICS	

NEO-PLATONISM

162–243) at first adhered. The Catholic movement to oust the "pseudo-gnostics" from the church was successful and Ammonius thereafter united with the Judæo-Pythagorean-Platonic school of Maximius above mentioned. He gathered up, in fact, all that was left outside Catholic Christianity into one system of teaching and called to his aid some notable disciples, the two Origenes, Herennius, and, lastly, Plotinus of Lycopolis (A.D. 204–270), a man descended from Roman stock settled in Egypt for several generations. This disciple, after being eleven years with his teacher, left him at the age of thirty-nine and attempted to reach Persia and India in the wake of the army of the Roman Emperor Gordianus, but not being successful, returned to Rome where he settled down as a teacher of philosophy, the acknowledged "Platonic Successor" of the day. He died at the age of sixty-six.

3. A FAMILY TREE OF PHILOSOPHY

For the convenience of my readers I have attempted to summarize the foregoing paragraphs in diagrammatic form.

It must, of course, be remembered that, in addition to the five great philosophic schools existing side by side with the now growing Christian Church, Græco-Roman religions together with Oriental cults—such as that of Mithra—flourished in different parts of the Empire; to these, at various times and in various degrees, the Neo-Platonists were the intellectual patrons.

4. THE INFLUENCE OF PHILO

Philo has a special interest for us because he was the contemporary of Seneca, the Roman Stoic, Apollonius of Tyana, the Neo-Pythagorean, and Jesus, the founder of the Christian movement; but beyond that he has another interest, in so far as he undoubtedly influenced the Neo-Platonic school, especially in the person of Plotinus, and possibly also Sakkas. According to Philo we are to believe in the Divine Infinity. God is unknowable, ineffable and infinite. The Greek philosophers before him had not thought thus; the most they had taught was of the infinity of the physical elements and their qualities. Even the thought of Plato was not precise, and Aristotle remained a dualist. All this changed when the Greek genius made contact with the Hebrew religion which had already elevated the idea God to great heights. For moral and political reasons the Hebrew people had attained to a rigorous monotheism which affirmed the Divine Almighty with a force that has never been surpassed. They had raised God to such a height above man that to regard Him under any form whatever was a kind of sacrilege. Jewish thought was therefore obliged to institute a series of intermediaries to connect the world to a God so perfectly conceived, namely The Powers. But this conception progressed at the same time in the direction of emptying from itself all anthropomorphic elements. Philo, in belief a Jew, in education a Greek, introduced in concise form the idea of the Logos as chief intermediary between an infinite God and imperfect man. In speculation regarding Divine Infinity he writes:

> The Universal Intelligence is very pure . . . more so than Virtue, Science and even the Good . . .
> It is more beautiful than Beauty; its felicity surpasses all felicity . . .
> No name can express even what it is . . . but only the Powers that surround it. . . .
> God is without qualities . . .
> (Herriot's *Reminiscences de Philon.*)

To his speculation we must add Philo's psychological experience of ecstasy, an experience in which the soul ceases to be itself (finite) and becomes ineffable, unknowable and infinite like God, thus reaching its fullest felicity. These ideas are found fully developed in Plotinus who had similar experiences and spoke of them in similar terms.

NEO-PLATONISM

5. AMMONIUS SAKKAS

Of the actual founder of the school in Alexandria we know very little; it may be said, however, that while Philo contributed the element of *religion* to the new group, Sakkas handed on the chief conceptions of *philosophy*. There are two interesting fragments of his writings preserved, the larger one by Nemesius quoting his very lucid teaching on the immateriality of the soul and its union with the body. The kernel of the passage is contained in the words:

> In her union with the body, therefore, the soul undergoes no alteration. . . . What proves that the soul does not form a " mixture " with the body is the soul's power to separate from the body during sleep. . . . This appears again when the soul gathers herself together to devote herself to her thoughts; for then she separates herself from the body as far as she can, and retires within herself better to be able to apply herself to the consideration of intelligible things. . . . She remains without alteration as two things that are placed by each other's side. . . . She modifies that to which she is united, but she is not modified thereby.
>
> (*On Human Nature*, 2. In Guthrie's *Plotinus*.)

In the writings of Plotinus we shall find these doctrines elaborated. That Sakkas was a very great personality in the chain of philosophy may be learned from a short passage by Hierocles (about A.D. 430) preserved by Photius which I quote in full:

> Then shone the wisdom of Ammonius, who is famous under the name of " Inspired by the Divinity." It was he, in fact, who, purifying the opinions of the ancient philosophers, and dissipating the fancies woven here and there, established harmony between the teaching of Plato, and that of Aristotle, in that

which was most essential and fundamental. . . . It was Ammonius of Alexandria, the " Inspired by the Divinity," who, devoting himself enthusiastically to the truth in philosophy, and rising above the popular notions that made of philosophy an object of scorn, clearly understood the doctrine of Plato and of Aristotle, gathered them into a single ideal, and thus peacefully handed philosophy down to his disciples Plotinus, Origen Minor and their successors. (*Biblioteca*, 127, 461.)

6. THE NEO-PYTHAGOREANS

During the century immediately preceding the Christian era a considerable revival occurred of the Pythagorean philosophy. Belonging to this school was the prophet Apollonius of Tyana, who was born in the year 4 B.C., thus precisely contemporary, as is now believed by historical critics, with Jesus Christ. He is said to have reached the age of a hundred years, a great part of which was spent in travel. He visited all the important cities of the Græco-Roman world besides the distant Taxila (in the Panjab) and Spain in the west ; he also went to Egypt and conversed with the ascetics at the Nile cataracts. We have two sources of information about the teaching : in his life by Philostratos, the elder, of Lemnos (died about A.D. 250) and a series of letters from the hand of the prophet himself. The biography devotes great attention to the supernormal powers of Apollonius to which the letters, however, make no reference or claim ; it is difficult to determine how far we can place reliance on the work of Philostratos, who, not a Pythagorean or a philosopher himself, seems to have produced a romance out of materials supplied to him by his imperial patroness, Julia Domna, the wife of the Emperor Septimus Severus. Putting documents and tradition together we can, however, gain a picture of a man of remarkable influence among people, priests and rulers of his day, his chief claim to notoriety being his austere ascetic life and the theurgic powers he learned from the Brahmins of India. We are probably right in attributing to him little direct influence on Neo-Platonism.

It is otherwise, however, with Numenius who was much more of a philosopher than Apollonius. He was a voluminous writer, and his disciple Amelius was later for many years the secretary of Plotinus, whose writings contain frequent reference to his doctrines, both agreements and refutations. The essential difference between Pythagoreans and new Platonists was on the doctrine of Matter. The former were dualists like the Gnostics and Zoroastrians; the latter were moving in the direction of monism, and, in the person of Plotinus, realized it to the full.

7. PLOTINUS

The life of Plotinus has been told by Porphyrius, one of his intimate disciples, and is easily accessible. From it we gain the impression of a man of great personal charm and unique spiritual experience, while deficient, nevertheless, in those masterly qualities of mind which had distinguished Plato and Aristotle—the sublime artist and the keen scientific observer—his predecessors. Plotinus had sat at the feet of Sakkas, had read Numenius and Philo, and, having absorbed and sifted the material of Greek philosophy, he reinterpreted it in terms of his own religious experience. It was this fact which made the "restored" Platonism of Numenius into the "new" Platonism of which we write. It was the formulation of the philosophic life as the pathway to Religion or union with God. The fifty-four treatises which he wrote at the instance of his disciples Amelius, Porphyrius and Eustochius read like reports of casual lectures and have little organic relation to one another. Each is a miniature philosophy, and many of his prime doctrines are repeated again and again. The student of Plotinus, therefore, has the liberty to begin where he likes.

The supreme purpose of life, according to Plotinus, is

ecstasis or "standing out" of our normal self-consciousness; it is the vision of God—nay more—the union with Him. *Henosis*, or "becoming one," and *haplosis*, "simplification," are other terms to describe this state in scientific phraseology; poetic and rhetorical terms abound in Plotinus, who is a master of analogy. I will now quote a few passages from the Enneads, which I take from an excellent translation, the first complete English version, by Dr. Kenneth Sylvan Guthrie, of New Jersey, U.S.A.

The supreme Purpose of Life is the Ecstatical Vision of God.

Thus in her ascension towards divinity, the soul advances until, having risen above everything that is foreign to her, she alone with Him who is alone, beholds, in all His simplicity and purity, Him from whom all depends, to whom all aspires, from whom everything draws its existence, life and thought. He who beholds Him is overwhelmed with love; with ardour desiring to unite himself with Him, entranced with ecstasy. Men who have not yet seen Him desire Him as the Good; those who have, admire Him as sovereign beauty, struck simultaneously with stupor and pleasure, thrilling in a painless orgiasm, loving with a genuine emotion, with an ardour without equal, scorning all other affections, and disdaining those things which formerly they characterised as beautiful. This is the experience of those to whom divinities and guardians have appeared; they reck no longer of the beauty of other bodies. Imagine, if you can, the experiences of those who behold Beauty itself, the pure Beauty which, because of its very purity, is fleshless and bodiless, outside of earth and heaven. What beauty could one still wish to see after having arrived at vision of Him who gives perfection to all beings, though Himself remains unmoved, without receiving anything; after finding rest in this contemplation, and enjoying it by becoming assimilated to Him?

(*Enneads*, I. vi. 7.)

This treatise, the first from the pen of Plotinus, is a sermon on a text supplied by Plato in his *Symposium*. Plato had made Diotima tell Sokrates of the Beautiful Itself as the object of all love, and now Plotinus carries the idea forward into the realm of mystical experience. Moreover, this vision of and union with divinity gives us a new and corrected estimate of the value of all other beauty, as the following passage shows:

The method to achieve Ecstasy is to close the eyes of the body.

How shall we start and later arrive at the contemplation of this ineffable beauty which, like the divinity in the mysteries, remains hidden in the recesses of a sanctuary, and does not show itself outside, where it might be perceived by the profane? We must advance into this sanctuary, penetrating into it, if we have the strength to do so, closing our eyes to the spectacle of terrestrial things, without throwing a backward glance on the bodies whose graces formerly charmed us. If we do still see corporeal beauties, we must no longer rush at them, but, knowing that they are only images, traces and adumbrations of a superior principle, we will flee from them to approach Him of whom they are merely the reflections.

Whoever would let himself be misled by the pursuit of those vain shadows, mistaking them for realities, would grasp only an image as fugitive as the fluctuating form reflected by the waters, and would resemble that senseless Narcissus who, wishing to grasp that image himself, according to the fable, disappeared, carried away by the current. Likewise he would wish to embrace corporeal beauties and not release them, would plunge, not his body, but his soul into the gloomy abysses, so repugnant to intelligence; he would be condemned to total blindness; and on this earth, as well as in hell, he would see naught but mendacious shades.

(I. vi. 8.)

The experience of Ecstasy leads to Questions.

On waking from the slumber of the body to return to myself, and on turning my attention from exterior things so as to concentrate it on myself, I often observe an alluring beauty, and I become conscious of an innate nobility. Then I live out a higher life, and I experience atonement with the divinity. Fortifying myself within it, I arrive at that actualisation which raises me above the intelligible. But if, after this sojourn with the divinity, I descend once more from intelligence to the exercise of my reasoning powers, I am wont to ask myself how I ever could actually again descend, and how my soul ever could have entered into a body since, although she actually abides in the body, she still possesses within herself all the perfection I discover in her.

(IV. viii. 1.)

Here is again a proof of a speculation following an experience. The answer is a theory of "the descent of the soul into the body" which requires a pre-existence in a heavenly sphere, the development of self-will—away from divine control. It also leads to the more emphatic statement that heaven, not earth, is our true home, and that earth-experiences must be interpreted accordingly. Although such ecstasies are very rare and their memory fades, yet their influence is life-long and beneficent.

The Trance of Ecstasy.

As this vision of the divinity did not imply the existence of two things—and as he who was identical

NEO-PLATONISM

to Him whom he saw, so that he did not see Him, but was united thereto—if any one could preserve the memory of what he was while thus absorbed into the Divinity, he would within himself have a faithful image of the Divinity. Then, indeed, had he attained at-one-ment, containing no difference, neither in regard to himself nor to other beings. While he was thus transported into the celestial region, there was within him no activity, no anger, nor appetite, nor reason, nor even thought. So much the more, if we dare say so, was he no longer himself, but sunk in trance or entheasm, tranquil and solitary with the divinity, he enjoyed an imperturbable calm. Contained within his own "being," or essence, he did not incline to either side, he did not even turn towards himself, he was, indeed, in a state of perfect stability, having thus, so to speak, become stability itself.

(VI. ix. 11.)

The outward symbolism of religion, if it be wisely framed, serves to remind us of the inner spectacle which is directly unrepresentable by word or form. All philosophy on its intellectual side, all morality on its ethical side, all art on its expressive side, should lead us to this goal, and, having led us truly, should thereafter remind us of the truth they have been able to reveal. So thinks Plotinus.

8. SUBSEQUENT ECSTATIC EXPERIENCES

Before obtaining the vision of the Divinity, the soul desires what yet remains to be seen. For him, however, who has risen above all things, what remains to be seen is He who is above all other things. Indeed, the nature of the soul will never reach absolute nonentity. Consequently, when she descends from the vision she will fall into evil, that is, nonentity, but not into absolute nonentity. Following the contrary, upward path, she will arrive at something different, namely, herself. From the fact that she then is not anything different from herself, it does not result that she is "within" anything, for she remains in herself. That which, without being in essence, remains within itself, necessarily resides in the Divinity. Then it ceases to be "being," and so far as it comes into communion with the Divinity it grows superior to "being" —it becomes *supra-being*.

Now he who sees himself as having become Divinity, possesses within himself an image of the Divinity. If he rise above himself, he will achieve the limit of his ascension, becoming as it were an image that becomes indistinguishable from its model. Then, when he shall have lost sight of the Divinity, he may still, by arousing the virtue preserved within himself, and by considering the perfections that adorn his soul, re-ascend to the celestial region, by virtue raising to Intelligence, and by wisdom to the Divinity Himself.

(VI. ix. 11.)

This "image of Divinity" appears to me to be God conceived of as transcendent and external and God loved as a personality which our finite minds can embrace. It is only in higher mystical experiences that we get beyond the finite mind's power and realize God as within and identical with the soul. The "image" therefore, as said above, is useful as *attracting* us to and *reminding* us of its Reality.

Mechanism of the Ecstasy.

The ecstasy operates as follows :—When a man is entranced by the Divinity, he loses consciousness of himself. Then, when he contemplates the Divine spectacle which he possesses within himself, he contemplates himself and sees his image embellished. However beautiful it be, he must leave it aside, and concentrate upon the unity, without dividing any of it. Then he becomes simultaneously one and all with this Divinity, which grants him His presence silently. Then is the man united to the Divinity to the extent of his desire and ability. If, while remaining pure he return to duality, he remains as close as possible to the Divinity, and he enjoys the Divine presence as soon as he turns towards the Divinity. (V. viii. 11.)

9. THE MORAL VALUE OF ECSTASY

The advantages derived from this conversion towards the Divinity are first self-consciousness,—so long as he remains distinct from the Divinity. If he penetrate into his interior sanctuary, he possesses all things, and renouncing self-consciousness in favour of indistinction from the Divinity, he fuses with it. As soon as he desires to *see* something, so to speak, outside of himself, it is he himself that he considers, even exteriorly.

The soul that studies the Divinity must form an idea of Him while seeking to know Him. Later, knowing how great is that Divinity to which she desires to unite herself, and being persuaded that she will find beatitude in this union, she plunges herself into the depths of the Divinity until, instead of contenting herself with contemplating the intelligible world, she herself becomes an object of contemplation, and shines with the clearness of the conceptions whose source is on high. (V. viii. 11.)

Plotinus dwells much on "the virtues" which in his day were still discussed in the Platonic manner. Rarely in any literature can a more lucid and concise statement be found (than in Plotinus) of the ethical consequences which should follow the vision of God. "If we are in unity with the Spirit we are in unity with each other and so we are all one." This is his doctrine of the metaphysical basis of morality.

Metaphysical Basis of Morality.

In this way, we and all that is ours are carried back into real Being. We rise to it, as that from which originally we sprang. We think intelligible objects, and not merely their images or impressions, and in thinking them we are identified with them. And the same is the case with the other souls as with our own. Hence, if we are in unity with the Spirit, we are in unity with each other, and so we are all one.

When, on the other hand, we carry our view outside of the principle on which we depend we lose consciousness of our unity and become like a number of faces which are turned outwards, though inwardly they are attached to one head. But if one of us (like one of these faces) would turn round either by his own effort or by the aid of Athené, he would behold at once God, *himself* and the *whole*. At first, indeed, he might not be able to see himself as one with the whole; but soon he would find that there was no boundary he could fix for his separate self. He would, therefore, cease to draw lines of division between himself and the Universe; and he would attain to the absolute whole, not by going forward to another place, but by abiding in that principle on which the whole Universe is based.

(VI. v. 7.)

This was, in point of value, the last word of Neo-Platonism, though the school continued thereafter to flourish in the charming moralities and biographies of Porphyrius, the spiritistic disquisitions attributed to Jamblichus, the bathos of the Emperor Julianus, the majestic treatises by Proclus, and the pathetic "*Consolation of Philosophy*" by Boëthius. Neo-Platonism did not die; it handed on its mystical

NEO-PLATONISM

light to the growing Christian Church which in Pseudo-Dionysius, Augustine, Scotus Erigena, the Victorines and Eckhart kept the flame alive.

10. THE THREE GREAT SCHOOLS

From the death of Plotinus in A.D. 270 to the edict of Justinian against Greek philosophy in A.D. 529, two-and-a-half centuries flowed by. It has been asserted that in this long period, although there were philosophers there was little philosophy; with equal truth it might be said that there was philosophy but no original philosophers. Such contradictory generalizations help to explain the nature of this period of human thought, a period characterized by the wide diffusion of serious philosophic study, though devoid of the brilliant personalities of former generations.

The dissemination of philosophy in the Græco-Roman world was conducted on well-known principles. Before Plato and Aristotle philosophy hardly existed in organized form and, except for Pythagoras, brought into being no teaching institutions. This great man followed in the steps of the Orphic and Dionysian brotherhoods. Plato and Aristotle were the first to found regular schools in settled places, but their originality consisted in the subject matter chosen—namely philosophy—rather than in the nature of the institution itself; there were already schools devoted to rhetoric and similar arts. The really new feature in the Academy and the Lyceum founded by Plato and Aristotle respectively was their permanence. Plato's nephew, Seusippos, was his successor, and after him an unbroken line of scholarchs presided over the academy for nearly a thousand years. The scholarchs were not always Athenians; they were drawn from all parts of the world; but they took up their residence in the city, administered the instruction and controlled the endowments of the school. There were times when the schools sank into unimportance and times when, under the guidance of some man of genius, they

I.—THE ALEXANDRIAN-ROMAN SCHOOL.

Ammonius Sakkas (A.D. 162-243)

Plotinus (A.D. 204-270) — Origen Minor — Origen, the Christian (A.D. 184-254) — Herennius — Olympius and Antoninus

Amelius — Porphyrius and Eustochius (A.D. 253-304) — Longinus (A.D. 213-273)

Geladius — Erasthenes — Chrysaorius — Aristeides — Ptolemy — Anatolius and Abammon

II.—THE SYRIAN SCHOOL.

Jamblichus (A.D. -330)

Themistes — Euphrasius — Hierus — Sopatros of Apamea

Maximus of Ephesus (A.D. -370) — Adesius and Theodorus

Priscus — Chrysanthius and Eusebius of Sardis

Hypatia of Alexandria (A.D. -415)

Eunapius of Sardis

Emperor Julianus (A.D. 332-363)

III.—THE ATHENIAN SCHOOL.

Synesius

Plutarch of Athens (A.D. -433).
Hierocles and Syrianus (A.D. -450)
Proclus of Byzantium (A.D. 410-485) and Hermias
Marinus of Neapolis, Ammonias and Asclepodotus
Isidorus and Johannes Philopon
Syrianus Minor and Damascius (A.D. -529)   Boëthius in Italy (A.D. 470-526)
Simplicius of Cilicia and Theodotus
Priscianus

(The School was closed by order of the Emperor Justinian)

NEO-PLATONISM

rose again into life. From them, with missionary zeal, scholars would find their way to distant places to found there daughter schools. Many of these naturally—perhaps all of them—tended to become independent in spirit, and after some centuries it would have been difficult to trace their family connections: even more difficult is it at this distance of time to do so with certainty. The three great schools of the Neo-Platonists of which I have now to write were not *institutions* like those established by Plato and Aristotle, but groups or generations of teachers and disciples. In the first part of this section I have given the genealogy of thought which led to the founding of a teaching centre in Alexandria under Ammonius Sakkas. It was Plotinus who shifted its location to Rome; hence it is called the Alexandrian-Roman School. When Jamblichus, of Chalcis, became the leading light of this group, he, being a Syrian, moved the centre of its influence eastwards, and thus there came into existence what is called the Syrian School; this ran its course until Plutarch of Athens was found to be the leading man and Neo-Platonism returned, as it were, to its long-lost home at Athens to find the Platonic Scholarchs steadily pursuing their philosophical activities. On the preceding page will be found a diagram showing the relationship of the more important of the numerous adherents to those three schools which for our purpose will not be further divided. The learned critics are not yet agreed as to how far we are authorized in separating the schools. It is sufficient to say here that no less than sixty names of philosophers are included in the lists compiled in ancient and modern times, and that many of them were great personalities whose original works and commentaries exercised an important influence on their own times.

11. AMELIUS GENTILIANUS

Amelius, the first secretary of Plotinus, had, earlier in his life, been an ardent disciple of Numenius the Neo-

Pythagorean and, on attaching himself to Plotinus about the year A.D. 246, he both influenced and was influenced by his new master. It is, however, as a Neo-Platonist that we have to consider him briefly. A point of disagreement between Plotinus and Amelius is of considerable interest, namely, concerning the relations between the individual soul and the universal soul. Plotinus had formulated his doctrine that the soul of the world—the third of his hypostases—was the principle of individuation though itself indivisible. It was only when in relation to bodies that it could be, as it were, divided into a multiplicity. Souls, inasmuch as they are of the intelligible order, could, according to him, be at the same time the whole and a part. This gave rise to the doctrine of the unity of all souls, so reminiscent of the oriental Vedānta philosophy. For Amelius the world soul is one in number and absolutely indivisible. He founded on this opinion his doctrine that the human soul is nothing, at bottom, than the sum of its actions—an opinion which strongly resembles one that has reappeared in our own time—that the soul is no longer a substance, but the system of psychic and mental manifestations linked together. The logical conclusion of this thesis was either that matter is the true principle of individuation, or that individuality is but the result of diverse relations in which the world soul can place itself, relations which *seem* to divide it and to multiply it. Individuality is thus nothing but a phenomenon, a pure appearance.

Amelius is also responsible for the statement of a doctrine of the "three reasons," which he calls the "Three Kings," namely, (1) reason which *is*; (2) reason which *possesses*, and (3) the reason which *sees*. The first creates only by will, the second by order, and the third by active operation. These three reasons, considered in their unity, constitute the Demiourgos, who is the *paradeigma*, the system of pre-existent Ideas.

In conformity with the doctrine of Plato, but in opposition

NEO-PLATONISM

to Plotinus, Amelius admits into his system the Ideas of original forms not only of the genus, the species and the individuals, but of all things, even the rational principle of evil. Unfortunately also he continued to teach the incomprehensible theory of numerology, supposed to be derived from Pythagoras, though finding in the writings of Plotinus no warrant for so doing.

As an illustration of the friendly intellectual relations subsisting between disciples and teacher, I quote parts of a letter written by Amelius to his colleague Porphyrius:

> You may be sure that I did not have the least inclination even to mention some otherwise respectable people who, to the point of deafening you, insist that the doctrines of our friend Plotinus are none other than those of Numenius of Apamea. . . . Possessed with the desire to rend Plotinus to pieces, they dare to go as far as to assert that he is no more than a babbler, a forger, and that his opinions are impossible. But since you think that it would be well for us to seize the occasion to recall to the public the teachings of which we approve in Plotinus's system of philosophy, and in order to honour so great a man as our friend Plotinus by spreading his teachings—although this really is needless, inasmuch as they have long since become celebrated—I comply with your request and, in accordance with my promise, I am hereby inscribing to you this work. . . . I am sure you will have the goodness to correct me if I happen to stray from the opinions of Plotinus. As the tragic poet says somewhere, being overwhelmed with the pressure of duties, I find myself compelled to criticism and correction if I am discovered in altering the doctrines of our leader. You see how anxious I am to please you. Farewell.
>
> (*Porphyrius' Life of Plotinus* in Guthrie.)

12. PORPHYRIUS THE PHILOSOPHER

The second secretary and chief disciple of Plotinus was a man of superior type, of profound and extended erudition, of wise and sensible mind. He displayed in his numerous writings an elegance of style, a simplicity, a clearness and, above all, a correctness and care which was not always noticeable in the philosophic authors of the day. The literary output of Porphyrius was considerable. The first writings were introductions and commentaries on the chief works of Aristotle. Next we have *The Abstinence from Flesh Food, An Epistle to Marcella*, and *The Cave of the Nymphs*. Two valuable biographies also came from his pen, one of Pythagoras and the other of Plotinus; the first drawing on the collected tradition about the ancient philosopher, and the second from first-hand knowledge. These five works exist in English translations.

A book on the sayings of the philosophers is cited at considerable length by Eusebius, but Porphyrius went a step further and compiled one on the sayings of the gods! His collection of *Oracles of Apollo and other Divinities* had for its end to demonstrate the power of these divine revelations and to encourage the study of the fount of wisdom which he, for the first time, called *Theosophia*. It is thus to the Neo-Platonist that we of this generation owe this word, which in the course of time was adopted by certain mediæval students, notably by Jacob Boehme, whose translators gave it its English form. It is worth while remembering the original significance of this exalted word, and perhaps even now not too late to attempt to restrict it to the body of divine wisdom which the gods enjoy; it is hardly right to use the same word to denote both their wisdom and ours. If it can refer to theirs, it cannot be appropriate for ours.

Seven other treatises, some of them lengthy, are known by name and by citations of later authors; they are

NEO-PLATONISM

concerned mostly with philosophical and psychological discussions. Porphyrius' fourteenth and fifteenth works merit special mention; the one known by its Latin title *De regressu animæ* deals with the important question as to whether or not the human soul descends to the level of the animals in its many incarnations; I will refer to it shortly. The other work, known as *Against the Christians*, consisted of fifteen books, in one of which he made the first attempt at the "higher criticism" of the Old Testament, pointing out, for instance, what is now universally admitted, that the Book of Daniel was written after the events which it appears to predict apocalyptically. His judgment of the character of Jesus Christ is very interesting and deserves to be known.

13. PORPHYRIUS AS EDITOR AND CRITIC

Very important in its contents and results was the letter to Anebo the Egyptian priest, for in the first place it reveals Porphyrius as very sceptical of theurgy or religious magic professed in the temples, and in the second it called forth a reply which is known as the *Mysteries of the Egyptians and Chaldeans*, which I shall deal with in its proper place.

Above all—and perhaps this was his most important work—Porphyrius induced Plotinus to commit his lectures to writing, which in his turn he preserved and edited. Without effecting any change in the teaching of his master, and in contenting himself by putting them in a clear and beautiful order, Porphyrius imprinted upon them a very practical character and, as far as he could, gave them a specifically religious turn. He accentuated the metaphysical spiritualism, found in philosophy a place for moral asceticism as leading to the purification and salvation of the soul—the true object of philosophy in his opinion. The cause of evil lies not in the body as such but in the soul; in its desires for base and inferior things, that is to say for corporeal things. For the salvation of the soul man must be ready to sacrifice the body which leads us on to a magic illusion, γοήτευμα. Such, in a few words, is the point of view of Porphyrius.

14. HIS ETHICAL SIGNIFICANCE

All his writings, though many of them are speculative in relation to metaphysics and psychology, have a strong ethical tendency. I quote a few passages from his commentary on Plotinus:

> There is a difference between the virtues of the citizen, those of the man who essays to rise to contemplation, and who, on this account, is said to possess a contemplative mind ; those of him who contemplate intelligence ; and finally those of pure Intelligence, which is completely separated from the soul. The civil virtues consist of moderation in passions and in letting one's actions follow the rational laws of duty. The object of these virtues being to make us benevolent in our dealings with our fellow human beings, they are called civil virtues because they mutually unite citizens. . . .
>
> The virtues of the man who tries to contemplate consist in detaching oneself from things here below ; that is why they are called "purifications." They command us to abstain from activities which overrate the organs, and which excite the affections that relate to the body. The object of these virtues is to raise the soul to genuine existence. While the civil virtues are the ornament of mortal life, and prepare the soul for the purificatory virtues, the latter direct the man whom they adorn to abstain from activities in which the body predominates. . . .
>
> The civil virtues moderate the passions: their object is to teach us to live in conformity with the laws of human nature. The contemplative virtues

obliterate the passions from the soul : their object is to assimilate man to the divinity. . . .

There is a third kind of virtue, which is superior to the civil and purificatory virtues, the " virtues of the soul that contemplates intelligence." . . .

There is a fourth kind of virtue, the " exemplary virtue," which resides within intelligence. Their superiority to the virtues of the soul is the same as that of the type to the image : for intelligence contains simultaneously all the " beings " or essences which are the types of lower things.

(Guthrie, *Works of Plotinus*.)

15. FREE-WILL AND FATE

In agreement with the whole school of Plato, Porphyrius professed the belief in the free-will of man, and he essayed to reconcile it with fate or the universal bond uniting causes and effects throughout the world. The web of destiny relates only to corporeal relations, within which the will of the soul exercises, with varying degrees, its own proper force. Moral responsibility rests upon the freedom of the will, and moral excellence depends upon the extent to which the free-will develops power to overcome the obstacles provided by corporeal existence. It is not the body which is culpable and responsible, but the soul.

The document which most clearly reveals the character of Porphyrius and his philosophy is his short unfinished epistle to his wife, Marcella, from which I will now quote :

There are four first principles that must be upheld concerning God—faith, truth, love, hope. We must have faith that our only salvation is in turning to God. And, having faith, we must strive with all our might to know the truth about God. And when we know this, we must love Him we do know. And when we love Him, we must nourish our souls on good hopes for our life, for it is by their good hopes men are superior to bad ones. Let then these four principles be firmly held.

Next, let these three laws be distinguished. First, the law of God; second, the law of human nature; third, that which is laid down for nations and states. The law of nature fixes the limits of bodily needs, and shows what is necessary to these, and condemns all striving after what is needless and superfluous. Now that which is established and laid down for states regulates by fixed agreements the common relations of men, by their mutual observance of the covenants laid down. But the divine law is implanted by the mind, for their welfare, in the thoughts of reasoning souls, and it is found truthfully inscribed therein. The law of humanity is transgressed by him who through vain opinions knows it not, owing to his excessive love for the pleasures of the body. And it is broken and despised by those who, even for the body's sake, gain the mastery over the body.

(*Epistle to Marcella*, pars. 24 and 25.)

The resemblance to Christian ethic is remarkable, and it still remains a matter of regret that the Christians and the non-Christians of this period did not co-operate with one another for the redemption of the world rather than seek each other's overthrow. At this distance of time their mutual polemics and apologies seem futile and irrelevant.

16. REINCARNATION IN NEO-PLATONISM

It will be convenient at this point to consider the question of cardinal importance in Neo-Platonic doctrine called in Greek *metempsychosis* or *metensomatosis*, and in Latin *transmigratio*. All three words signify the same idea expressed by the Indian word *Samsāra*.

The belief in transmigration is entirely foreign to native Greek, Egyptian and Jewish religions in their pure and

NEO-PLATONISM

original forms. Students of these faiths will know that in various ways the future destiny of the soul is otherwise explained; the early Greeks were not even certain about immortality, and the Jews were in the same case, though the later generations of thinkers, in common with the Egyptians, looked for a resurrection. It was doubtless from Indian sources that the Orphic brotherhoods received the idea and disseminated it among the Hellenic peoples in different parts of the world—Egypt, Italy and Asia. In this way it was probably accepted by the Pythagoreans, though there are no reliable texts on the subject. The first of the Greek philosophers to record his belief in it was Empedokles, and he was followed by Pindar the poet; both of them were men of priestly families. Though Sokrates (in Plato) talks a good deal about it, we can hardly say he believed it, and when he came to die he expected to go to live with the gods and divine and happy men. Sokrates and Plato had to contend with a powerful scepticism which doubted even the existence of the soul. It is Plato's use of the idea of reincarnation in several of his myths which has led many in ancient and modern times to declare, rather loosely, that he *taught* it. I have no space here to show that this is a mistaken view. His myth of Er uses the doctrine as part of an effort to prove, *a priori*, the moral responsibility of man, and elsewhere he introduces rather humorously the idea of the descent of the souls of men into the bodies of animals—wolves, asses, bees, and wasps. I have no doubt that Plato's references as well as the presence of the teaching in many schools after his time led to its official incorporation in Neo-Platonism. Plato's dialogues were gaining the position of infallible scriptures. In Plotinus at last it arrives at definiteness, and thereafter remains, receiving, as it were, an additional element of authoritativeness from the great man. Unfortunately, however, the texts of Plotinus simply restate in dogmatic form the substance of the Platonic myths, including the categorical statement of the descent into the bodies of animals and insects.

We may now return to Porphyrius who maintains that all human souls, immortal as to essence, pass after death from one body to another in order to undertake the eternal circle of life in the sensible world ; it is for this that they desire to have a body. He interprets the mythological and dogmatic dicta of Plato and Plotinus respectively by saying that human souls never sink into the bodies of animals, but can descend into the level of lower irrational species while remaining human. The souls of man can *resemble* those of animals ; this is the most that Porphyrius will allow, and perhaps it may strike the reader as a nice point—a distinction without a difference. If when the soul abandons its terrestrial life free of its earthly body it be absolutely purified, all its irrational faculties become detached, and it re-enters completely the life of the One from which it had been separated. But after periods not determined by the philosopher the soul returns again and again eternally. There does not appear, in his view, the conception of a final liberation known to the Indians as *Mōksha* ; it may, of course, have been in his lost works.

17. JAMBLICHUS

We are ignorant of the precise birth-date of Jamblichus ; he was a native of Chalcis in Cœle-Syria. His first instructor was Anatolius, but it was Porphyrius himself, also a Syrian, who completed his philosophical education. Upon the departure of the philosopher the mantle of leadership fell upon Jamblichus. According to the testimony of later writers his was a noble personality bearing the titles of " the divine " and " the great," a man of superior intelligence, of deep learning, a brilliant writer and an eloquent theologian. In conformity with the tendency, already marked in previous writers of the school, he developed to a high degree the symbolic interpretation of Plato and the Greek myths,

NEO-PLATONISM

discovering some significance for philosophy in every trivial detail. This abandonment of criticism for the charms of symbolism—a movement full of subtle dangers—drew the school in the direction of ritualism and the absorption of practices foreign to the spirit of Plato. Nevertheless, Jamblichus cannot be accused of departing from the teaching of Plotinus ; being a priest himself he combined side by side both the philosophic and priestly interests. He was a voluminous writer, but nearly all his works have perished. He wrote extensive commentaries on Plato and Aristotle, a work entitled *The Perfect Theology of the Chaldeans*, of which citations alone remain. We have in our hands his *Life of Pythagoras, A Stimulus to Philosophy*, a work on *Mathematics*, and another on *Arithmetic*. He also wrote a work *On the Soul* and one on *The Migration of Souls*. Both are almost wholly lost. The philosophic reputation of Jamblichus has suffered much from the attribution to him of books which he never wrote, notably *The Mysteries of the Egyptians, Chaldeans and Assyrians*. We may judge of his philosophic character from the following citation made by Proclus :

> How the gods have created the body, how they have put life into it, are things which our reason cannot conceive of, and which remain to us unknowable. That all things subsist from the gods we can affirm in attributing the facts to their bounty and to their power ; but how these effects come forth from their cause we are incapable of understanding.
>
> (Chaignet, *Histoire de la Psychologie des Grecs*.)

Jamblichus considered that his predecessors had erred in regarding the soul as an absolutely pure essence incapable of sin, a stranger to the passions and evil. The facts of consciousness and experience spoke to the contrary, he thought. It therefore became necessary for him to expound a theory of the nature, migration and destiny of the soul in rather fuller detail than Porphyrius or Plotinus had done. I will endeavour to condense this into the minimum of words.

Below the soul lies the generated, divisible, corporeal world, and above it the ungenerated, indivisible, incorporeal essences—according to Plotinus—the World Soul, the Nous or Spirit and the One or God. The peculiar function of the human soul is to be an intermediary between the two systems : to possess the plenitude of the system living and complete, the pleroma of universal Ideas : τὸ πλήρωμα τῶν καθόλου λόγων; to be the minister of the creation of things after the pattern of the Ideas (or true forms). Thus the soul is an essence which cannot be declared pure because of its attraction to things which are below it. This intermediary position of the soul gives it the possibility of desiring and receiving the inspiration of the Divine Mind (Nous or Spirit) ; or, on the other hand, by plunging into commerce with sensation, to turn away from a higher form of life. In this the soul is entirely free—but not free from the *consequences* of its own choice. This is the synthesis of Freedom and Fate—strictly in accord with Plato's *Er*.

Needless to say, the higher world is eternal without change, and the life of the lower world eternal in its own peculiar way ; the intermediary soul linked to both of them is also eternal, though subject to continual change as to its will and experience. Part of this change is the repeated phenomenon of death which provides opportunity for fresh choice, a fresh exercise of will either upwards or downwards, the path of destiny leading in both directions. But death always leads the soul to a new body which is appropriate to the dominant desire generated during any given life. This *metensomatosis*, however, does not permit a man to become a beast ; he can at most become bestial. To this changing of bodies is linked the punishment, or recompense which the soul merits during its life, and thus *metensomatosis* belongs to the moral order and forms part of the system of Divine Justice.

NEO-PLATONISM

Jamblichus also teaches, as a new opinion, the progressive growth of human personality by the preservation of faculties wisely exercised ; thus death does but change the residence but not the nature of the man ; man does this latter himself, for better or for worse.

18. CONDITIONAL IMMORTALITY

Almost from the beginning of Greek philosophy there had been, as it were, a pendulum movement between the view of the human soul as substantive and its view as qualitative. After much debate Plato decided for the former, and Aristotle, in his turn, for the latter. The soul, said Aristotle, is the *entelecheia* or completion of the body. In his *Nicomachean Ethics* he concludes a majestic chapter on Contemplative Happiness with the remarkable aphorism that it is man's chief duty " to make himself immortal." This is the crowning idea of his grand philosophy of development. The Neo-Platonists—who were quite as much Neo-Aristotelians—swerved from side to side on this question and, as we have seen, Amelius held to the tentative opinion " that the soul is identical with its functions." Jamblichus had very strong views as to the progressive development of these functions, regarding the souls of men as differing in rank because they differed in function. The highest in rank are those who, though pure, descend voluntarily in order to save, purify and perfect the beings here below,[1] while the lowest descend involuntarily to submit to chastisement and constraint.

After many generations of thought we arrive at a synthesis of the apparently opposing doctrines of Plato and Aristotle. The soul is indeed individual and substantive. Endowed with free-will exercised in the environment of fate, she strives either for the higher or the lower, and, life after life, gains or loses powers and functions accordingly. Psychology is the understanding of these powers ; ethic is their

[1] Compare the Bodhisattvas of Mahāyāna Buddhism.

proper exercise; not in one life only, but in the whole life-cycle, at the end of which is an immortality gained, not by chance or by destiny, but by effort; in a word, *conditionally*.

Such were the views held with increasing definiteness by the whole school.

19. ABAMMON AND HIS BOOK

And as, from time to time, priests of the various Græco-Roman cults were attracted by the leading expositors of the philosophy, it was natural that they should not altogether abandon their former interests—spiritistic, divinatory, theurgic and magical. In this way we must understand the remarkable book, so long erroneously attributed to Jamblichus, entitled the *Mysteries of the Egyptians*. Its contents as well as its title show that it is the reply of Abammon to the inquiries of Porphyrius addressed to Anebo. The letter of Porphyrius, as I have remarked above, reveals the official and critical attitude of the school to the so-called Mysteries, and the reply is an *apologia* for the sacred rites long practised in the various temples. The book is so well known and available in two translations—the dignified and rather pedantic version of Thomas Taylor and the careless "good readable English" of Alexander Wilder—that I need not attempt to analyse it. I venture to give, however, a rendering of a portion of Abammon's *Reply*, which illustrates its style and purpose.

> In the first place you say "it must be granted that there are Gods." It is not right to speak thus on this mighty subject, for an inborn knowledge of the Gods is co-existent with our very being, and this kind of knowledge is superior to all deliberate choice and judgment; it subsists prior to the processes of reason and demonstration. . . . Indeed, if we must speak accurately, the contact with divinity is not "knowledge," for

NEO-PLATONISM

knowledge implies a separation or otherness [of subject and object]; but prior to knowledge, as one being knows another, is the uniform connection of the soul with divinity. It is dependent upon the Gods; it is spontaneous and inseparable from them.

Hence it is not proper " to grant that there are Gods " as if it might not be granted, nor to admit it as doubtful. . . .

I say the same regarding the more excellent Genera, which come next in order after the Gods; I mean the Spirits, demi-Gods and undefiled souls. For we must understand that there is always in them one definite form of being, and not the indefiniteness and instability incident to human condition. Also we must not suppose that they [like men] incline to one side of an argument rather than to another, resulting from the balancing employed in the rational process. For this kind of thing is foreign to the principles of pure reason and life, and only belongs to beings of secondary nature, and to such beings as belong to the realms of generated existences.

So the human soul is conjoined to the Gods by a " knowledge " due to the law of similarity of subsistence, not gained through conjecture, or opinion or a syllogistic process, all which originate in time, which controls them, but by the pure and faultless intuitions which the soul received in Eternity from the Gods in virtue of being conjoined to them. . . . For knowledge of divine nature is different from that of other things, and is separate from all antithesis, it is not derived from " being granted," nor does it " come into existence "; but on the other hand is from Eternity uniformly co-existent with the soul.

(*Mysteries of the Egyptians*, Ch. III.)

The reader of this book will notice that " the gods "

are not any longer the divine hypostases of Plotinus, but the innumerable denizens of a heaven upon which spiritists of all times have drawn. This book is important as illustrating the movement of Neo-Platonic philosophy generally towards the older Hellenic religion. Not satisfied with having produced a philosophy of religion—as Plotinus had done—the Syrian School, from Abammon down to Julianus, combined the two to the detriment of philosophy; and when the leadership passed back into the hands of the Athenian scholarchs, philosophy and its great figures of the older time were interpreted in the terms of the mystery religions. The student has become an "initiate," Aristotle's teaching is the "lesser mysteries" revealed in the adytum of the temple. Plato is the "hierophant" and his teaching is the "greater mysteries" revealed in the holy of holies. A rigorous asceticism, which was supposed to precede and accompany the mystery teaching, was practised by Plutarch, Syrianus, Proclus, and their philosophic disciples. A further consequence of this movement was the development of a dogmatic theology comparable to that which was being debated in the Christian church at the time. For Plutarch there were already nine hypostases, five of which were "gods." Syrianus and Proclus added to their number and expounded their hierarchical relationship. In a certain sense Proclus was the greatest scholar of the whole movement. His immense researches embraced not only the Greek philosophies and religions, but turning eastwards included those of the Chaldeans and Zoroastrians. Of the forty works known to have been composed by him nineteen are preserved, and many translated into English. It would require more space and labour than I can at present devote to deal adequately with the attainments of this great man who regarded Philosophy herself as the only hierophant capable of initiating the human race into the knowledge of God. He performed for Platonism the task of placing it, as he conceived, on a sure foundation of logical and scientific

NEO-PLATONISM

certainty. The very title of Thomas Taylor's *History of the Restoration of the Platonic Theology by the Later Platonists* is significant. It may seem cruel to say so—but I think it is true—that they " restored " what had never been lost, because it had never existed ! Plato devoted all his efforts to stimulating personal, social and political righteousness—*Dikaiosune*. Rising in his youth from practical problems of conduct pointed out in a hundred ways by Sokrates, he entered the heaven of metaphysical principles for light and truth and, in descending towards the earth again, applied them rigorously to the affairs of men in states, his large and last work being called *The Laws*. I cannot resist the thought that the Emperor Justinian, the maker of the famous Code and silencer of the School of Athens, was, unconsciously, the true Platonic Successor ; for Plato had desired that kings should become philosophers, and philosophers, kings.

XVII : *Between the Testaments*

A STUDY OF THE PERIOD IMMEDIATELY PRECEDING THE COMING OF CHRIST

IN his symbolical topography of the earth's surface Dante places Jerusalem at the centre of the world then known to him—between Tagus and Ganges. This ancient city, indeed, has some claim to such distinction, and, in preference to Athens or Rome, will be used as our meridian for an historical survey of the period " between the Testaments." Standing on its sacred hill in the year 333 B.C. and looking towards the East, we see the whole of Asia to the waters of the Jaxartes and the Indus under the dominion of the Persian kings ; looking also to the West, Egypt and Asia Minor to the coasts of Hellas are included in that immense domain, geographically the largest empire of the ancient days. But in that year also began the short, energetic and successful effort of Alexander, King of Macedon, to conquer the Persian empire ; and when he died in 323 B.C. his newly-seized empire fell into its many constituent parts, the two most important being Syria and Egypt, ruled respectively by the Seleucids and the Ptolemies. It was the fate of Palestine, and its capital-city, Jerusalem, to be on the borders of these two contending Greek kingdoms, each of which comprised large non-Greek populations over whom the veneer of Hellenism was gradually being spread. The story of the resistance to Hellenic influence is a tragic one, and includes a record of the origins of many ideas which appeared in their fully-developed form in the pages of the New Testament.

BETWEEN THE TESTAMENTS

1. RACE AND RULE

We must make a distinction between the actual *distribution of races* over the surface of the world we are considering and *political rule* or power.

Political rule, after many changes, had reached new conditions. All the ancient empires—Babylon, Assyria, Media, Persia and Egypt—had entirely collapsed, the two last-named under the assaults of European races, and the political centres of gravity had shifted to Alexandria, Antioch and Rome; new Oriental powers had risen on the ashes of the dismembered empire of Alexander.

For more than 100 years the Greek dynasties ruling at Antioch and Alexandria had been in active rivalry, and Palestine was the cockpit of their endeavours to overwhelm each other. In 202 B.C., Antiochus III. occupied Coele-Syria and Palestine and took possession of Jerusalem. An Egyptian army was sent under Scopas to recover these provinces; but though successful at first, this officer was in 198 defeated at Paneion, near the sources of the Jordan, and afterwards, when he had withdrawn to Sidon, obliged to surrender. The sufferings of the Jews during these years were considerable, as Josephus tells; whichever side prevailed for the time, their country was burdened by the presence in it of an invading army, and many in addition were carried off as slaves, or took refuge in flight. In the end, however, the Jews gave their support to Antiochus III, welcomed his troops into Jerusalem, and assisted in the ejection of the Egyptian garrison which had been left in the citadel by Scopas. In return for this support, Antiochus, in a letter written to his general, Ptolemy, directed many privileges to be granted to them; contributions were to be made, on a liberal scale, towards defraying the expenses both of the regular sacrifices, and of the repair of the Temple, till the country should have recovered its losses.

2. CRADLE AND ROOF

In the year 200 B.C. we again take our stand, as before suggested, but for a closer inspection, in the city of Jerusalem; the people of Jewry have contact with Alexandria through their dispersed brethren there, and with Babylon for the same reason : they represent the vigorous life-force of the older Semitic peoples in conflict with the newer Greek culture. From time to time and in various places they fall before the powerful intellectual influences of Greek philosophy or the more subtle Oriental ideas absorbed in Babylon ; nevertheless, there and in Palestine they maintain a vigorous struggle to remain " unspotted from the world," to keep their Law intact, their prophecy pure, their customs unchanged, and from 142 to 63 B.C., under almost miraculous conditions, they gain political independence of the surrounding rule of Greek, Roman and Arabian powers. It is not too much to say that the converging pressure of the world for two centuries forced the Jews, unknown to themselves, to prepare the cradle in which Christianity was born. Pushing the simile a point further, we may think of the Roman empire as the house under whose roof the infant faith was brought to maturity.

3. RELIGIOUS LITERATURE

We must remember that the Canon of the Jewish scriptures had by 200 B.C. been " closed " for a hundred years, but the religious genius of the race continued to produce works of great importance and variety, some reflecting the blend of Judaism and Hellenism, some affected by contact with the East ; but the most remarkable and influential are the product of the resistance to Greek culture of which I have spoken. For the convenience of the reader I give a table of these works arranged in the order in which it is believed that they were compiled.

It will be noticed that the first column contains the bulk

Date.	Apocalyptic Books.	Religious Romances.	Philosophical and Ethical.	Historical.
200 B.C. to	The Apocalypse of Weeks (Enoch I.) The Book of Noah (Enoch I.) The Book of Daniel (O.T.) The Dream Visions (Enoch I.)	Tobit	Ecclesiasticus	
150 B.C. to	The Book of Jubilees The Heavenly Luminaries (Enoch I.) Sibylline Oracles III.	Bel and the Dragon		
100 B.C. to	The Similitudes (Enoch I.)	Susanna	Testaments of the XII. Patriarchs Many of the Psalms	Maccabees I. Maccabees II. Maccabees III.
50 B.C. to	The Rest of Enoch I.	Judith	Psalms of Solomon Wisdom of Solomon	
A.D. 1 to	Esdras I. The Assumption of Moses The Secrets of Enoch (Enoch II.) The Apocalypse of Baruch		(Rabbi Hillel)	
A.D. 50	Esdras II. The Martyrdom of Isaiah Sibylline Oracles IV.		(Philo Judæus)	Maccabees IV.

of the religious writing of the Jews during this period, and that for the most part—excepting *Daniel*, in fact—these books are little known to the general public, even the religious public. This deficiency is being rapidly made good by the admirable series of translations issued by the S.P.C.K. It is not too much to say that since the recent study of the subject, led by Archdeacon Charles, of Westminster, an entirely new light has been shed on the New Testament which cannot properly be understood unless a fair knowledge of the pre-Christian Jewish literature is gained.

4. WHAT IS APOCALYPTIC?

The origin of Jewish apocalyptic literature is of great historical interest, and its religious effects are almost incalculable. Designed for a definite purpose this literature gradually secured very different ends, and the tradition started by some obscure Jews of 200 B.C. has dominated religious writings down to the present day. We must therefore endeavour to understand the facts aright.

The Hebrew prophets, as distinct from the priests, fell naturally into two groups depending largely on the political vicissitudes of the nation. One group was led to criticize the rulers with great severity and the other the enemies of Israel : individual prophets had done both. But among the many predictions standing to their credit—and not so many as once generally supposed—those stood out which foretold the restoration of the political power taken away from them by Assyrians and Chaldeans respectively. Jeremiah had been understood to say that the captivity in Babylon would last for seventy years, and others had told of a glorious return. In the main, however, it must be admitted—in spite of several remarkable exceptions—that prophecy had failed to attain that degree of realization which was expected of its oracles. The outstanding fact for Israel was a Gentile oppression lasting for more than five hundred years. Since the fall of Samaria in 721 B.C., Assyrian, Chaldean, Persian

BETWEEN THE TESTAMENTS

and Greek power had possessed their land and persecuted their people. Jeremiah's seventy years had been multiplied many times over, but still there was no sign of political restoration. What could be said in face of such an evident failure of Jehovah's prophets, and even of Jehovah himself, to deliver? More than that: for generations, reaching back to patriarchal times, the people had been encouraged to believe that earthly prosperity and happiness followed naturally as a reward for good deeds. Their history had seemed to show this; but now, for centuries, many eminently "righteous men" had, by their sufferings and their fate, provided evidence that conflicted with the early tradition. It was "the wicked" who prospered.

This serious dilemma called for new ways of escape. The philosophic endeavour of the book of *Job* was one way out of the difficulty—faith in God in spite of the inscrutability of His ways. The pessimism of *Ecclesiastes*, the Stoicism and resignation of *Ecclesiasticus* and *Wisdom* helped some men through the age of storm. But a new way was to be found by which God could be justified in the face of the seeming failure of His cause on earth, and this was the production of a new and deeper philosophy of history and life. It was expressed in a form which gave its name to this species of literature.

In the earlier prophetic writings there are occasional instances where the seers enjoy symbolic visions from some lofty eminence, and in *Ezekiel* (written in Babylon during the captivity) we have the frequent and significant phrase describing how the prophet was lifted up by the hair of his head and placed upon a high mountain whence he was able to discern the historical landscape of the immediate future. An "apocalypse," then, is the *revelation* or *uncovering* of something by the expedient of obtaining a point of view from which it can be seen in its true significance (*apo*—removal from a place; *kalupto*—to envelop, to conceal, to darken). Not only is the seer removed from the *place* he normally occupies on the earth, but in the order of *time* also—and this is its special feature—he is removed backwards to a period so remote that he is able thence to look forward over the whole expanse of history, past, present and to come. In doing this he gains an understanding of the events of recent and present occurrence and sees them in a perspective which makes known to him their relation to the past and the future. History and life are "uncovered," "revealed" for him, and God is justified!

No one can deny that the Jews of 200 B.C. and onwards needed such a revelation; their faith was weakening, their patience exhausted, their hopes unfulfilled. To their rescue came fresh prophets who by fresh means sought to revive their drooping faith, to sustain them in yet more suffering and to assure them that the godly life would be rewarded here or hereafter; if not on earth, then in heaven. This new race of prophets were really philosophers who, by a wider survey of earthly history, saw in it a preparation for a life that was more than earthly. They were also dramatic poets, for they looked upon life as a long process which could only be understood in its totality, not in its fragmentary aspects. For them there were grand and majestic beginnings, terrible mistakes and sins, titanic struggling between good and evil forces, in heaven, on earth and in men's hearts. All this was accompanied by suffering which became explicable only when seen in its relation to human destiny.

5. THE LAST THINGS

By some of the prophets the drama was conceived to have reached its closing stages; the last things (*Eschata*) were about to be witnessed; and then, according to the particular view of the writer, the rosy future was depicted in encouraging and sometimes magnificent language. Their flights of vision indicate to us how much they believed men capable of suffering and what triumphs of faith and lofty spirituality they might attain before complete salvation at the hands of God or his anointed messengers.

I may mention in passing the singular difference between the philosophy of history as expressed by these pious Jews and that held by contemporary Greeks. The one is a moving panorama of cosmic events against whose background man appears and takes his appropriate share; it has its tense moments and dramatic climaxes, in which God, his Messiah, his Archangels, and his Spirits take part continually, working towards an inevitable, though delayed victory for the Divine purposes. What value such a conception gives to creative personality and to life—even to our brief span! On the other hand, the Greeks, under the influence of Parmenides and Plato, see through the vicissitudes and mists of life to a static calm and beauty which represents Reality to them. Stoical endurance, philosophic withdrawal and a personal life of sanctity befitting a heavenly destiny is *their* deduction from what they discern. The one is active and heroic, the other passive and contemplative. Christianity came, in time, to combine the two into a higher and finer synthesis.

Here I may be permitted to remark that it is a matter of regret that the generation of Theosophists who have written and spoken most of Christianity have identified it with the *blasé* mysticism and pseudo-gnosis of Hellenized Alexandria rather than with the virile apocalyptic of Galilee. I am not exaggerating when I say that almost every word in the synoptic gospels (Mark, Matthew and Luke) is apocalyptic in form or in essence; the atmosphere in which Jesus delivered His message was apocalyptic and it was this that made it appropriate that what He said should be called "good news"—there had been bad news for long enough! Even the gospel of John, based on the idea of the coming of the Logos, puts that great being directly into the apocalyptic panorama as the chief personage beside the Divinity.

"For God so loved the world that he sent His only-begotten Son, that every one who believes in Him may not perish but have Immortal Life. For God sent not His Son into the world to condemn the world but that the world through Him might be saved."—

(*John* iii. 18, 17.)

These words concentrate into themselves the process, the machinery, the purpose of three centuries of Jewish apocalyptic writings and carry them to the sublimest height.

6. SOPHIA AND LOGOS

It has often been argued that the Johannine conception of the Logos referred to in the introductory passage to the fourth gospel and the epistles gives to Christianity and to Christ a specially Greek orientation, depriving the Galilean-Jewish school of the credit derived from a beautiful and profound doctrine. But this is quite a mistake. The doctrine of the Logos, though employing a Greek term, was nine-tenths Jewish; the Greeks had hardly any part in its origin and formulation. In the "Wisdom Literature" of the Old Testament we can trace the growth from small beginnings—thoughts having to do with cosmogony—of the conception of Wisdom as a power or attribute of God. *Job*, certain *Psalms*, and parts of *Proverbs*, *Ecclesiasticus* and the *Wisdom of Solomon* gradually, but surely, built up a figure into a Divine Being at the right hand of God. This figure is called *Hokba* in Hebrew and *Sophia* in Greek, consequently feminine. The doctrine of Sophia in this literature exists for two purposes: (1) to explain the process of creation as founded on a structure of Reason, and (2) to explain the possibility of Divine Communion with men, psychologically.

Parallel to this Jewish formulation there was a Greek doctrine of Logos appearing in Herakleitos (500 B.C.) as

BETWEEN THE TESTAMENTS

Divine Law, Will of God, energy of the Cosmos; in Anaxagoras as intermediate between God and the world, the regulating principle of the universe, the Divine Mind. In Plato there is hardly any place for the Logos, but in the Stoics the term reappears in two forms—" the potential " and the " expressed-in-action "—like Thought and Word. The complete personification of Sophia, however, in the Jewish writings had gone much further than the Greek Logos and at length came Philo the Jewish philosopher of Alexandria, immersed in Plato as to his mind, and in Moses as to his heart. It was he who put forward the fully-developed doctrine of the Logos as the Second God, the intermediary between perfect God and imperfect Man— the ray of light shining from the central sun into the darkened soul of man—bestowing the masculine name Logos upon the feminine divinity Sophia. It was he, the Jew, looking for world-salvation through his race, who in a hundred passages strengthened and clarified the idea of the Logos. It was perfectly easy, therefore, for John, or Cerinthus, if he wrote the fourth gospel—to point his finger to Jesus and say, simply: *Behold the Logos!* His opening words combine the apocalyptic figure of the Messiah with the Sophia of earlier Jewish writers. His gospel, is in fact, based on the symbolism of Philo:

> In the beginning the Logos was
> And the Logos was with God
> And the Logos was Divine . . .
> Through him all things came into being . . .
> That which came into being in him was life
> And that light was the light of man
> And the light shines into the darkness
> And the darkness never overpowers it.
>
> * * * * *
>
> And the Logos became Man and dwelt among us
> Full of love and truth . . .

Out of his fulness we have all received some gift,
Gift after gift of Love.
For the Law was given through Moses,
Love and truth came through Jesus Christ.
(*John* i. 1-17.)

In a sentence we may say that the Only-begotten Logos-Son is the masculine of the Unique-Sophia-Daughter. Whichever term we use we see in it the figure represented in the pure Jewish apocalyptic of the two centuries before our era. I summarize this sub-section by a diagram.

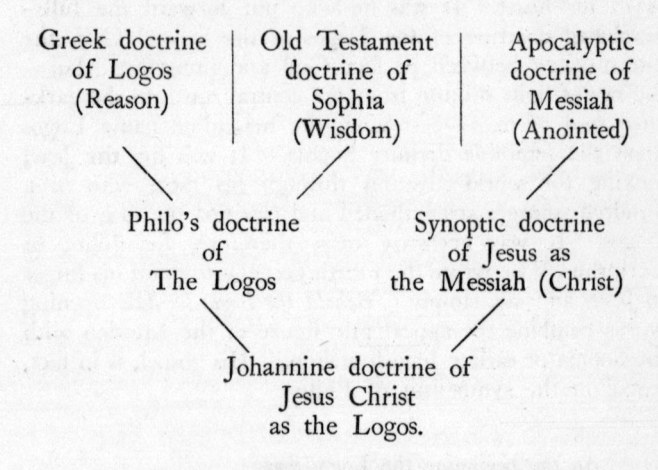

```
Greek doctrine    │  Old Testament   │  Apocalyptic
  of Logos        │   doctrine of    │   doctrine of
  (Reason)        │     Sophia       │    Messiah
                  │    (Wisdom)      │   (Anointed)
         \                  |                 /
          \                 |                /
           Philo's doctrine         Synoptic doctrine
                  of                   of Jesus as
              The Logos              the Messiah (Christ)
                     \                  /
                      \                /
                     Johannine doctrine of
                         Jesus Christ
                         as the Logos.
```

7. CHIEF APOCALYPTIC DOCTRINES

My space will not permit an attempt to give an exhaustive account of the pre-Christian " Christian " doctrines, but a few of them can be referred to in detail; nevertheless, it will be useful to give here a list of those familiar figures, incidents and teachings which, while appearing with apparent suddenness in the New Testament, have their origins in the " main stream " flowing towards it. Old Testament incidents, of course, are found abundantly there also.

BETWEEN THE TESTAMENTS

1. A fully-developed doctrine of angels of varying species and moral power.
2. The fallen angels as the initiators of evil in the world.
3. The course of evil as exhibited in human history.
4. The successive "Judgments" upon the world, beginning with the Deluge, ending with the last judgment.
5. The topography of the Heavens, the Underworld and Hell : Gehenna.
6. The "Kingdom of the Heavens" "the Kingdom of God."
7. The destruction of the world and salvation of the righteous.
8. The Resurrection of the righteous dead, and a general Resurrection.
9. The Messiah : the Anointed, the Christ, the Elect One, the Son of Man ; His function of Judge, Saviour and King.
10. The World-war and the Millennium.
11. Requisite exalted ethical ideas.
12. Authors of Apocalyptic Literature.

I propose to say a few words about points 6, 8, 9, and 12.

8. THE KINGDOM OF GOD AND THE RESURRECTION

The phrase "The Kingdom of God" has its origin in the book of *Daniel* (165 B.C.), but the idea is, in various forms, older. The apocalyptic writers by no means agree as to its nature except in one thing : that it belongs to the moving drama of the world : that it is an incident that occurs in the order of time. Its location and duration, too, are differently regarded. Some teachers thought of Jerusalem as its capital, some of the land of Israel as its limit ; others, who held that the world must perish, transferred it to the security of the Celestial World. Thus we have the origin of the two New Testament terms "The Kingdom of God" and "The Kingdom of the Heavens." No apocalyptic writer ventured to think of it as beyond time, and psychological in its character. It was left to Jesus to perceive and to say: "*not here, not there, with observation . . . but within you.*" On this doctrine was based all his specifically original teaching; though he used the apocalyptic language throughout, yet he had for it a much deeper meaning.

The doctrine of the Resurrection has its origin in a logical necessity and a spiritual longing—an intuition of immortality. Men saw around them and in their past history the triumph of the wicked and the humiliation of the righteous. Successive teachers and writers of these works—mostly Chassidim or Pharisees—found themselves oppressed by Greeks, by Hellenized Jews, by the Herodian party, or by Sadducees, according as each gained power. The terrible persecutions of Antiochus IV. led the writer of *Daniel* to affirm that this could not always be so: the grave would at last open and the righteous be rewarded with a life of happiness denied to them on earth, while the wicked would be punished in a terrible form.

This is a convenient place to say that the doctrine of bodily resurrection, long known to Egypt and probably familiar to the Jews from that direction, entirely precludes a doctrine of Reincarnation. No shred of evidence can be found to show that *the Jews* believed in Reincarnation; their eschatology and apocalyptic theories make it impossible, and we need not be surprised when we fail to find a single reference to it among the orthodox Palestinian Jews. Only where Hellenism had done its work—in Egypt and Upper Syria—could any Jew or Semite be found to hold such a belief; these people at once become heretics.

My readers will ask themselves how it is possible to reconcile reincarnation with any of the following forms of

BETWEEN THE TESTAMENTS

resurrection held from 200 B.C. onwards:—Resurrection could be attained in the body of the righteous—and of such wicked Israelites as had not been punished in life—on the advent of the Kingdom, says the writer of *Enoch* I.; but *Maccabees* II. thinks all Israelites will rise again, and they alone. Another writer in *Enoch* believes that there will be a resurrection of righteous Israelites only, and that their bodies will be subsequently transformed.

A new idea appears during the first century B.C. under the pressure of spirituality; it is the *spirit* of the righteous which rises again to life, not the body, and this at the close of the Messianic Kingdom. This idea appears in the *Psalms of Solomon* and *Enoch* I.; it is carried a step further by those who declare that the spirit of the righteous will rise from the grave clothed in a body of glory and light and those of the wicked for judgment and a second death. Other voices speak of a resurrection of the righteous, after a final judgment without a body, and still others of a spiritual body; *Enoch* II. and Josephus hold this view. The apocalypse of *Baruch* and *Esdras* for the first time think of a universal resurrection in the body of all mankind, and a new element is introduced by Alexandrian Judaism which hopes for a spiritual resurrection of the righteous immediately after death. This is found in *Wisdom*, Philo and *Maccabees* IV. No wonder the opinions held in New Testament times are uncertain, confused and contradictory!

9. THE MESSIAH

The first person in the Old Testament to be greeted with the title "Messiah" was Cyrus, the King of Persia; the liberator of the Jewish captives in Babylon. This fact is typical, for thereafter it is applied to a good number of persons—Prophets, High Priests and military heroes. There is nothing extraordinary in this, as the term meant no more than "anointed" by God for a special service to be performed. Thus there could be, and were, many such persons.

The transcendental figure to whom the term Messiah came to be applied by certain influential writers in *Enoch* is the centre of the whole scheme of world judgment and salvation. He is not a "World teacher" or founder of a new religion. He is a world ruler, a judge, a deliverer, a divine vice-regent on Earth and in Heaven. Many titles were bestowed upon him in pre-Christian times, including the two most notable, "The Son of Man," and "The Son of God." He was certainly not a "suffering God" or a "dying God," and there is no thought in these writings of an atoning sacrifice for the sins of mankind. These are Pauline additions to the virile drama of Jewish apocalyptic which marches on to victory in quite another manner. There is no connection with the Egyptian Osiris or the Persian Mithras—the creation is entirely Jewish in every feature.

10. THE APOCALYPTIC WRITERS

Not one of the authors of these works is known to us by name; and this is naturally so. As I have explained in sub-section 4, the real author is standing in the midst of his contemporaries witnessing their shortcomings and understanding their problems, and takes upon himself the name of some great man of an older day. Enoch "who walked with God" was thought to be an appropriate choice for the beginning of this kind of literature. He was already in that place from which the course of the world's history could be seen as a whole; he was not in the grave. He had but to write a book containing his revelation and to "seal it up" until the generations to come. This is the literary artifice adopted by all the writers. Noah, Moses, Daniel, Esdras, Baruch, Isaiah, Solomon, and the twelve Patriarchs were similarly chosen. It is impossible to believe that there was purposeful deception here; there was the impressive atmosphere of mystery and authority; the real author was able to remove his known personality from the message and, indeed, to rise to a higher one in the composition of his work. A prophet has not honour in his own day and land, but he may add to the honour another enjoys. These writers did this to the full.

In some cases we know the schools or sects from which these works emanated; with a fair degree of accuracy we know their dates, and in some cases the places in which they were written and circulated. *Enoch* was written, probably, by Galileans living at the foot of Mount Hermon, on to whose slopes descended the rebellious angels " in the days of Jared," whence began the long struggle between good and evil for the world. It was entirely in accord with this impressive philosophy of history that Jesus declared "*Repent, for the Kingdom of God is at hand.*" He was immediately understood though few believed Him. He called humanity to the point of decision, but, like his many predecessors, He was despised and rejected. Men are not willing to learn by the study of history that their miseries are self-inflicted, their hopes self-destroyed. The Kingdom of Heaven suffers from violence and the violent keep it away by force.

XVIII : *The Eucharist*

I THINK I can best serve readers who are interested, many are, in the question concerning ceremonies, ritual, and sacraments, by recounting in simple form the facts that are known about the early history of what is called the Eucharist.

1. FROM SACRIFICE TO SACRAMENT

In the first place the Christian ritual—if we may call it such—appeared on a background of Semitic ideas associated with sacrifices. The Old Testament is full of the records and the supposed significance and efficacy of sacrifices of the bodies of animals and the fruits of the earth. The writings of the prophets, beginning with Jeremiah (the initiator of personal religion in Judaism) and the Psalmists, contain explicit rejection of blood sacrifices and insistent demands for a sacrifice of the heart—" What does the Lord require of thee but to do justice and to love mercy ? "—the fat of rams and the blood of beasts, the burning of incense were rejected by the prophets as unsuited to the nature of a Spiritual God. True, Judaism as a whole never accepted to the full this prophetic teaching, but many of the finest of the race did, and the idea of making of one's body and heart a sacrifice unto the Lord, sweet smelling and acceptable, was thoroughly understood by them. It meant, of course, a complete moral regeneration. In this way the word " sacrifice " remained in spite of the fact that in the best of old Judaism and the new Christianity, the actual burnt offering had ceased to be given. The first Christian community in Jerusalem instituted the common purse and the common meal, partly due to the pressure of necessity and partly due to the impulses of compassion, and what each brought to it was in fact and in name his " sacrifice."

THE EUCHARIST

In the second place we know that a custom of meeting together for a common meal on special and regular occasions can be found in several religions contemporaneous to that of the Christian among whom it became known as the Agape, literally " Love," but understood to mean " love-feast." Of the origin of these Agapæ I do not now inquire because it is of no importance at the moment ; I merely want to establish the fact, attested to in the writings of St. Paul, of the custom of love-feasts as part of the consequences of Christian association. The " Last Supper," with all its surroundings of tragic beauty, was such a love-feast, and was easily and reasonably taken as the type for all others held by the followers of the Lord. Leaving aside, therefore, all earlier or collateral types of Agapæ, I direct my readers' attention to those which flowed from the example set by the Master when He ate his last meal—a real one—with His loving friends. It was at their love-feasts, held every Sabbath, that the devout adherents of the Name *remembered* their Lord with special emphasis.

I give in tabular form for convenience of reference the books which should be consulted, and I have added the dates (generally agreed) of their composition. As time proceeded the subject became a favourite and important one with Christian writers, but I have confined myself to the earliest books which lie within the compass of a century and a half after the death of Jesus.

1. Mark's Gospel — after A.D. 55
2. 1 Corinthians — about A.D. 58
3. Matthew's Gospel founded on Mark — ,, A.D. 60
4. Luke's Gospel ,, ,, ,, — after A.D. 60
5. Ignatius' Epistles — about A.D. 108
6. The Didache — ,, A.D. 130
7. Justin Martyr — ,, A.D. 139
8. Marcion's Gospel, founded on Luke — ,, A.D. 140
9. Tatian's Diatessaron — ,, A.D. 170

I will now consider the passages in their correct order and make such necessary comments as will connect them together.

2. DIVERGENT VIEWS

We must remember that Jesus and His friends are engaged at a meal which He knows, and they suspect, is a specially solemn one—probably the last they will eat together. He was the host, the Lord of the feast.

> And as they were eating, he took bread, and when he had blessed, he brake it, and gave to them, and said, Take ye : this is my body. And he took a cup, and when he had *given thanks*, he gave to them ; and they all drank of it. And he said unto them, This is my " blood of the covenant," which is shed for many.
>
> (*Mark* xiv. 22–24.)

The situation is tense with emotion, and Jesus so makes sacred this meal, that hereafter *every* common meal shall be made sacred in a similar manner. He first of all gives thanks to God, then He shares the bread and the wine with His disciples *symbolizing* the fact that He is about to make sacrifice of His body and blood. What more simple or impressive ceremony could have accompanied the act? Special emphasis should be laid on the Greek word in verse 23 for " had given thanks "—*eucharistesas*. It is, in some respects, the key-word to the problem. It is the word which belongs to a part of the ceremony natural to the occasion, but which later came to apply to the whole of it, but in a different sense.

The Apostle Paul might have had access to the written record of Mark, but that is very unlikely, yet his version is substantially identical. But he, too, adds a feature of interest ; he makes the ritual *commemorative*—" this do in remembrance of me."

THE EUCHARIST

The Lord Jesus in the night in which he was betrayed took bread ; and when he had given thanks he brake it, and said, This is my body, which is for you : this do in remembrance of me. In like manner also the cup, after supper, saying, This cup is the new covenant in my blood ; this do, as oft as ye drink it, in remembrance of me. (1 *Cor*. xi. 23–25.)

Matthew's version is almost literally identical with Mark's except that it adds the imperative "Eat" and "drink ye" and the significant words in reference to the blood "shed for many *unto the remission of sins*." We see the germ of a theological doctrine in these words, although we can be sure that there was none such connected with the original event. It is the beginning of the long-drawn-out process of interpretation.

Luke's version appears to be written in the presence of Mark and 1 Corinthians whose features it combines, although it is believed by some critics that the Pauline phrases were not in the original work of the evangelist ; no fresh feature is introduced.

3. SYMBOLISM AND MAGIC

It is certain there was a fluid verbal tradition of this Last Supper in circulation years before the words were crystallized into writing, and we would give a good deal to know just what this tradition was. There is a possibility of knowing something about it, as I shall shortly explain, but just here I want my readers to imagine this verbal tradition finding its way into the various Christian communities, becoming cherished and loved, and *then* being overtaken and, as it were, corrected by the written tradition as to the nature, ritual and significance of the ceremony in existence during the first and second centuries and possibly more. The tendency was for the written word to gain for itself the final authority over the unwritten tradition.

As Ignatius, the Bishop of Ephesus, was on his way to Rome to embrace a martyr's death, he addressed several epistles to sister Churches; in these are found some new features. I will quote the passages:

> Seek, then, to come together more frequently to give thanks (*eucharistian*) and glory to God. For when you gather together frequently the powers of Satan are destroyed, and his mischief is brought to nothing by the concord of your faith.
> (Ignatius, *Ep. to Eph.* xiii.)

> Be careful therefore to use one Thanksgiving (*eucharistia*)—for there is one flesh of our Lord Jesus Christ, and one cup for union with his blood, one altar, as there is one overseer with the elders and the deacons my fellow servants,—in order that whatever you do you may do it according unto God.
> (*Ep. to Phil.* iv.)

> [Some Heretics] abstain from Eucharist and prayer, because they do not confess that the Eucharist is the flesh of our Saviour Jesus Christ who suffered for our sins, which the Father raised up by his goodness.
> (*Ep. to Smy.* vii.)

There are now several new features introduced. Firstly, the word *Eucharist*, thanksgiving, is becoming technical and general for the whole ceremony; it has its origin in Mark's word which was as a separate act, clearly no more than a kind of " grace after meals " as we should say. Secondly, not only is the thanksgiving rendered to God as a duty to Him, but in the congregational meeting together the powers of evil are destroyed and a spiritual security attained. Thirdly, Ignatius lays stress on uniformity of ritual, with rhetorical rather than logical force; and fourthly, we are told quite clearly that there are some Christian heretics who " do not confess that the Eucharist is the flesh of our Saviour Jesus." This admission is important for

THE EUCHARIST

two reasons : it shows that the Ignatius tradition was leading towards transubstantiation but that another tradition would not hear of such a thing.

We now come upon the track of what I referred to as the hitherto unwritten tradition about the Eucharist. It is contained in a small but important book called *The Didache* ("The Teaching" of the twelve Apostles) dated about A.D. 130. It appears to have been composed in presence of the Gospels, which it frequently quotes. It is a manual of church instruction as to conduct, worship, baptism, fasting and the Eucharist.

> And concerning the Eucharist, hold Eucharist thus : First concerning the cup, "We give thanks to thee, our Father, for the Holy Vine of David thy child, which thou didst make known to us through Jesus thy child ; to thee be glory for ever." And concerning the broken Bread : "We give thee thanks, our Father, for the life and knowledge which thou didst make known to us through Jesus thy child. To thee be glory for ever. As this broken bread was scattered upon the mountains but was brought together and became one, so let thy Church be gathered together from the ends of the earth into thy kingdom, for thine is the glory and the power through Jesus Christ for ever." But let none eat or drink of your Eucharist except those who have been baptised in the Lord's name. (*Didache* ix. 1–5.)

Here the actual meal takes place and we read further :

> But after you are satisfied with food, thus give thanks : "We give thanks to thee, O Holy Father, for Thy Holy Name which thou didst make to tabernacle in our hearts, and for the knowledge and faith and immortality which thou didst make known to us through Jesus thy Child. To thee be glory for ever. Thou, Lord Almighty, didst create all things for thy

Name's sake, and didst give food and drink to men for their enjoyment that they might give thanks to thee, but us hast thou blest with spiritual food and drink and eternal light through thy Child. Above all we give thanks to thee for that thou art mighty, to thee be glory for ever." (x. 1–4.)

4. EMERGENCE OF THE TRUE VIEW

The ritual included the use of the Lord's Prayer in which occurs the petition " Give us each day our super-substantial bread" which doubtless is the "spiritual food" referred to above. Material bread has already been distributed.

This passage throws a tremendous flood of light on the ceremony it is referring to. At the table in the upper chamber Jesus, presumably, " gave thanks " to God for the elements of the meal, in accordance with the Jewish custom ; but now something greater is the object of thanksgiving of the Christians of a hundred years later. They, in partaking of the cup, thank God for " the Holy Vine of David " now made known through Jesus. We still do not know what the symbol hides beneath its suggestive words, though we can perhaps guess. The term " Holy Vine of David " is most probably derived from the Gospel phrase " I am the true vine " and may be a mystical name for Jesus. Clement of Alexandria later uses the words " This is he who poured out for us the wine, the blood of the Vine of David." In breaking the bread they gave thanks "for the life and knowledge" made known through Jesus. Again, the bread symbolizes *not* the body of the Lord, but the body of the Christian community, aforetime scattered as individual grains on the hillside, now kneaded into one society.

We observe, too, that this Eucharist is not to be taken by those unbaptized. It is clear also that it is not a ritual meal, nor a ritual instead of a meal, but a ritual at a real meal—" after you are satisfied with food thus give thanks." Further gratitude is then expressed for the dwelling of

THE EUCHARIST

God's name in the hearts of the worshippers, for knowledge, faith and immortality, for spiritual food and drink and eternal light. A significant sentence is "But suffer the prophets to hold Eucharist as they will," showing that some were already liberated from the conformity to ritual, or that they have never come under its influence.

In a very important section of his first apology Justin Martyr is explaining the origin of the rite of baptism; it is performed, he says, "over him who chooses to be born again," proving conclusively that it is outwardly *symbolical* of that changed life on which the convert has embarked and *not magically efficacious* in itself. He continues:

> But we, after we have thus washed him who has been convinced and has assented to our teaching, bring him to the place where those who are called brethren are assembled, in order that we may offer hearty prayers in common for ourselves and for the baptised person. . . . Having ended the prayers, we salute one another with a kiss. There is then brought to the president of the brethren bread and a cup of wine mixed with water; and he taking them, gives praise and glory to the Father . . . and *offers thanks* at considerable length for our being counted worthy to receive these things at His hands. And when he has concluded the prayers and thanksgiving, all the people present express their assent by saying Amen. . . . And when the president *has given thanks*, and all the people have expressed their assent, those who are called by us deacons give to each of those present to partake of the bread and wine mixed with water over which the thanksgiving was pronounced, and to those who are absent they carry away a portion.
>
> And this food is called among us *Eucharistia*, of which no one is allowed to partake but the man who believes that things which we teach are true and

who has been washed with the washing that is for the remission of sins, and unto regeneration, and who is so living as Christ has enjoined. For not as common bread and common drink do we receive these. . . .
(*Justin I. Ap.*, lxv., lxvi.)

The closing words emphasize the nature of the distribution of this food. It is not *common* bread and wine, such as people would eat *individually* and, so to speak, separately; it is that part of a meal which is partaken of *communally*, and is *made sacred*.

So far, Justin may be supposed to agree with the fuller account of the rite given in *The Didache*, of which only *one* interpretation is possible; but now he introduces the Ignatian concept in his explanation of the ritual actions. He has before him the Gospel words, "this is my body, this is my blood," and he appears to interpret them literally, instead of symbolically as he might have done. This shows that Justin had received and accepted the idea of Ignatius whose teaching had begun to triumph over the simpler form of *The Didache*. He says:

We have been taught that the food which is blessed by the prayer of His word, and from which our blood and flesh by transmutation are nourished, is the flesh and blood of that Jesus who was made flesh.

Marcion's *Gospel of the Lord* is very generally agreed as being a reconstruction of Luke's or, if we do Marcion the justice he desired, the original edition of Luke. In any case it is worth noticing that his version is almost literally that of our third Gospel, which I will now quote.

And he said unto them, With desire I have desired to eat this passover with you before I suffer. And he received a cup, and when he had given thanks, he said, Take this, and divide it among yourselves. . . . And he took bread, and when he had given

THE EUCHARIST

thanks, he brake it and gave to them, saying, This is my body which is given for you : this do for my remembrance. (*The Gospel of the Lord*, xix. 16–18.)

There is no new feature, but the appearance of Marcion's Gospel at this time might emphasize the Ignatian tendency to literal interpretation. It must be remembered, however, that Marcion could not wish to adopt the view of Justin, for he denied the reality of the bodily life of Jesus. He could not believe in transubstantiation because he held the view that Jesus was a spiritual phantom only. He could only interpret the Gospel words as referring to participation in the divine *life* of the Son of God.

Tatian's *Diatessaron* combined and harmonized the version of Mark, 1 Corinthians, Matthew, and Luke, but introduced nothing new ; I mention it for this reason only.

5. CONCLUSION

I need go no further ; the continuation of the doctrinal history of the Eucharist takes us into ecclesiastical disputes which even yet have not died down. I do not, of course, wish to add to the controversy of ages which has resulted in wide divergence of interpretation and practice, nevertheless I think it will be useful if I draw together what appears to me to be the threads of the great age-long debate. None of the passages I have quoted can be regarded as inspired or authoritative in the absolute sense and I should not think it right in a matter of this kind to stand or fall with them ; nevertheless, they are of the nature of evidence which we may now look fairly in the face. They establish the following facts : at a love-feast, in the real and untechnical sense of the word, Jesus used a simple, intelligible and significant ritual of *Communion*, illustrating the very words he had used (according to John's Gospel) about His being in union with His disciples and they in union with Him, and with one another. The meal at which this was done was a real meal and was elevated by Him into a *Sacrament*—in the untechnical sense of a common thing made sacred or consecrated. This consecration of common things was symbolic of the New Life He was endeavouring to introduce into the world. Further it was, as He said, a *New* covenant replacing the old Jewish sacrificial ritual of blood and flesh; it consequently symbolized the abandoned rite and thus stood in place of a *Sacrifice*. A special part of the whole ceremony, not new but quite conventional, was the *Thanksgiving*—and this part has fortunately preserved in its name the heart and soul of the ritual.

We do not know the exact method of holding the love-feast immediately after the departure of Jesus. Possibly some time would elapse before the little community would be able to fix for itself a commemorative ceremony; however this may be, we must now admit a new and inevitable element into it, namely, *Commemoration*—which I take to be a "common memory" of the event. We may well suppose that for some time the common practice would not show much divergence, but certainly the *interpretation* was not uniform. The two early distinct types are *Ignatius-Justin* and *The Didache*, the one seeming to be literal and therefore difficult, the other symbolical and therefore thoroughly understandable.

To me, the critical issue seems to lie between that view which makes the Eucharist to be a *magical process* of efficacy in itself and that other view which makes it a *symbolical representation* of a spiritual state to which the worshippers have attained or to which they aspire. Obviously, the doctrine of the Transubstantiation of bread and wine into flesh and blood is a magical conception and the participation of the elements is supposed to produce magical results. For myself, I decide against the interpretation of the rite as magic and prefer the reasonable and beautiful conception expressed in *The Didache*.

A further question which lies beyond the field of study

THE EUCHARIST

in which I move, in this Section, is that concerned with the supposed obligation upon Christians to use the Eucharist. Any one who decides in favour of the rite as symbolism will at once perceive that it cannot be obligatory for him. Only those use a symbol to whom it means something and who cannot do without it. If they *can* do without it it is because doubtless they value highly and realize keenly what formerly the symbol reminded them of. To put it tersely, the man who has "*chosen* to be born again" is not *obliged* to be baptized; the man who makes his every meal, his every deed, sacred, who lives " in the perpetual presence of God" needs no special ritual to induce a consciousness that has happily become normal for him.

Consequently the saying of *The Didache* is germane for us to-day : " But suffer the prophets to hold thanksgiving as they will."

XIX : "*The Unpardonable Sin*"

IT is probable that thousands of sermons, articles and commentaries have been composed around the obscure words that occur in the Gospels of Mark iii. 28–29, and Matthew xii. 31–32. Here the Christ is supposed to have said something important about the forgiveness of sins and to have made a reservation in a special case. Popularly we have in our minds three persons of a Divine Trinity, and we seem to learn from the saying that though men may be forgiven for sin and blasphemy, against "the Son of Man," yet if directed to the third person of the Trinity, it will never be forgiven. One would have thought that long ago there would have been doubts as to the true meaning of these words, that people would have asked the reason of this permission to expect forgiveness after having blasphemed the Father and the Son, but not to expect it after blaspheming the Holy Ghost.

I know that long ago, by avoiding too close a scrutiny of the text itself, it was rationalized to mean that a man must not "sin against the light within him." Of course he must not ; but when that is said, we have not cleared up the chief difficulty.

Some years ago, when studying the Christian Teaching about "spirit," I became convinced that this view was entirely unfounded ; or rather, that it was based, not on a wrong translation of the Greek text, but on a misunderstanding of the words of Jesus, so complete and so early, that it must have been present in the minds of the Evangelists themselves. Yet the true meaning of the words is not difficult to recover, for the misunderstanding displays itself quite nakedly in the documents ; and when the mystery

THE UNPARDONABLE SIN

has been unravelled, we find that Christ's dictum has nothing whatever to do with the so-called "unpardonable sin."

In my present study I shall employ the Greek text of Dr. Eberhard Nestlé of Maulbronn, who has collated the recensions of Tischendorf, of Westcott and Hort, and of Bernhard Weiss. The text is published by the British and Foreign Bible Society, of London, in handy form.

1. THE GOSPEL PHRASES

I quote from the revised version the two passages in question, printing that of St. Mark first, in accordance with the usual critical custom.

> Verily I say unto you, all their sins shall be forgiven unto the sons of men and their *blasphemies* wherewith soever they shall *blaspheme* : (v. 29).
> But who shall however *blaspheme* against the Holy Spirit hath never forgiveness, but is guilty of an eternal sin.   (*Mark* iii. 28–29.)

> Therefore I say unto you, every sin and blasphemy shall be forgiven unto men ; (but the blasphemy against the Holy Spirit shall not be forgiven) (v. 32).
> And whosoever shall *speak a word* against the Son of Man, it shall be forgiven him ; but whosoever shall *speak against* the Holy Spirit, it shall not be forgiven him, neither in this world nor in that which is to come.
>   (*Matthew* xii. 31–32.)

The two passages are roughly parallel, and have a common source, which shows the words in brackets in Matthew to be an interpolated repetition. Verse 32 of Matthew, I believe, has preserved the form derived from the original spoken word, while verse 29 of Mark, by substituting the word "blaspheme," has started all our troubles.

I am convinced that the Christ never used these words, and now propose to show the extraordinary process by which what He did say has been so seriously misunderstood.

We must remember that the vulgar tongue of the day was Palestinian Aramaic, a first cousin, according to the latest research, to Hebrew; its nearest surviving affinity is Syriac. Tradition has it that Matthew recorded the "Sayings" in Hebrew and that the Gospels were written originally in Greek, although a certain learned authority now argues that the fourth Gospel was composed in Aramaic. Certain crucial words occur in the passages, and it must be understood that they would be affected by translation from a spoken language into a written one. These words are: "forgive," "Son of Man," "blaspheme" or "speak against," "sin," and "holy spirit."

2. THE FIVE KEY-WORDS

(1.) We do not know the Aramaic word used by Christ rendered by us "forgive"; the Greek word is *aphiemi*, which equals "to send forth," "to discharge"; the Latin equivalent is *emittere*; or, in the secondary sense, "to send away," "to let go," "to throw away," of which the Latin equivalent is *dimittere*. The word *forgive* does not appear under this article in Liddell & Scott's *Lexicon*, but under the word *pariemi*, whose Latin equivalent is *condonare*, to pardon.

(2.) The popular term in the Aramaic for "man" is *bar nasha*; and in Hebrew, too, there is a similar term; both of them, which occur commonly in the Old Testament, mean "son of man," or, as we might say, "a member of the human family," or simply a man, as distinguished from the angels or "sons of god." Another way in which this term is used has altogether a different significance. "The Son of Man" was the title of a transcendental figure who first appeared in the visions contained in the *Book of Enoch* (160 B.C.). These two terms, representing respectively, an ordinary man, and, on the other hand, a unique individual, have several times become confused in the pages of the New Testament, and the same Greek term has been used for them; unhappily this has occurred here also.

THE UNPARDONABLE SIN

(3.) In classical Greek the word *blasphemeo* has no special theological significance; it means "to speak ill of" or "to the prejudice of" one, and *blasphemia* simply means "slander"; here, however, there is a confusion between "to blaspheme" and "to speak against" (in Matthew's version), *eipei logon kata* meaning, as I shall show, to speak a word of magical power over against some spiritual entity. This is not equivalent to blasphemy, but is of the nature of exorcism.

(4.) The word "sin" (*hamartia*) is a difficult word, but it has to be understood in the sense of a state of corruption, an infestation; it is not an act; acts of sin or sins are called *hamartémata*, and they proceed from men who have in them the corruption which is their source.

(5.) The word "spirit" in the Bible is a translation of the Hebrew *ruah* and the Greek *pneuma*, both of which originally meant breath. Spirit, as the New Testament shows, regarded as the innermost life of man, can be either good or bad; there are evil spirits and there is holy spirit, the latter is identified with the Divine, and had been said, from old prophetic days, to be communicable to men.

3. SIN AND EXORCISM

I am aware that in the five paragraphs above I have introduced a great deal of matter for controversy, but it is necessary that I should get my readers to understand the sense in which I use these crucial words. There is one more remark of a general character which students of the New Testament will appreciate. The Semitic people, and the Jews no less than the other races, constantly thought and spoke in spiritistic terms, and, as the discourses of Christ show, disease, infirmities and mental deficiency were supposed to have been caused by evil spirits. I do not go so far as to say that He Himself had no higher view than this, but in the cases I am now about to quote, the language, at least, is spiritistic. I only need say that, in order to bring out what I believe to be the true sense of the discourses, I have not followed strictly any particular translation, and have introduced emendations of my own here and there ; the passages constitute a paraphrase and an interpretation of what I believe to have been a connected spontaneous discourse.

4. THE CURE OF THE MAN POSSESSED

Just as they were going out some people brought to Jesus a man *possessed by a demon* ; he was both blind and dumb. And Jesus cured him, so that the man who had been dumb both talked and saw. At this people were astounded, and exclaimed : " Nothing like this has ever been seen in Israel "—" Can it be possible that he is the 'Son of David' spoken of in our traditions ? "

(Founded on *Matt.* ix. 32, 33 ; *Mark* iii. 22 ; *Matt.* xii. 23, 24.)

The Pharisees also heard of this, and gave their usual explanation : " He has Beelzebub in him, and drives out demons only by the chief of the demons."

(*Mark* iii. 22 ; *Matt.* ix. 34 ; *Matt.* xii. 23, 24.)

(*a*) *Of the Divided Kingdom.* Jesus, however, being made aware of what was passing in their minds, said to them : " Any kingdom divided against itself falls to ruin, and in the same way, if Satan is opposed to himself, and has driven a demon from a man, then *his* kingdom is divided, it cannot last, his end has come. In this case it is well.

" But if you do not agree to this and if you still say that I drive out demons by the power of their chief, I ask you by whose power is it that your sons *drive them out* ? Let your own people be your judges in this matter."

(*Matt.* xii. 25–28 ; *Mark* iii. 23–36 ; *Luke* xi. 17–20.)

THE UNPARDONABLE SIN

(*b*) *Of the Strong Man's House.* " Now if, on the other hand, it be that I drive out demons by the Spirit of God, then the rule and kingdom of God must be already upon you ! For consider : How can any one break into a strong man's house, who is keeping guard over his property, fully armed, unless he be *stronger* than the strong man ? Only then can he plunder his goods ; so I cannot drive out evil except by a force that is greater than evil."

(*Matt.* xii. 29 ; *Mark* iii. 27 ; *Luke* xi. 21–22.)

(*c*) *Who is not for is against.* " And remember that he who is not on my side, is opposed to me ; he who does not help me to gather is scattering, and he who is not on the side of the spirit which is holy is on the side of the spirit which is evil."

(*Matt.* xii. 30 ; *Luke* xi. 23.)

5. SUGGESTED RECONSTRUCTION OF THE PASSAGE

(*d*) *The Law of the Expulsion of Evil.* " Therefore I truly say to you that all sin and slander can *be sent forth* from the sons of men, no matter how much they may have sinned. And if any one [being possessed by the Spirit which is holy] should *speak a word* over against a man, it [sin] will be sent forth from him. But whosoever should *speak a word* over against the Spirit which is holy, *it will not be sent forth*—no, neither in this age, nor in that to come."

(*Matt.* xii. 31–32 ; *Mark* iii. 28–29.)

I have italicized the significant words in this passage, which is, in my view, the true meaning of Mark iii. 28–29, and Matthew xii. 31–32, though hardly recognizable in its new form.

(e) *The Possible Return of Evil.* " But when an evil spirit has been *driven forth* from a man it is like a robber who has been expelled from a house, he goes into the wilderness in search of rest. Not finding it he says : ' I will go back to the house which I have left.' If, arriving there, he finds the house unoccupied, clean, and put in order, then he goes and brings with him seven others more wicked than himself, and they go in and make their home there. [Thus, if a man merely abstains from committing sinful acts and has not received into himself the Spirit that is Holy, his state, when the evil returns to him, is worse than it was at first."]

(*Matt.* xii. 43–45 ; *Luke* xi. 24–26.)

(f) *Causes may be Judged by Effects.* " Your contentions are not sound ; you must assume either that both the tree and the fruit are good, or that both the tree and the fruit are worthless—that is, either that what I have done is good and proceeds from a good source, or that it is evil and proceeds from an evil source : for by its fruit the tree is known. Do people gather grapes from thorns, or figs from thistles ?

" But—you brood of vipers !—how can you, being so evil, say what is good ? For what fills the heart rises to the lips. Remember, a good man out of his stores of good produces good things, while an evil man out of his stores of evil produces evil things."

(*Matt.* xii. 33 ; *Matt.* vii. 16–20.)

(g) *The Pharisees' Charge Refuted.* " If therefore you agree that I have driven evil out of this man, it is only by the force of the Spirit which is holy that I have done so, and not, as you say, by the force of Beelzebub. All this was said in reply to the charge that he had a foul spirit in him."

(*Mark* iii. 30.)

THE UNPARDONABLE SIN

I must not lengthen this section by going so fully into another case (that of the paralytic referred to in Mark ii. 5, and Matt. ix. 1), but if my readers will consult the passages they will see that here also the Greek word has been rendered " forgiven " instead of " expelled " or " sent forth." And what is most significant is that at the end of the cure the people " praised God for giving such power *to men*," that is, the power to send forth from their fellows the evil spirit and its concomitant disease by the strength of a spirit which is holy.

6. DEFENSIVE POWER OF THE SPIRIT

It is clear to me that we must abandon the belief that in the sentences quoted there is any teaching whatsoever about the " unpardonable sin." The Christian doctrine with regard to sin falls into two divisions ; the first is the good news that *hamartia*, the root of all sins, can be eradicated, and the second that a man must pardon the *hamartémata*, sins or offences of others in order himself to be pardoned. In this way only, by mystical and moral processes, can sin be destroyed. It will perhaps help us to dismiss the " unpardonable sin " from our minds if we remember that Christ taught this science and art of the eradication of all evil.

Having rid ourselves of the old, inexplicable and illogical view, we may find ourselves provided with a new view which is, though more intelligible, not to our liking. I am prepared to admit that " exorcism " seems to be a primitive conception belonging to the old spiritistic view of life, and I should not care to maintain that Christ adopted it as the final explanation of his cures. Yet he had no alternative but to use the language current in his day ; and this was spiritistic. Language, however, lags behind thought, sometimes for centuries, and I think we may be safe in saying that Christ used the spiritistic language to describe psychological changes which, even yet, are hardly understood. In the majority of instances the condition precedent of His cures was not His own power—He sometimes confessed Himself impotent—but His patient's faith. "Thy faith hath made thee whole" is crystal clear and astonishingly modern. The "evil spirit" which infests the unhappy and the unhealthy lurks in the depths of the Unconscious Mind. It is not an entity but, none the less, a force more powerful for harm than the seven devils of older belief. On the other hand, the great, the good and the pure are—in the language of the discourse quoted above—" filled with the Spirit which is holy." They harbour no evil thought or feeling, and they know the power this gives them to evoke faith in others. When they speak the word of power over against one who has faith, the old inner state passes away and gives place to a new state The phenomenal change—the "cure," the "miracle"—if it be possible and reasonable, follows on the psychological change; for the Unconscious, ever alert and at work on the body, handles its material more deftly than drug, priest or physician can do.

The general conclusion from the passages considered is simple to understand if too great to believe: all offences (*hamartémata*) are pardonable by those who have sufficient love. Sin (*hamartia*) is eradicable by those who have sufficient faith. Love and Faith are gifts of the Spirit.

XX : *The Ethic and Psychology of Forgiveness*

1. TWO DOCTRINES

SERIOUSLY, I suggest that the time has come in the world's history to consider the question of forgiveness as a practical necessity. We gladly supersede manual labour by machinery, steam by electricity, coal by oil and petrol as soon as we realize the practical advantages of doing so. May it not be that, now, the hitherto-practised motives of justice and revenge are both ready for abandonment if but we had to our hand an instrument more potent for human needs, more appropriate to human nature as it is or, at least, as it is struggling to become?

Forgiveness has been taught in the world under two aspects ; (1) as a divine attribute it takes the form of a theological doctrine which is a well-worn subject of dispute and upon which various schools have as yet hardly reached agreement ; (2) as an ethical doctrine it is humanistic and more easily understood ; it comes immediately within our sphere of influence, irrespective of the theological doctrines of Divine Forgiveness. To a certain extent the two doctrines, theological and ethical, are intertwined, but they can be separated, the first being put on one side and the second examined alone.

So far as I am aware a doctrine of divine forgiveness of man or one of man's forgiveness of his fellows is not found in specific form in the great world religions other than Judaism and Christianity. Owing to their peculiar view of evil as objective and remorseless in its consequences, the non-Christian thinkers of antiquity had other means of dealing with it than forgiveness, specially considered. I do not mean that Indians, Buddhists, Chinese, Greeks and Egyptians did not forgive one another or seek forgiveness (or its equivalent) from Heaven; they must have done. But the process of obtaining what we may call forgiveness either from God or from man was deeply wrapped up in magical practices. It was so indeed in the early days of the Hebrews whose legislators and ritualists elaborated formulæ to exemplify it: some of the sacrifices and the scape-goat, for instance. The " wiping out " of sin was no easy attainment.

The history of human forgiveness can best be studied in isolation from the pages of the Bible with the addition of kindred religious literature, but before I turn to that I must revert to the point made above, namely, that the theological and ethical doctrines are closely connected; the connection must be recognized first before it is broken and we shall then be able to learn the precise background against which the ethic of human forgiveness arose.

2. INESCAPABLE NEMESIS

The old ideas of evil held all over the world picture a kind of inescapable Nemesis of three kinds : (1) that administered by God or Nature (e.g. the Indian doctrine of Karma, or the significance of deeds; the Greek doctrine of Moira or Destiny; and the Hebrew doctrine of Divine retribution); (2) the Nemesis administered by man for God; and (3) the Nemesis administered by man on his own account, namely, private revenge. This last had two bases, first the natural *feeling* of resentment following injury and second the *idea* of the rightness of retaliation. In the hard days of old, men lived in perpetual fear of nemesis of one sort or another which must have been terrible to bear. It was, I believe, due to the weight of this burden that personal ethic on the one hand and political ethic on the other were called into being by the leaders of the race. To the Indians belongs the credit of having elaborated a doctrine and practice of morality which, while it included forgiveness implicitly, aimed at a gradual shifting of the burden of evil deeds by a life of discipline. To the Babylonians belongs the credit of having made the first grand code of laws aimed at the restriction and reduction of private and indiscriminate revenge. "Nemesis administered by Nature," said the Indian teachers of Karma, "can be escaped by living the good life"; "Nemesis administered by man's private impulse," says Khammurabi of Babylon in effect, "can and must be regulated, reduced, transmuted into newer forms." This was the beginning of Justice, or political ethic. But neither Karma nor Justice disposed of Nemesis altogether; the first led a man to endeavour to liquidate his own misdeeds for his own sake in a somewhat distant though certain future; it did not negotiate any welfare directly for one's neighbour, one's enemy or oppressor. Forgiveness in the sense of helping him was not part of the discipline of Karma; only indirectly, in a general diffusion of well-doing radiated from the practising moralist, did other people benefit. Each had to seek his own salvation. In the same way Justice did not altogether get rid of the weight of Nemesis; it brought it down from Heaven to Earth so to speak; it legalized and crystallized revenge, sanctifying it with the state's authority and attributing it to the Divine decree. It really made forgiveness impossible because it left nothing to the kind heart, rather insisting on the exact measurement of punishment allowed.

3. FORGIVENESS OVERCOMES NEMESIS

As we shall see shortly, forgiveness does attempt to do what Karma and Justice fail to do. It helps to relieve the ill-doer of the fateful consequences of his actions by removing the antipathy which he rightly might otherwise dread; it removes the objective consequences by an act of pardon and thus makes Nemesis a negotiable foe. My aim here is to show that forgiveness receives its significance when we

MYSTICISM OF EAST AND WEST

realize the double background against which it rises in opposition, namely, against inescapable Divine or natural Nemesis on the one hand and against human Justice on the other. Forgiveness is part of that Mercy which transcends Justice in the same way that Justice is superior to indiscriminate private Revenge.

4. KHAMMURABI'S CODE

I have a suspicion that my readers may need further demonstration before they will accept the briefly-stated conclusion above ; and I will now supply the facts in detail regarding the ancient institution of Justice. In the British Museum may be seen a replica of the basalt stele of the Babylonian King. It is most impressive to contemplate its cuneiform writing and learn the secret it contains :

The Code reads :

> Ana and Bel delighted the flesh of mankind by calling me, the renowned prince, the god-fearing Khammurabi, to establish Justice in the earth, to destroy the base and the wicked, and to hold back the strong from oppressing the weak.

After the terse recital of 283 laws, the King concludes with a commendation of his code, containing these words :

> It is I that the great Gods have elected to be the Shepherd of Salvation, whose sceptre is just. I throw my good shadow over my city. Upon my bosom I cherish the men of the lands of Sumir and Akkad. By my protecting genius, their brethren in peace are guided : by my wisdom are they sheltered. That the strong may not oppress the weak ; that the orphan and the widow may be counselled ; in Babylon, the city whose head has been lifted up by Ana and Bel.

The code of Babylon is the oldest and most perfect specimen of the principle of retaliation adopted as a method of

PSYCHOLOGY OF FORGIVENESS

maintaining social order, and therefore has a singular interest for us in that it is the original of the law that Christ essayed to abolish. If any one should doubt this, let him read these words of Khammurabi :

> If a son has struck his father, his hand shall be cut off.
> If a man has destroyed the eye of a free man, his own eye shall be destroyed. If he has broken the bone of a free man, his bone shall be broken. . . .
> If he has destroyed the eye of a plebeian, or broken the bone of a plebeian, he shall pay one mina of silver. If a man has knocked out the teeth of a man of the same rank, his own teeth shall be knocked out. . . .
> If a man strike the daughter of a free man, and that woman die, his daughter shall be slain. . . .
> If a builder has built a house for a man, and his work is not strong, and if the house he has built falls in and kills the householder, the builder shall be slain. If the child of the householder be killed, the child of that builder shall be slain.

Lex talionis imposes a discipline upon private revenge ; it restricts the amount of punishment which may be inflicted by the injured party ; further, by the institution of monetary compensation in a large number of its laws it eliminates the violent and uncertain consequences which might have otherwise followed robberies and material damage.

5. THE MOSAIC CODE AND ITS REJECTION

The various instalments of the Jewish legal code follow in general the principle of Khammurabi, but in some cases seem to go beyond him in severity. He is drawing up a system of permissive revenge which the Jews transmute into imperative inflictions. I quote the relevant passages :

> He that smiteth his father, or his mother shall surely

be put to death. And he that curseth his father, or his mother shall surely be put to death.
(*Exodus* xxi. 15–17.)

If a man has struck a woman and any mischief follow, then thou shalt give life for life, eye for eye, tooth for tooth, hand for hand, foot for foot, burning for burning, wound for wound, stripe for stripe.
(*Exodus* xxi. 23–25.)

And behold if a witness be a false witness, and hath testified falsely against his brother, then shall ye do unto him as he had thought to do unto his brother; so shall thou put away the evil from the midst of thee. . . . And thine eye shall not pity, life for life, eye for eye, tooth for tooth, hand for hand, foot for foot.
(*Deut.* xix. 18–21.)

And if a man cause a blemish in his neighbour, as he hath done so shall it be done to him, breach for breach, eye for eye, tooth for tooth; as he hath caused a blemish in a man, so shall it be rendered unto him.
(*Leviticus* xxiv. 19–21.)

Terrible as is the dictum "thine eye shall not pity," yet it is the beginning of the biblical history of human forgiveness inasmuch as it thereby recognizes the possibility of, even the predisposition to, pity. We are now able to discern the tender form of Pity rising up against Justice, challenging her, resting upon a doctrine and practice that became increasingly strong, until at last, in opposition to the Law (ὁ νόμος) given by Moses came the Kindness and Truth (ἡ χάρις καὶ ἀλήθεια) through Jesus Christ. The struggle between Justice and Mercy has been a long one and is not yet determined. We shall do well to mark the stages by which the motive of forgiveness transcends that of legal revenge. I shall quote the passages with as little comment as possible.

6. THE REJECTION OF NEMESIS

First may be noticed the recognition of inescapable Nemesis as administered by man for God in the case of the Canaanitish King Adoni-bezek, whose feet and hands were mutilated by his conquerors; he says: "Three score and ten Kings having their thumbs and their great toes cut off gathered their meat under my table; as I have done, so God hath requited me." This is *lex talionis* regarded as a Divine ordinance. It and the foregoing Mosaic code are explicitly negatived by the writer of *Proverbs*:

Say not thou, I will recompense evil;
Wait on the Lord and He shall save thee.   (xx. 22.)

Say not, I will do so to him as he hath done to me;
I will render to the man according to his work.
                                            (xxiv. 29.)

Positive form is given to the new command:

If thine enemy be hungry, give him bread to eat,
And if he be thirsty, give him water to drink;
For thou shalt heap coals of fire upon his head.
And the Lord shall reward thee.   (xxv. 21, 22.)

Then comes the general dictum, "Vengeance is mine and recompense," which relieves the sufferer from participation in the punishment of his injurer. Highest of all in the Old Testament is the passage:

Thou shalt not hate thy brother in thine heart: thou shalt surely rebuke thy neighbour, and not bear sin because of him. Thou shalt not take vengeance nor bear grudge against the children of thy people, but thou shalt love thy neighbour as thyself.
                                (*Leviticus* xix. 17, 18.)

Ben Sirach has the following:

> Man cherisheth anger against a man,
> And doth he seek healing from the Lord?
> Upon a man like himself he hath no mercy,
> And doth he make supplication for his own sins?
> He being flesh nourisheth wrath:
> Who shall make atonement for his sins?
>
> (*Ecclesiasticus* xxviii. 3–5),

He asks consistency in our seeking and granting mercy (cp. the Unforgiving Servant). The whole of the *Testament of Gad* may be read with profit here, but particularly the passage which teaches unconditional and complete forgiveness accompanied by tactful address:

> And now, my children, I exhort you, love ye each one his brother, and put away hatred from your hearts, love one another in deed, and in word, and in the inclination of the soul. For in the presence of my father I spake peaceably to Joseph; and when I had gone out, the spirit of hatred darkened my mind, and stirred up my soul to slay him. Love ye one another from the heart; and if a man sin against thee, speak peaceably to him, and in thy soul hold no guile: and if he repent and confess, forgive him. But if he deny it, do not get into a passion with him, lest catching the poison from thee he take to swearing and so thou sin doubly.... And though he deny it and yet have a sense of shame when reproved, give over reproving him. For he who denieth may repent so as not to wrong thee again; yea, he may also honour thee, and fear and be at peace with thee. But if he be shameless and persisteth in his wrongdoing, even so forgive him from the heart, and leave to God the avenging.
>
> (*Testaments of the XII Patriarchs: Gad* vi. 1–7.)

PSYCHOLOGY OF FORGIVENESS

These words must have been familiar to our Master when he taught in Palestine His own doctrine of forgiveness.

Forgive us our debts, as we also have forgiven our debtors. . . . For if ye forgive men their trespasses, your heavenly Father will also forgive you. But if ye forgive not men their trespasses, neither will your Father forgive you. . . . Whensoever ye stand praying, forgive if ye have ought against any one. . . . How often shall my brother sin against me and I forgive him? Until seven times? . . . Until seventy times seven. . . . If thy brother sin against thee go and show him his fault between him and thee alone; if he hear thee thou hast gained thy brother. . . . If thy brother sin rebuke him; and if he repent forgive him. And if he sin against thee seventy times in a day, and seven times turned again to thee, saying, I repent, thou shalt forgive him.

The Talmud has a terse and useful phrase among many on the subject of forgiveness: "Who is strong? He who turns an enemy into a friend."

7. FORGIVENESS AND PARDON

Forgiveness in its elementary form is a mitigation of justice, more properly called "pardon." God, a Judge or a man is conceived to have the right to punish the guilty, but under certain conditions does not do so. The conditions are various: God is said to impose humiliation and repentance—one cannot give God anything objectively. Man, however, grants pardon on condition of restitution, substitution or compensation. Pardon thus is only a part of forgiveness; it is objective and requires no psychological change in the person administering it. Forgiveness in full is both objective and subjective, essentially requiring psychological change in both the offender and his victim. In its highest form taught by Christ it is universal and unconditional.

8. THE PSYCHOLOGY OF FORGIVENESS

Although the word " forgive " occurs many times in the Old and New Testaments, it is significant that a knowledge of its meaning is assumed; here, I think, the Scriptures go too far, at least, for us Europeans who have been struggling with " Justice " since the days of Rome, our teacher in this respect. We must endeavour to penetrate to the heart of forgiveness if we wish to make it ours. I now propose to make this endeavour.

Forgiveness appears to me to be no simple and facile act but a difficult and complex process or concatenation of elements which interact upon each other in such a manner that the forgiveness becomes a rich and blessed state. These elements may be discerned as follows:

(1.) *Perception of the injury* done to oneself or another as the subject of forgiveness. To ignore an offence is not to forgive: such is the policy of the ostrich which produces an illusion of self-deception.

(2.) *Perception of the consequences* of the offence to the evil-doer and to his victim, so that by forgiveness, if possible, these may be turned aside. One hopes to " gain " a brother, to turn an enemy into a friend.

(3.) *Tactfulness* in approaching the offender, rebuking him privately, speaking to him peacefully is more likely to reach his heart than public railing and exposure. Moreover, we must not " rub it in " lest he falls into greater anger; having spoken clearly we must " give over reproving him," as Gad says. Rebuke must have the same quality and aim as the forgiveness which is to follow it.

(4.) *Sincerity*. Forgiveness must be " from the heart," not from the lips only nor of the hands. It must not be condescending patronage which offends, but gracious and attractive which compels. "In thy soul hold not guile."

(5.) *Goodwill* is essential to forgiveness, for one desires the good of the offender, to remove for him the consequences, objective or subjective, of the evil he has done; to save him from further suffering or at least to mitigate it or support him in the endurance of it if it cannot be avoided.

(6.) *Compassion* is part of forgiveness; the great truth that we are all one, closely knit together as members of one body, is demonstrated when we feel compassion for one who has injured us. If there be this sensibility of metaphysical identity with the evil-doer it makes forgiveness easier.

(7.) *Imagination* is necessary to forgiveness; we have to put ourselves in the place of the offender. "*As thyself*," says Leviticus; "*As ye would*," says the Golden rule. If we cannot make that effort of the imagination we hardly know how to forgive, especially on the objective and practical side of the process.

(8.) *Faith* is a strong element of forgiveness, which can hardly be regarded as genuine if based on fear. We cannot be assured in our inmost hearts that our forgiveness will be effective, will stop the persecutor, assuage the enemy, heal the injury. This *uncertainty* constitutes the heroic element of forgiveness. We have the mysterious encouragement to "forgive and thy sins will be loosed from thee," "with what measure ye mete," etc. Forgiveness involves risks or seems to do so; hence we must have faith to try it, in the absence of certain "sight."

(9.) *Persistency*. Oft-times our faith may seem to be unjustified and the offender offends again. Nevertheless, says Jesus, "forgive seven times a day, seventy times seven"—to infinity. And Gad says: "if he perisheth in his wrong-doing, even so forgive him from the heart and leave to God the avenging." This is of course reasonable, for to take back our forgiveness is to deny its significance. Even if our enemy can gain no good from our forgiveness, at least we can do so ourselves, in which case the injury he has done becomes an occasion for a kind of good other than that of which he has robbed us.

(10.) *Logical integrity.* Forgiveness is in itself a necessity if we would ourselves be forgiven. This is a profound truth, as yet unplumbed. "Upon a man like himself he hath no mercy," says Ben Sirach, "and doth he make supplication for his own sins?"; and we have the telling parable of the unforgiving servant who had already been much forgiven. So long, therefore, as we have any need of forgiveness ourselves we must consistently forgive others. The truth of this is felt intuitively with great force; indeed, a man who does not forgive will hardly ask forgiveness.

(11.) *Action.* The immediately practical side of forgiveness is perhaps the least difficult to understand; the other elements coalescing, as it were, create naturally the appropriate action. Here the imagination is a ready guide and the teachers supply only formal indications; such as food and drink to the enemy. The emphasis, however, is on the word Do. Forgiveness from the heart must have an objective outlet.

(12.) *Oblivion.* The old saying "forgive and forget" might equally be rendered "forget and forgive." The most mysterious element is the oblivion that comes to him who cultivates the habit of forgiveness. Dante tells of how on the edge of the Earthly Paradise he was bidden to drink of two rivers, Lethe and Eunöe; the one which takes away all memory of ill and the other which restores the memory of forgotten good. Both rivers flow from the fountain of God's heart; of both waters we must drink, says Dante, before we can enter the celestial realm. This is a true parable of forgiveness; we cannot forgive and *remember* the evil. The mind must be so preoccupied with good that evil memories cannot rise above its threshold.

9. THE WORLD'S EXHAUSTION

The brief history and rough analysis of the subject that I have given above may be enough to induce my readers to consider the real significance of the phenomenon of Forgiveness and its promise for the future. We carry on our worldly affairs by means of the conception of Justice and have hardly ever asked ourselves whether the basis is adequate to human needs. And yet if Justice be sufficient, why did Forgiveness ever come into being? And further, since it has come into being, what is the need of continuing to rely on motives which it transcends so completely and satisfactorily? The fact is undeniable—when it is faced honestly—that if men did not already, in hundreds of minor matters, daily resort to Forgiveness and Forgetfulness, their lives would be choked up with poisonous memories and antipathies which Justice would be unable to dispose of. Any person who looks back upon an average uneventful life will recognize that normal progress is only possible by disposing of the accumulations and difficulties by the practice of Forgiveness. Indeed, I affirm that it is far more *natural* to forgive than to resort to Justice; it requires powers of the more ordinary kind possessed by nearly everybody, even without their being aware of the fact; whereas the judicial qualities are very rare and not always present where they are most needed.

I confess I see no light ahead of humanity unless we now resort to the only avenue of escape open to us—Universal Forgiveness. Society will not collapse; the world will not stand still. On the contrary, Forgiveness is the lubricant that will ease the creaking and rusty machinery by which we carry on our myriad affairs.

It is no part of my present purpose to indicate the countless problems that are even now susceptible of solution by Forgiveness in greater or less degree; to do so would make a very long catalogue and perhaps discourage the endeavour

I am desiring to stimulate. Yet I say that such a catalogue of personal, economic, industrial and political difficulties, which any one of general knowledge could draw up for himself, would terrify the bravest heart if he felt he had no other instrument to his hand than the vengeful impulses rising from our egoism or the legalized revenge which we call Justice.

The world is well-nigh exhausted; it has tried everything; it has asserted rights, and claimed privileges *ad nauseam*. It has passed through Hell, suffered—as yet in part only—the cleansing Purgatorial fires. It stands near—nearer than it knows—to the rivers of Lethe and Eunöe, "forgetfulness" and "good-mindedness." But our old world has no present guide, as Dante had, to tempt us to take the plunge. We are proud and stubborn; we crave for victory over our enemies both great and small; nothing satisfies us so much as the " triumph of Justice." If Dante be right it is worth our while to hesitate no longer. He says:

> If, reader, I had greater space for writing, I would sing at least in part, of the sweet draught which never would have sated me; I came back from the most holy waves, born again, even as new trees with new foliage, pure and made ready to mount to the stars.

* * *

Who is there, with sure steps, to guide us to those shores?

INDEX

of Works and Authors quoted and referred to in the text.

Achārānga Sutra (S.B.E.), 118, 221

Ambattha Sutta, Rhys Davids, 129, 134, 136

Amelius, quoted by Guthrie, 287

Ammonius Sakkas, quoted by Guthrie, 273

Ananda Mettayya, quoted, 189

Ancient History of China, by Hirth (Columbia Un. Press), 82

Anguttara Nikāya in *The Word of the Buddha*, and Warren's *Buddhism in Translation*, 179, 204, 217, 218, 219

The Antichrist, by Nietzsche (Foulis), 196, 197

Apocalyptic Books, list of, 305

Apology, The, Plato, 264

Āranyakas, or Forest Books, 92, 159

Artha-sāstra, by Chānakya, translated by Shamasastry, 120, 121, 122, 123, 192

Asoka, by Vincent Smith, 155

Augustine of Hippo on *the Manichæan Heresy*, 79, 80

Beyond Good and Evil, by Nietzsche (Foulis), 205, 206

Bhagavad Gita (S.B.E.), 159 ff.

Bibliotheca, Hierocles quoted in Guthrie's *Works of Plotinus*, 273

Book of Kindred Sayings (Pali Text Society), 150

Brahma-jala Sutta, Rhys Davids, 103, 104, 108, 116, 148

Brihadāranyaka Upanishad (S.B.E.), 75, 87, 88, 89, 213, 228, 229

Buddha, *Life of the*, by Rockill ('Trübner's Oriental Series), 78

Buddhism in Translation, by Warren (Harvard Oriental Series), 153, 177, 178, 217, 218, 219

Brāhmanas, or Commentaries, 89, 90, 92, 159

Corinthians, I Epistle to the, 321

Chāndogya Upanishad (S.B.E.), 75, 90, 101, 115, 172, 212, 228

Chinese Philosophy, by Paul Carus (Open Court Publishing Co.), 42

Chwang-tze (S.B.E.), 31, 32, 33, 36, 38, 39, 42, 62

353

INDEX

Crito; Plato; Translated by Carey, 260

Dante's Purgatorio, 352
Deuteronomy, R.V., 344
Dhammapada (S.B.E.), 181
Dhamma Sangani, by Mrs. Rhys Davids (Pali Text Society), 180
Dialogues of the Buddha, by Rhys Davids (Oxford University Press), 103, 104, 105, 106, 107, 108, 110(n.), 116, 129, 132, 133, 134, 136, 137, 139, 148
Diatessaron, Tatian, 319, 327
Didache (Löeb Library), 323, 329
Discourses of Gotama, by Sīlācāra (Luzac), 117, 149, 201, 208

Exodus (R.V.), 333, 344
Ecclesiasticus (R.V.), 346
Enoch, Book of, translated by Charles, 71, 72
Epistle to Marcella, Porphyrius, 291
Esdras II (R.V.), 74

First Outlines of a Systematic Anthropology of Asia, by Giuffrida-Ruggeri (Calcutta University), 128

Gaudapāda, 97
Genealogy of Morals, by Nietzsche (Foulis), 191
Genesis (Addis' Translation), 71
Giles, Dr.; *Chuang-tzu*, 44

Gorgias, Plato, translated by Jowett, 252, 253, 254
Gospel of John, 310, 311
Gospel of the Lord, Marcion, 326
Gospel of Mark, 320, 331, 334, 335, 336
Gospel of Matthew, 331, 334, 335, 336
Greek Thinkers, by Gomperz, 245

Hierocles, quoted by Guthrie, 273
Histoire de la Psychologie des Grecs, by Chaignet, 295
Horæ Hellenicæ, by Blackie, 249
Hsün-tze (described as Seun K'ing in Legge's *Chinese Classics*), 63

Ignatius, *Epistles of* (Loeb Library), 322

Jamblichus, list of writings, 295
Jātaka, or Birth Stories of the Buddha (in Warren's *Buddhism in Translation*), 178
Joyful Wisdom, The, by Nietzsche (Foulis), 195, 196, 198, 202, 203
Justin Martyr's I Apology, 325, 326

Katha Upanishad (S.B.E.), 88
Kaushītaki Upanishad (S.B.E.), 87
Khammurabi's Code (Chilperic Edwards' Translation), 342, 343

INDEX

Kritānga Sūtra (S.B.E.), 104, 105, 144, 221
Kūtadanta Sutta, Rhys Davids, 137
Lakkhana Suttanta, Rhys Davids, 132
Li-Chi (S.B.E.), 32
Lieh-tze (Wisdom of the East Series), 35, 43
Legge's *Chinese Classics*, 47, 60, 61, 63
Leviticus (R.V.), 344, 345

Maccabees II (R.V.), 269
Mahābhārata, 160
Mahāvagga (S.B.E.), 145, 177
Majjhima Nikāya in *Discourses of Gotama*, 117, 147, 149, 185, 201, 208, 216
Maitrāyana Upanishad (S.B.E.), 102
Manichæan Heresy, The, St. Augustine (T. & T. Clark), 79, 80
Memorabilia of Sokrates, Xenophon, 262, 263
Meng-tze, *Chinese Classics*, 60, 61
Milinda Panha (S.B.E.), 153, 183, 184
Mysteries of the Egyptians, by Abammon, 295, 298

Oldest Book of Hebrew History, by Addis (David Nutt), 71
On Human Nature, Ammonius Sakkas in Guthrie's *Works of Plotinus*, 273

Peloponnesian War, Thucydides, 250
Plotinus, Works of, by Guthrie, 276 ff.
Porphyrius, quoted by Guthrie, 290, 291
Porphyrius, list of his writings, 288
Proverbs, 345

Reminiscences de Philon chez Plotin, by Herriot, 272
Republic, Plato, translation by Jowett, 256, 257, 258, 259, 260, 265
Restoration of the Platonic Theology by the Later Platonists, by Thomas Taylor, 301
Rig Veda, Hymns of the, 92, 159

Saddharma Pundarīka (S.B.E.), 187, 188
Sāmanna-phala Sutta, Rhys Davids, 105, 106, 139, 152
Samyutta-Nikāya, in *Word of the Buddha*, 76, 116, 154, 216
Sānkhya-Kārikā, 97, 99
Sankhya-Pravachana-Bhāshya (Trübner), 97, 99, 100
Sarvadarsana-Samgraha (Trübner), 112
Satapatha Brāhmana (S.B.E.), 89, 90
Sonādanda Sutta, Rhys Davids, 133

Tao-teh-King (S.B.E.), 31, 37
Tattva Samāsa, 95, 100

INDEX

Testaments of the XII Patriarchs (S.P.C.K.), 346
Tevijja Sutta (S.B.E.), 117, 134, 148
Theognis, translated by Frere (Routledge), 244, 246
Theosophia, origin of the word, 288

Udana, 186

Vedānta Sutras (S.B.E.), 109, 171

Vinaya Texts in *Word of the Buddha*, 135

Will-to-Power, by Nietzsche (Foulis), 194, 199, 207
Word of the Buddha, by Nyāntiloka (Luzac), 76, 135, 147, 179, 185, 216

Yang Chu's Garden of Pleasure, 34, 47, 48, 49, 51, 52, 53, 54, 55, 57, 58, 59